D1065423

For Herbert and Mary Lou Brewer

To Win the Peace

Susan A. Brewer

To Win
the Peace

BRITISH PROPAGANDA
IN THE UNITED STATES
DURING WORLD WAR II

Cornell University Press · ITHACA AND LONDON

First published 1997 by Cornell University Press.

Printed in the United States of America

Cornell University Press strives to utilize environmentally responsible suppliers and materials to the fullest extent possible in the publishing of its books. Such materials include vegetable-based, low-VOC inks and acid-free papers that are also either recycled, totally chlorine-free, or partly composed of nonwood fibers.

Cloth printing   10 9 8 7 6 5 4 3 2 1

Library of Congress Cataloging-in-Publication Data

Brewer, Susan A. (Susan Ann), 1958–
To win the peace. : British propaganda in the United States during World War II / Susan A. Brewer.
p. cm.
Includes bibliographical references (p.) and index.
ISBN 0-8014-3367-3 (cloth : alk. paper)
1. World War, 1939–1945—Propaganda.   2. Propaganda, British—United States—History—20th century.   3. Neutrality—United States.   4. World War, 1939–1945—United States.   I. Title.
D810.P7G7218   1997
940.54'88641'0973—dc21   97-15057

For Herbert and Mary Lou Brewer

CONTENTS

Illustrations

ACKNOWLEDGMENTS

The whereabouts of the records of the American Division of the Ministry of Information are unknown; apparently they were misplaced by the British government shortly after the war. Professor H. G. Nicholas of Oxford University, who spent his war years at the American Division, believes the loss of those particular MOI records may have been deliberate. He also recalls, however, that filing was not a high priority at the American Division and that the staff tended to keep important documents in or on their desks. Fortunately, for those of us interested in British propaganda in the United States, this gap in the documentation is partially filled by the records of the Foreign Office, other divisions of the Ministry of Information, the Colonial Office, and the Board of Trade, at the Public Record Office in Kew; the British Broadcasting Corporation Written Archives Center in Caversham Park; and manuscript collections at the Bodleian Library, Oxford University, and the Churchill College Library, Cambridge University. In Ottawa, I found excellent material at the National Archives of Canada. In the United States, I have relied on the National Archives, the Library of Congress, the Franklin Delano Roosevelt Presidential Library, the Harvard University Archives, the Richard B. Russell Library for Political Research and Studies at the University of Georgia, the Seeley G. Mudd Manuscript Library of Princeton University, the State Historical Society of Wisconsin, and the Manuscripts and Archives collection of Yale University Libraries. I am most grateful to the archivists and librarians who assisted me in my research.

I thank Oliver E. Allen, Peter R. Clapper, A. M. Farrer, the executors of the Richard B. Russell estate, Irene M. Spry, the Borthwick Institute of Historical Research at the University of York, the Seeley

G. Mudd Manuscript Library of Princeton University, and Yale University Library for granting me permission to quote from unpublished papers and correspondence. I quote from the BBC Written Archives with the BBC's kind permission.

I want also to express my appreciation for the generosity of Sir Isaiah Berlin, Graham Hutton, Herbert G. Nicholas, Dean Rusk, Arthur Schlesinger Jr., Eric Sevareid, and Irene Spry, the veterans and witnesses of the propaganda campaign who shared their memories with me. I am grateful to the Cornell University Graduate School, the Franklin and Eleanor Roosevelt Institute, the National Endowment for the Humanities, and the University Personnel Development Committee of the University of Wisconsin–Stevens Point for financial assistance. In addition, I wish to thank Christine Neidlein and the staff of the University of Wisconsin–Stevens Point Interlibrary Loan office for their skill, efficiency, and perseverance.

I deeply appreciate the time and efforts of friends and colleagues who read and commented on my manuscript. I am most indebted to Walter LaFeber, who supervised this project in its early stages and provided wise and generous counsel. I cannot thank him enough. I am exceedingly grateful to Emily Rosenberg and Allan Winkler for their close reading of the manuscript, thoughtful criticisms, and excellent advice. James Baughman, Anne Greer Kishmir, and Diane Kunz read the entire manuscript and made discerning and helpful comments with enthusiasm and good humor. I received stimulating commentary on portions of my work from Patricia Clavin, Carole Fink, Isabel V. Hull, Theresa Kaminski, Gordon Martel, Thomas Risse-Kappen, Sally Kent, Mitchell Robinson, Robert Schulzinger, Duane Tananbaum, Michael Logan-John Wilson, and Robin Winks. I want to thank Paul Kennedy for inviting me to speak at the International History symposium of the International Security Program at Yale. I am grateful to Donald Cameron Watt for introducing me to the topic of Anglo-American relations in his postgraduate seminars at the London School of Economics and Political Science. I thank Nicholas Cull and Caroline Anstey for generously sharing resources and ideas on British propaganda. I am also indebted to my fellow historians at the University of Wisconsin–Stevens Point who inspire and encourage with their exemplary commitment to scholarship and teaching. To Eric Yonke, Sarah Elkind, and Charles Clark, I offer my thanks for compassionate computer counseling. I am especially grateful to Leslie Midkiff-DeBauche for reading, listening, and talking through problems of research and writing as well as other concerns of life as we know it.

I wish to extend my thanks to Peter Agree, my editor at Cornell University Press, for his interest and advice, and to Kay Scheuer, Carol Betsch, and Wendy Jacobs for their care and attention.

Over the years of working on the book, many gracious people offered me food, shelter, and great conversation. I thank Sheila Ferguson, Lady Liddell Hart, Lori and Dave Snyder, Dafydd Ellis Thomas, and Marjorie Thompson on the British side of the Atlantic, with particular gratitude to Janet Powney and Jeremy Mitchell. In the United States, I am grateful to Thomas and Claudia Risse-Kappen, Mitchell and Mary Robinson, and for years of friendship, Christopher Bort, Linda Nemec, Anne Greer Kishmir, and Maxim Kishmir. To Robert Erickson, I express my gratitude for his constant encouragement. Lastly, I want to thank my family, especially my parents, for their love and support.

S. B.

Amherst Junction, Wisconsin

ABBREVIATIONS

BBC WAC	British Broadcasting Corporation Written Archives Center
BIS	British Information Services
BPS	British Press Service
BSC	British Security Coordination
BT	Board of Trade Records
CAB	Cabinet Records
CO	Colonial Office Records
CPI	Committee on Public Information
FBIS	Foreign Broadcasting Intelligence Service
FDRL	Franklin D. Roosevelt Presidential Library
FO	Foreign Office Records
INF	Ministry of Information Records
IO	India Office Records
MOI	Ministry of Information
NA	National Archives of the United States
NAC	National Archives of Canada
OF	Official Files of President Roosevelt
OGR	Office of Government Reports
OWI	Office of War Information
PPF	President's Personal Files
PREM	Prime Minister's Records
PRO	Public Record Office
PSF	President's Secretary's File
PWE	Political Warfare Executive

To Win the Peace

Introduction: The Mission

> So in order to commend ourselves to the U.S. public
> through publicity we have to demonstrate with grim repeti-
> tion how great a contribution Britain has made in the fight
> against the common enemy. . . . We have to proclaim the
> [r]enaissance of Britain in this war.
>
> In this respect, publicity can be a servant of highest value
> to policy. For if we do not correct, through publicity, the
> illusion of many Americans that this country is doomed to
> be a satellite power, a poor relation, a sort of Uncle James
> who worked hard in his day, but is now past it, poor old
> fellow, and must be pensioned off, then our Government
> will have a tough time.
>
> —ROBIN CRUIKSHANK, MINISTRY OF INFORMATION,
> 1943

During the Second World War, while the Allies clashed with Axis
forces in Africa, Asia, and Europe, a small British army campaigned
on the battlefield of American public opinion. Recruits discreetly conducted reconnaissance missions. Officials in London debated strategy
and tactics and dispatched orders to their representatives across the
Atlantic. The troops, who before the war had been journalists, business executives, professors, and writers, carried out operations from
New York to Los Angeles, from St. Paul to Houston. Their mission
was the creation of a "special relationship" or informal partnership
between Britain and the United States. The weapon was propaganda.

The propagandists conducted their campaign with urgency. They had tried and failed to pull the neutral United States into the European War when Britain faced Nazi Germany alone in 1940–1941. Britain's plight had earned it sympathy and supplies from the American nation, where most people believed that Germany must be defeated, but a consistent 80 percent of the public told George Gallup's pollsters that the United States should not declare war on the Axis powers. When the Japanese attack on Pearl Harbor in December 1941 brought the United States into the war, an ebullient Prime Minister Winston Churchill went home and "slept the sleep of the saved."[1] While the Allied military forces took on the terrific job of salvation, officials in London turned their attention to the problems that might follow victory. They concluded that there would be no real security for Britain in the postwar world without an American commitment to maintaining the peace. The United States, they believed, must be persuaded to take on international leadership, ideally based on a partnership between the United States and Britain that would outlast the war and win the peace.

The British government's wartime attempt to create a "special relationship" signified a transition of power from the global leadership of Pax Britannia to the "American Century." Relations between the former thirteen colonies and the "mother country" had become less antagonistic at the close of the nineteenth century. "We are kin in sin," pronounced Mark Twain in December 1900. The author and anti-imperialist praised common Anglo-American ideals, religion, and representative government but condemned Britain's war against the Boers in South Africa and the United States's battle with nationalists in the newly acquired Philippines. Twain made these remarks as he introduced to a New York audience the twenty-six-year-old Winston Churchill. The future prime minister, on a lecture tour to promote a book about his South African adventures, defended British policy and thus began his famous courtship of the United States.[2] In

1. George H. Gallup, *The Gallup Poll: Public Opinion, 1935–1948* (New York: Random House, 1972), 133–257; Winston S. Churchill, *The Grand Alliance* (Boston: Houghton Mifflin, 1950), 608.

2. Mark Twain, "Introducing Winston S. Churchill," in Jim Zwick, ed., *Mark Twain's Weapons of Satire: Anti-Imperialist Writings on the Philippine-American War* (Syracuse, N.Y.: Syracuse University Press, 1992), 9–11; Bradford Perkins, in

the pivotal decades of the early twentieth century, American and British champions of Anglo-American cooperation would emphasize the element of "kin," extolling principles of democracy and civilization, while critics would raise the issue of "sin," denouncing the exploitations of imperialism and industrial capitalism.

At the heart of the kin or sin contest was the question of how Americans should use their growing power. The United States had become, to quote Twain, a "planetary swell," a rival that shared Britain's interest in a stable world order. When World War I threatened that order, the two nations had combined temporarily to restore it. The destruction of the fragile peace by the Axis powers brought the United States and Britain closer than ever before. The exceptional World War II alliance, as the excellent studies by William Roger Louis, David Reynolds, Christopher Thorne, and Randall Bennett Woods have shown, was one in which contentions over empire and economies persisted.[3]

The propaganda campaign took place at the intersection of foreign relations with American politics and culture. Its mission reflected the British government's recognition of the significance of domestic influences on the foreign policy of the United States. Propagandists therefore were not only concerned with the transition of power from Britain to the United States but also with the transformation of

---

The Great Rapprochement: England and the United States, 1898–1905 (New York: Atheneum, 1968), and Lloyd Gardner, in *Safe for Democracy: The Anglo-American Response to Revolution, 1913–1923* (New York: Oxford University Press, 1984), discuss the growth of common interests between the United States and Britain in the early twentieth century.

3. William Roger Louis' *Imperialism at Bay, 1941–1945: The United States and the Decolonization of the British Empire* (New York: Oxford University Press, 1978) is a masterful account of conflicting interests within the alliance; in *The Creation of the Anglo-American Alliance, 1937–1941: A Study in Competitive Cooperation* (Chapel Hill: University of North Carolina Press, 1982), David Reynolds explores the reluctance of the Chamberlain government to seek American assistance in the late thirties, even though it recognized that in total war U.S. involvement would be vital to Britain; Christopher Thorne, in *Allies of a Kind: The United States, Britain and the War against Japan, 1941–1945* (New York: Oxford University Press, 1978), reveals that while the United States and Britain agreed on the importance of maintaining white, western dominance in Asia, they competed for control; in *A Changing of the Guard: Anglo-American Relations, 1941–1946* (Chapel Hill: University of North Carolina Press, 1990), Randall Bennett Woods shows how the United States dominated Anglo-American efforts to shape the postwar international economy.

American political culture from a tradition of isolationism and independent international action to global leadership and cooperation. Their goal was to make an Anglo-American partnership politically acceptable to the U.S. government and to the American people.

This book analyzes the propaganda policy of the British government as it attempted to create the "special relationship" from 1942 to 1945 and American responses to those attempts. The task of building a consensus for postwar Anglo-American cooperation was a daunting one. The British campaign—a highly plotted, well-orchestrated endeavor with concrete goals—was conducted in a wide-open country of diverse population, disparate regions, and divided political power. Propagandists studied American opinion, set up discreet organizations, identified target audiences, defined themes, considered language, and chose methods of dissemination. American political culture, therefore, played a role in shaping the development of Britain's propaganda campaign, a campaign dedicated to influencing American opinion.

The British had learned following World War I that Americans resented being the target of propaganda. Propaganda, defined as the deliberate attempt by the few to influence the many by the manipulation of ideas, facts, and lies, had been condemned as mostly lies after "the war to end all wars."[4] Its disgrace, however, did not discourage the development of new methods of mass persuasion during the interwar period. With great care, as I show in Chapter 1, the British in 1940–1941 attempted to persuade the Americans to abandon neutrality.

Propagandists, well aware that they could risk sabotaging the "special relationship" by getting caught trying to create it, adopted the "strategy of truth." They presented fact-based news and information incorporating propaganda messages. The method, if not the messages, was familiar to the U.S. government. In World War II, as in World War I, democratic governments relied on domestic propaganda to mobilize the public. The British Ministry of Information (MOI), organized in 1939, and the American Office of War Information (OWI), set up in 1942, referred to their propaganda by the

---

4. Terence H. Qualter, *Opinion Control in Democracies* (New York: St. Martin's Press, 1985), 124. Another useful study of propaganda is Garth S. Jowett and Victoria O'Donnell, *Propaganda and Persuasion* (Beverly Hills: Sage Publications, 1986).

more neutral term "information." These agencies promoted enlistment, rationing, morale, and war aims. Democratic governments preferred to apply the term "propaganda" to enemy activity or to Allied psychological warfare against the enemy.[5] Among themselves, British officials used the words "propaganda," "information," and "publicity" interchangeably. Later, many of their policy papers would be listed in the index to Foreign Office correspondence under "Propaganda in the U.S." Therefore, to avoid the false neutrality of "information," as well as to encompass its variations "misinformation" and "disinformation," I use the term "propaganda."

London charged a diverse group of experts and amateurs with the task of launching a circumspect invasion, as I discuss in Chapter 2. The diplomats and career civil servants of the American Department of the Foreign Office and the British embassy in Washington oversaw propaganda policy developed by the MOI's American Division and the U.S.-based British Information Services. Programmers at the North American Service of the British Broadcasting Corporation (BBC) contributed to propaganda policy, as did special committees in Whitehall. For shorthand purposes, I refer to these people as propagandists, with apologies to those whose responsibilities went far beyond propaganda policymaking. All of them, of course, took pains to avoid such a label.

Propagandists perceived a two-tiered American audience. The first tier consisted of opinion leaders, such as university administrators and professors, business leaders, politicians and government officials, and most important, journalists, broadcasters, editors, and publishers of the news media. The second tier consisted of the general public.

5. Propaganda scholars have distinguished between "black" and "white" propaganda. In the "black" propaganda of psychological warfare (or "political warfare" as it was called in Britain), the source was disguised and the content was creative. Propaganda among allies usually fell into the category of "white" propaganda, in which the source was known and the content was generally accurate. This distinction about content tends to break down because so-called black propaganda sometimes incorporated facts, whereas so-called white propaganda sometimes relied on falsehoods and half-truths. See, for instance, Daniel Lerner, *Psychological Warfare against Nazi Germany: The Sykewar Campaign, D-Day to V-E Day* (Cambridge: MIT Press, 1971), 323–346. MOI's domestic propaganda is covered in Ian McLaine's *Ministry of Morale: Home Front Morale and the Ministry of Information in World War II* (London: George Allen and Unwin, 1979). Allan Winkler analyzes the OWI's domestic and foreign activities in *The Politics of Propaganda: The Office of War Information, 1942–1945* (New Haven: Yale University Press, 1974).

Here, on more unfamiliar territory, the British encountered American ethnic and racial identifications, regionalism, religions, and party affiliations. Although propagandists never lost sight of the general public and indeed made it a deliberate target for films and radio shows, they focused their efforts on opinion leaders. They found that, as Benjamin Page and Robert Shapiro noted in *The Rational Public*, the highly decentralized battlefield of opinion was dominated by "competing elites."[6] Once enough influential Americans had adopted the British view of events, propagandists believed, they would shape the opinion of the public at large and influence government policymakers.

Propagandists designed themes that combined an appeal to American principles and pragmatism. As I cover in Chapter 3, the democratic theme of "the people's war" and the teamwork theme of "the war effort" presented Britain as a valuable partner of the United States. Compelling narratives drew on history, myth, and Hollywood. Propagandists studied American beliefs and attitudes in order to identify themselves with the same values or to take care not to tread on them.

A common language both united and divided the two nations. Certainly, common language did not ensure common understanding. George Orwell, whose wartime work for the Ministry of Information inspired his creation of "newspeak" in *Nineteen Eighty-Four*, believed that to control language was to control thought.[7] The Ministry of Information's control over language and thus its audience was not as absolute as that of Orwell's fictional Ministry of Truth. Rather, the MOI attempted to choose language that would best further its goal of linking British and American interests. According to Garth Jowett and Victoria O'Donnell, propagandists know that "the persuader is a voice from without speaking the language of the au-

---

6. Benjamin I. Page and Robert Y. Shapiro, *The Rational Public: Fifty Years of Trends in Americans' Policy Preferences* (Chicago: University of Chicago Press, 1992), 365, 381; Ralph Levering cites education, media usage, ethnicity, and party affiliation as most influential in shaping opinion on foreign policy with religion, regionalism, and economic status as less helpful. British analysts used all of these categories. Ralph B. Levering, *The Public and American Foreign Policy, 1918–1978* (New York: William Morrow, 1978), 21.

7. George Orwell wrote and broadcast commentaries for the BBC under MOI guidance from December 1941 to February 1943. See W. J. West's introduction to W. J. West, ed., *Orwell: The War Commentaries* (New York: Pantheon Books, 1985).

dience's voices within."[8] For the British to speak the American language, they had to consider vocabulary, accent, and expression, but more important, the cultural assumptions underlying language.

The preferred and most common method propagandists used to reach their American audience was through the American media. As the principal link between the government and the citizens, the news media often determined the framework for discussion of public interests. The British aimed to use this agenda-setting function to influence public debates. Although diplomats, who prefer to maneuver in secret, and journalists, who seek to expose those maneuvers, share an antipathy of long standing, they depend on each other. As the Viennese satirist Karl Kraus observed, wars begin because diplomats tell lies to journalists and then believe what they read.

Propagandists relied on contacts with the American media for several reasons. First, they sought to allay American suspicions of the "insidious wiles of foreign influence" by shunning obvious propaganda and working through American reporters. Second, reporters and broadcasters could present the British message in an American voice and language familiar and attractive to the American audience. Third, using the media, with its focus on news, suited the information format of British propaganda. War correspondents sought facts to put into context, which the Ministry of Information was happy to supply. Yet the MOI had to contend with the skepticism toward government agencies reflected in such remarks as that of an American journalist who once said, "Always remember that the State Department is selling something; a good newspaperman must take the wrapping off."[9]

Propagandists worked within boundaries formed by the attitudes of the U.S. public and opinion leaders, the events that made the news, and the foreign policy goals of the British government. The "strategy of truth" left propagandists at the mercy of events. They scrambled to put the best possible face on bad news or inconvenient facts that contradicted their propaganda message. Propagandists also found that certain aspects of British foreign policy did not translate into appealing propaganda for the U.S. audience. The social scientist Har-

---

8. Jowett and O'Donnell, *Propaganda and Persuasion*, 28.
9. Bernard C. Cohen, *The Press and Foreign Policy* (Princeton: Princeton University Press, 1963), 78.

old Lasswell noted that, whereas policymakers require propaganda to further their goals, propagandists require policy goals that can be translated into effective propaganda.[10] On policies regarding the British Empire and Lend-Lease, British policy goals conflicted with U.S. policy goals. In Chapter 4, I show how U.S. sympathies for Indian independence alerted the British that their governing of the empire would now be under American scrutiny. Britain's propaganda policy for promoting the entire Empire and Commonwealth, based on persuading Americans to identify with the British rather than the colonial peoples, is covered in Chapter 5. Chapter 6 explores why Britain's need for economic aid and the United States's penchant for hard bargains made difficult the goal of proclaiming an equal partnership. Propagandists sometimes faced the task of promoting cooperation where little existed.

The effectiveness of the campaign remains difficult to measure, then and now. Propagandists relied on public opinion polls and press surveys. But it was impossible to draw direct correlations between favorable results and successful propaganda or unfavorable results and failed propaganda. Historians have access to additional sources, including the U.S. government's analysis of BBC broadcasts, the remarks of American officials and politicians who made U.S. foreign policy, and the memoirs and papers of American journalists and broadcasters who were the targets of British efforts. In these it is possible to trace the propaganda message as Americans adopted interpretations of events or narratives designed in London. Of course, no American would admit to being influenced by British propaganda. And the British themselves deftly appropriated the words and voices of "right-thinking" Americans to disguise their efforts. Nevertheless, propagandists left a trail showing how they exploited contacts with the media, effectively employed themes, and stretched the "strategy of truth."

One of the most significant indications of the campaign's success may be the fifty-year attempt by historians of Anglo-American relations to take the wrapping off of the "special relationship" in order to argue whether it indeed existed.[11] Winston Churchill drew on his

---

10. Harold Lasswell, *Propaganda Technique in World War I* (1927; Cambridge: MIT Press, 1971), xx.

11. See, for instance, Coral Bell, "The Special Relationship," in *Constraints and Adjustments in British Foreign Policy,* ed. Michael Leifer (London: George Allen and Unwin, 1972), 103–119; Max Beloff, "The Special Relationship: An Anglo-American

talents as orator, politician, writer, and historian to breathe time and glory into his influential version. He gave the "special relationship" an "if only" past in which an active Anglo-American alliance might have prevented the Second World War. He endowed the wartime comradeship with majestic heroism. And in 1944 he described its future role when he wrote, "It is my deepest conviction that unless Britain and the United States are joined together in a special relationship . . . another destructive war will come to pass."[12] Churchill's deliberate attempt to influence historical understanding obscured the work of propagandists. They, too, drew upon history to endow the "special relationship" with inevitability, but they directed their more subtle appeal to American strategic and economic interests.

Propaganda could not bridge the gap between Britain's loss of wealth and power and the United States's gain. Churchill himself knew this. Ten days after the Yalta Conference in February 1945, the prime minister mused about the "shadows of victory": "After this war," said Churchill, "we should be weak, we should have no money and no strength and we should lie between the two great powers of the USA and the USSR."[13] The prime minister and his successors would then call upon the Anglo-American partnership to protect Britain's interests. The United States would answer according to its own agenda.

The creation of the "special relationship" could not prevent the transition of power, but it helped make that transition work in Britain's interests. The propaganda campaign defined the role of the emerging superpower as the maintainer of the peace. It accentuated the basis for cooperation between the two democratic and capitalist countries and contained the troublesome issues of the future of the British Empire and Lend-Lease settlements.

The British propaganda campaign in the United States was an extraordinary undertaking. One of the most powerful countries in the

---

Myth," in *A Century of Conflict, 1850–1950: Essays for A. J. P. Taylor*, ed. Martin Gilbert (London: Hamish Hamilton, 1966), 151–171; William Roger Louis and Hedley Bull, eds., *The "Special Relationship": Anglo-American Relations since 1945* (Oxford: Clarendon Press, 1986).

12. Churchill to Richard Law, February 1944, PREM4 27/10, PRO. Christopher Thorne discusses Churchill's use of the "special relationship" in terms of historical lessons learned in *Border Crossings: Studies in International History* (Oxford: Basil Blackwell, 1988), 19.

13. John Colville, *The Fringes of Power: Downing Street Diaries, 1939–1955* (New York: Norton, 1986), 563–564.

world, no longer able to afford its own battles, sought to secure its position by shaping the opinion of a foreign population. Because the propaganda was done through the press, radio, film, speeches, and personal contact, and because it can be difficult to detect, given that it was designed to be undetectable, it would be easy to underrate the seriousness of the venture. But for Britain, it was a campaign for high stakes. Without American assistance, the British believed, they could neither win the war nor establish a favorable peace.

1 Precedent and Legacy: The "No Propaganda" Policy

> I would feel that our objectives, political and propagandist,
> vis-à-vis the U.S.A. should be maximum cooperation in all
> spheres and at all times between the peoples and govern-
> ments of the British Commonwealth and the United States,
> and that with this long term conception in mind we should
> in everything we say and do now take care to avoid what
> happened twenty years ago, when we got the short term ad-
> vantage of American assistance in the war at the expense of
> the long term advantage of American cooperation after the
> war.
>
> —Frank Darvall, Ministry of Information,
> January, 1941

From World War I, the British propagandists of World War II
learned that the propaganda that wins wars may lose the peace. They
contended with the perception that British propaganda from 1914 to
1917 had successfully manipulated the United States to abandon neutrality and enter the Great War. Consequently, the Americans, dis-
illusioned by their European venture, had rejected any commitment
to maintaining the Treaty of Versailles and had withdrawn into an
isolationism enforced by the Neutrality Acts of the 1930s. Although
this view of the results of World War I propaganda was distorted
and simplistic, the popular belief that Britain had duped the Americans nevertheless haunted London policymakers. Therefore, when
Europe went to war in September 1939, British officials, who once

again wanted American cooperation, refrained from any suggestion
of an aggressive propaganda campaign in the United States. This time
they needed a success that would not backfire on them. They created
the "no propaganda" policy based on the precedents of World War I
and its legacy of distrust.

Propaganda was "the task of creating and directing public opinion,"
stated Lord Beaverbrook, the Minister of Information in 1918.
"Since strength for the purposes of war was the total strength of
each belligerent nation, public opinion was as significant as fleets and
armies." For Britain, the total strength of the United States, including
its public opinion, grew increasingly significant as the Great War
between the Entente and the Central powers dragged on. The bloody
stalemate on the western front created a growing reliance on American production and the need for more manpower on the battlefield.[1]
British propagandists, accordingly, shifted from encouraging a
friendly American neutrality to promoting U.S. intervention in the
war. Their propaganda cast Britain as the upholder of democratic
values versus Germany, the violator of Belgian neutrality.

It was the dramatic theme of civilization versus barbarism, rather
than their fairly subtle method of cultivating elite opinion, which later
won British propagandists their reputation as sensationalist manipu-
lators. This method reflected an earlier analysis of American public
opinion by Lord Bryce, the historian, statesman, and highly regarded
ambassador to the United States (1907–1913), whose celebrated study
The American Commonwealth was first published in 1888 and revised
in 1910. Bryce divided American opinion into two categories: passive
and active. According to Bryce, nineteen out of twenty Americans fell
into the passive category as receivers rather than originators of opinion. The "masses" responded to issues with sentiment, not substance.
The 5 percent of Americans who made up active opinion included
statesmen, journalists, and lecturers, who "create and lead opinion"
through various organs, including the press. For Bryce, the way Amer-

1. Michael Sanders and Philip Taylor, *British Propaganda in the First World War,
1914–1918* (London: Macmillan, 1982), 254. For studies of Anglo-American relations during World War I, see Kathleen Burk, *Britain, America, and the Sinews of
War, 1914–1918* (Boston: George Allen and Unwin, 1984); Robert H. Ferrell, *Woodrow Wilson and World War I, 1917–1921* (New York: Harper and Row, 1985);
Gardner, *Safe for Democracy*; and Arthur S. Link, *Woodrow Wilson: Revolution,
War, and Peace* (Arlington Heights, Ill.: AHM Publishing, 1979).

ican opinion leaders tested views on the public before taking a position was the "most curious part of the whole process by which opinion is produced." This process, he noted, was unlike England's, where leaders merely expected the public to ratify their decisions. In the United States, Bryce observed, "a statesman is not expected to move ahead of [the people]; he must rather seem to follow." This process of American political leaders creating consensus while appearing to follow it was well established by World War I.[2] Propagandists appropriated it by presenting their version of events to the American statesmen and journalists who led opinion.

From 1914 on, the British dominated the war news received by the American public. First and most practically, Britain had cut the German trans-Atlantic cables and thus forced Americans to rely on direct cable communication from Britain. Second, censors removed from cables or mail any criticisms the government considered harmful. Official London could also manipulate the perception of events by timing the release of news. For instance, when Winston Churchill was First Lord of the Admiralty (1911–1915), he sometimes held back bad news on the chance that good news might come in. He could then release both at the same time to offset the bad with the good. Third, to fill the void left by the censor, the authorities provided the press with their version of events. The Foreign Office News Department supplied American journalists with news, opinions, and facilities. The only American correspondent accredited to the British Expeditionary Force in France was Frederick Palmer, a veteran war correspondent who had reported on the Boxer Rebellion, the Russo-Japanese War, and Gen. John Pershing's expedition into Mexico after Pancho Villa. Palmer received preferential treatment and wrote pro-British dispatches. The rest of the American war correspondents, chaperoned by diplomatic officers, were entertained and briefed at the headquarters château. Although American correspondents chafed at official control, they could either acquiesce to the limited conditions or go home. British analysts were therefore able to report regularly to the Cabinet that the American press was permeated by British influence.[3]

2. James Bryce, *The American Commonwealth*, vol. 2 (New York: Macmillan, 1910), 254–257, 284, 327; Robert C. Hilderbrand, *Power and the People: Executive Management of Public Opinion in Foreign Affairs, 1897–1921* (Chapel Hill: University of North Carolina Press, 1981), 201–202.

3. Sanders and Taylor, *British Propaganda in the First World War*, 170;

In addition to influencing the news of the war, a special American branch at the War Propaganda Bureau, known as Wellington House, directed propaganda to U.S. opinion leaders. At its head was Sir Gilbert Parker, the Canadian-born novelist and member of Parliament. Parker, pretending to be a private citizen, wrote to Americans using a mailing list of his own contacts and 260,000 addresses lifted from *Who's Who*. Parker described his audience as "influential and eminent people, university and college presidents, professors, and scientific men." In a tone designed to appeal to neutral Americans, he introduced his material on the war with the claim that it contained "the essential facts in the case" presented "in that objective scientific form which is alone suitable for serious and impartial study."[4]

The theme of German barbarism inspired the publication of reports of German atrocities in Belgium. The British government appointed an investigating committee under the chairmanship of Lord Bryce. It charged the Germans with being guilty of "murder, lust and pillage . . . on a scale unparalleled in any war between civilised nations during the last three centuries." The committee based its report on depositions collected from Belgian citizens, which it deliberately did not verify. The Bryce report presented the evidence in a legalistic, factual manner, yet it emphasized the sensational aspect of German brutality by focusing on crimes of rape and murder against women and children. The timing of the report's publication a few days after a German submarine sank the British passenger liner *Lusitania* reinforced the view that the Germans attacked the innocent. The Wellington House survey of the American press credited Lord Bryce's prestige for the absence of skepticism: "Even in papers hostile to the Allies, there is not the slightest attempt to impugn the correctness of the facts alleged." His report, Bryce learned, had "*swept* America."[5]

Lasswell, *Propaganda Technique in World War I*, 109; Phillip Knightley, *The First Casualty: From the Crimea to Vietnam: The War Correspondent as Hero, Propagandist, and Myth Maker* (New York: Harcourt Brace Jovanovich, 1975), 121, 124.

4. Sir Gilbert Parker, "The United States and the War," *Harper's*, March 1918, 522; Gary S. Messinger, *British Propaganda and the State in the First World War* (New York: Manchester University Press, 1992), 61.

5. "Report of the Committee on Alleged German Outrages Appointed by His Britannic Majesty's Government and presided over by Right Honorable Viscount Bryce, Formerly British Ambassador at Washington" (London: HMSO, 1915), 61; Trevor

Compared with Britain's successes, German propaganda appeared inept and less well-informed about American political culture. The German Press Bureau, which issued daily bulletins and photographs, naturally turned to a ready-made audience of German Americans, one of the largest immigrant groups in the United States. German propagandists, however, failed to foresee the danger in singling out German American ethnic groups and appealing to their loyalty to the "home" country. The Germans also misjudged their American audience by promising equal rights to African Americans when the Ku Klux Klan had been revived.[6] The Berlin government made a final blunder by inadvertently presenting the British with the gift of the Zimmermann telegram. Intercepted by British intelligence, the telegram from the German foreign minister to Mexico proposed that if the United States entered the war, Mexico would reconquer its former territories of Texas, New Mexico, and Arizona. The publication of the Zimmermann telegram in early 1917, shortly after Germany resumed unrestricted submarine warfare, increased anti-German sentiment. Germany's appeals to minority groups and its link with Mexico reinforced most Americans' identification with the British cause. By taking advantage of actual events—the invasion of Belgium, the sinking of the *Lusitania*, and the Zimmermann telegram—to illustrate the theme of civilization versus barbarism, British propagandists built a strong appeal to American interests and sentiments.

British propaganda did affect the way Americans perceived the war; it did not, however, manipulate the United States into World War I. American military and economic interests, as well as personal convictions, had influenced President Woodrow Wilson's attempt to act as an impartial mediator. His call for "peace without victory," however, was rejected by the belligerents. The United States severed diplomatic relations with Germany when it resumed unrestricted submarine warfare. The United States should go to war, President Wilson declared in his address to Congress on April 2, 1917, "to make the world safe for democracy" against autocratic powers. The president was convinced that America's war aims for a "just peace" were far superior to Britain's goals. Wilson insisted that the United States

---

Wilson, "Lord Bryce's Investigation into Alleged German Atrocities in Belgium, 1914–1915," *Journal of Contemporary History* 14 (July 1979), 370, 378.

6. Lasswell, *Propaganda Technique in World War I*, 149–154.

retain independence of action as an associated power, not an Allied power.

The assumption that the American version of civilization outshone any others was encouraged by the Committee on Public Information (CPI). Created by President Wilson to mobilize Americans for war, the CPI confirmed British methods of conducting propaganda in democracies. It preached "faith in democracy . . . faith in the fact," but resorted to atrocity stories and anti-German propaganda that inspired prejudice and in some cases violence against German Americans. The call for wartime unity and "100% Americanism" sanctioned repression and ignited hysteria. British propagandists had helped set the fire; American propagandists fanned the flames. Shared methods, however, did not mean shared goals. As the historian Stephen Vaughn concluded, the CPI functioned as a "nationalizing agent greatly enhancing nationalism during 1917–1918."[7] This nationalism would strengthen the American preference for freedom of action, rather than encourage international collaboration.

British observers of Anglo-American relations based in London and in the United States differed over the significance of growing American nationalism. With the goal of U.S. entry into the war accomplished, officials in London felt that the work of persuasion was done. Their propaganda should now merely inform the American public of British policy. The British government set up a formal propaganda agency in New York, the British Bureau of Information. The bureau, which later became the British Pictorial Service, eventually had branch offices in Washington, Chicago, and San Francisco and a staff of ninety-six. It arranged for articles to be published in American magazines, scheduled speakers, and circulated British films.[8] This more overt propaganda campaign, featuring British wartime exploits, reflected the assumption that the United States would continue to conform to Britain's lead.

The now-retired Sir Gilbert Parker confidently treated American nationalism as a sign that the United States was ready for Anglo-American solidarity. For the readers of the March 1918 issue of *Har-*

7. David Kennedy, *Over Here: The First World War and American Society* (New York: Oxford University Press, 1980), 63–75; Stephen Vaughn, *Holding Fast the Inner Lines: Democracy, Nationalism, and the Committee on Public Information* (Chapel Hill: University of North Carolina Press, 1980), 233.

8. Sanders and Taylor, *British Propaganda in the First World War*, 190–196.

per's magazine, Parker explained away a century and a half of historical misunderstanding between the United States and Britain. He assured Americans, without explaining why, that George III was unpopular in the Britain of 1918. Parker attempted to blame the conduct of the "wretched business" of the American Revolution on German mercenaries who, he claimed, were aided by only a handful of British army professionals. He did not use any numbers because at the height of the war for independence, the British had fifty thousand troops in the United States assisted by thirty thousand Hessians and half the British navy. After learning its lesson in the American Revolutionary War, Parker continued, Britain had secured the prosperity of the United States by making the Royal Navy the defender of the Monroe Doctrine and protector of the western hemisphere. Parker pronounced the days of willful misunderstanding to be over and predicted that when the terms of peace were signed the two democracies would be "working hand in hand for the political good of all the world."[9]

Less complacent than Parker, British propagandists in the United States urged London to make a concerted effort to win American cooperation. Lord Northcliffe, the journalist and publisher whose press empire included the *Times* and the *Daily Mail*, served as the head of the British War Mission in 1917. Northcliffe, whose fundamental premise was Britain's dependence on the United States, considered his chief concern to be propaganda. "The war can only be won from here," he reported to London.[10] The flamboyant newspaper magnate held press conferences and wrote articles to publicize the British war effort and the need for American matériel and financial support. He considered British propaganda to be most effective among the American upper classes but insisted it must reach the wider public through the American press.

At a luncheon Northcliffe publicly attacked fellow guest and pub-

9. Parker was not alone in attempting to revise history for the sake of Anglo-American relations. Pro-British Americans managed to blame the Germans for the "wretched business" of the Revolution by pointing out that George III himself was a German. See Dennis J. McCarthy, "The British," in *The Immigrant's Influence on Wilson's Peace Policies*, ed. Joseph P. O'Grady (Lexington: University of Kentucky Press, 1967), 100, 103–104; Parker, "The United States and the War," 528–530.

10. Arthur Willert, *The Road to Safety: A Study in Anglo-American Relations* (London: Derek Verschoyle, 1952), 115.

lisher William Randolph Hearst for his pro-German sympathies. Hearst retorted by offering Northcliffe the editorial page of the *New York American* for a day. Northcliffe smashed his fist on the table and declared, "Done." Afterward, Sir William Wiseman of the British Secret Service and Arthur Willert, a *Times* correspondent who also served as a propagandist, advised Northcliffe that his behavior was unacceptable for a senior British representative. Although Willert sided with Wiseman, he was more tolerant of Northcliffe, his boss. Willert thought Northcliffe was well liked and effective because he had much in common with "ordinary Americans." He belonged, Willert believed, "to the same stage of civilization." Although the Foreign Office preferred Gilbert Parker's method of cultivating elite opinion, Northcliffe and Lord Beaverbrook, the press barons who served as propagandists during the war, advocated propaganda for the masses, especially after the Bolshevik Revolution of November 1917.[11] Total war demanded total public involvement, and in a revolutionary era, it was perhaps no longer wise to rely on elite channels. Northcliffe returned to London to direct propaganda against enemy countries, to the relief of the Foreign Office and William Wiseman, who quietly pursued his own strategies.

Wiseman's methods were more in line with the use of personal contact among select circles preferred by the Foreign Office; like Lord Northcliffe, however, he was convinced that the United States had the power to insist on its own objectives. Wiseman had been an international banker with business interests in the United States and Mexico before the war. After he was gassed in Flanders in 1915, he was assigned by the British Secret Service to intelligence work in the United States. The thirty-year-old Wiseman developed the most useful of personal contacts by establishing a father-son relationship with President Wilson's closest adviser, Col. Edward M. House. He learned that the president and House disliked the obvious propaganda of Lord Northcliffe. Colonel House preferred influence by indirection. Prominent Americans and correspondents, he believed, should go overseas and then report home stories of British sacrifice and need. Americans could promote the British case more effectively than the British themselves. House took the same line that the Roo-

11. Ibid., 109, 115; Sanders and Taylor, *British Propaganda in the First World War*, 261.

sevelt administration would take during the Second World War when he suggested that the British leave the propaganda business to the American government. President Wilson told Wiseman that the people would accept the decisions of their leaders. Wiseman thought, somewhat inaccurately, that the administration was on the side of the British and that it would educate the Congress and the public about the demands of the war.[12]

Meanwhile, Wiseman tried to educate London about American politics and power. He referred to the potential danger of Britain's being tied too openly to powerful Republican circles in New York. The intelligence officer evidently was concerned enough about London's diplomatic habits that he found it necessary to remind the Foreign Office that President Wilson was a Democrat. Wiseman urged British officials to avoid party politics and to concentrate on two tasks. First, Britain must assist the United States to mobilize quickly its matériel and manpower resources. Second, Britain had to secure agreement between the two countries on war aims and peace terms. Wiseman warned that the first, short-range objective and the second, long-range objective were interdependent; an opportunistic push for the first might endanger the second.[13]

Wiseman believed that aggressive propaganda was needed only to soothe such thorny controversies as the issue of the British Empire. The most serious imperial issue, especially for 4.5 million Irish Americans, was Ireland. In 1916 the British had suppressed the Irish rebellion known as the Easter Rising. Without the benefit of public opinion polls, Wiseman estimated that 90 percent of the American people disapproved of Britain's Irish policy. He reported to London, "The more friendly look upon it as a grave political blunder; the majority regard it as a blot on civilization." To counter American sympathies for the Irish, the British discredited one of the rebellion's leaders, cultivated Irish Americans indirectly through the Catholic church, and highlighted links between Irish leaders and the Germans. The common enemy could be used as a temporary bond between the

---

12. William Wiseman, "Notes on Interview with the President," April 1, 1918, and "The Attitude of the United States and of President Wilson towards the Peace Conference" [c. October 20, 1918], in W. B. Fowler, *British-American Relations 1917–1918: The Role of Sir William Wiseman* (Princeton: Princeton University Press, 1969), 16–18, 74, 270, 290–291.

13. Fowler, *British-American Relations*, 62–65.

United States and Britain but would not erase the friction over the British Empire.[14]

The weaknesses in British propaganda strategy revealed themselves after the armistice was signed on November 11, 1918, and the enemy could no longer be used as effectively to unite the two countries. Although American and British propagandists had worked in tandem to vilify the Germans, they had not cooperated much on postwar issues. In London to promote American war aims, the CPI's representatives complained that the president's speeches were not surviving the British censors. Charles Edward Russell found that the British were not interested in American policies. Instead, as he discovered after dining with newspaper editors, they were obsessed with forming a permanent Anglo-American league to "control the world." John Balderston reported that American liberalism might win over the "moderate Tories," but the "High Tories" only wanted to use the United States to win the war and planned to "crush all our aims and ideals at the peace conference."[15] The impressions gathered by these Wilsonian crusaders showed that British and American propagandists did not agree on what form civilization should take once barbarism had been defeated.

Indeed, President Wilson's agenda for the peace contrasted with Britain's. Wilson offered the Old World a new order outlined in the Fourteen Points: freedom of the seas, free trade, disarmament, self-determination, and the League of Nations. Britain rejected the concept of freedom of the seas even before Wilson sailed for France to attend the peace conference. At the conference, British prime minister David Lloyd George worked to protect and enlarge the British Empire and leave Germany a lesser but stable power. The Allies did agree that Germany would be demilitarized and burdened with heavy reparations. The principle of self-determination was applied somewhat haphazardly to the creation of new countries in Central and Eastern Europe. By the end of the conference, Wilson had yielded on

14. Wiseman, "Attitude of the United States and of President Wilson," in Fowler, *British-American Relations*, 292; Sanders and Taylor, *British Propaganda in the First World War*, 199; Arthur Willert, *Washington and Other Memories* (Boston: Houghton Mifflin, 1972), 69.

15. James R. Mock and Cedric Larson, *Words That Won the War: The Story of the Committee on Public Information, 1917–1919* (Princeton: Princeton University Press, 1939), 298–299.

most of his Fourteen Points, but he preserved his main goal—the League of Nations.

Back in Washington, Wiseman noted that the president appeared to be ahead of general opinion on the League of Nations. Although the American people seemed more open to experiment than the British, Wiseman observed, a "new American national spirit" might lead the United States away from international commitments. The president, who had confidently told Wiseman that the people would follow him, neglected to win support for his policies among some crucial opinion leaders, including formidable opponents in the U.S. Senate. Belatedly, Wilson took his case "to the people." On a cross-country speaking tour, he tried to turn the "new American national spirit" his way. The president assured an audience in St. Louis that American financial, industrial, and commercial strength would make the United States the "senior partner." "The other countries of the world," declared Wilson, "are looking to us for leadership and direction."[16] Instead of seeing the United States as world leader, those opposed to the peace treaty feared that the United States would be compelled to defend the interests of European empires. When the final ballot was taken in March 1920, the Senate vote fell seven short of the two-thirds needed to ratify the treaty. The United States would not be the senior partner. It would be an economic giant without political commitments to keeping the peace.

The inability of Britain and the United States to achieve Wiseman's long-term objective of agreement on war aims and peace terms reflected the two nations' divergent priorities. President Wilson's failure to obtain support for the peace treaty and the U.S. Senate's use of its ratification power to prevent the United States from joining the League of Nations highlighted the significant role of public opinion and politics in American foreign policy. Wiseman's advice that British propagandists rely on the president to lead opinion was faulty on at least two counts: the president did not want what Britain wanted; moreover, he had failed to build a consensus in support of American commitments to maintaining the postwar peace.

16. Wiseman, "Attitude of the United States and of President Wilson," in Fowler, *British-American Relations*, 295; David Dimbleby and David Reynolds, *An Ocean Apart: The Relationship between Britain and America in the Twentieth Century* (London: Hodder and Stoughton, 1988), 71–72.

Propagandists had been more successful with Lord Bryce's 5 percent of opinion leaders than with the remaining 95 percent of the public. Gilbert Parker's appeal to opinion leaders strengthened ties with the social and economic elite, particularly in the northeastern United States. Many British officials believed that the cultivation of this powerful group was all that was necessary to ensure cooperation. As Lloyd George stated in 1921: "The people who govern America are our people. They are our kith and kin. The other breeds are not on top."[17] Yet this apparent partnership between classes rather than countries had not included enough members of the U.S. Senate. The stirring theme of civilization versus barbarism had been influential in persuading Americans to enter and fight the war but had failed to translate into common interests for the peace.

Propaganda, used to mobilize and unite the public for total war, left a legacy of suspicion. When the British government admitted that an infamous wartime report of a German corpse factory where human bodies were made into fat was a fabrication, it received a warning and advice from the *Times-Dispatch* of Richmond, Virginia. "The wholesale lying on the part of trusted governments" would be remembered, stated the *Times-Dispatch* in December 1925, and "in the next war, the propaganda must be more subtle and clever."[18]

Accordingly, British propagandists in the United States in the interwar period practiced circumspection. The wartime propaganda bureau in New York was renamed the British Library of Information. The branch offices were closed down. Angus Fletcher, the director of the library, supported a policy of discretion. Fletcher wrote to London in 1928 that the term "propaganda," a "good word gone wrong," should be avoided. To the American public, it meant "falsification or distortion of facts." The library carried on Gilbert Parker's method of providing information in an "objective, scientific form." It specialized in government publications on Britain and the empire, distributed only by request, and maintained a reading room and an inter-library loan service. Its restraint led Hamilton Fish Armstrong, the editor of *Foreign Affairs*, to say the library was

17. Reynolds, *Creation of the Anglo-American Alliance*, 12.
18. Kennedy, *Over Here*, 90–92; *Times-Dispatch* quoted in Arthur Ponsonby, *Falsehood in War-Time* (New York: E. P. Dutton, 1928), 112–113.

of no use to him because he had never gotten anything he wanted from it.[19]

The library, however, was useful to the Foreign Office, supplying it with analyses of how public opinion influenced U.S. foreign policy. It reported on the U.S. Senate's ratification of the 1928 Kellogg-Briand Pact, an international agreement that renounced war. According to the library, the senators' votes depended upon their perceptions of American opinion, which, in turn, would be shaped by the conduct of the negotiations. The British, who tended to blame America's isolationism for Europe's security problems, may have shared the widely held false hope that America's interest in the pact signaled a willingness to assume international political cooperation. The U.S. secretary of state, Frank Kellogg, endorsed the pact, as did forty-six other countries, because it contained no measures for enforcement and required no commitment.[20]

The British had not given up on influencing U.S. policy, however. Sir Robert Craigie of the Foreign Office suggested that London "could utilise the better elements in the United States for the purpose of advancing our world-wide interests."[21] The close ties established during World War I between promoters of the Atlantic community persisted, especially in the New York–based Council on Foreign Relations, whose members clearly qualified as the "better elements," and in the Royal Institute for International Affairs.[22] Arthur Willert, who had left the *Times* to be the head of the Foreign Office News Department from 1921 to 1931, avoided obvious propaganda by setting up his department as a news source. He designed his press releases to put across the British position to American journalists in

19. Philip M. Taylor, *The Projection of Britain: British Overseas Publicity and Propaganda, 1919–1939* (Cambridge: Cambridge University Press, 1981), 71–72; John Wheeler-Bennett, *Special Relationships: America in War and Peace* (London: Macmillan, 1975), 74.

20. B. J. C. McKercher, *The Second Baldwin Government and the United States, 1924–1929: Attitudes and Diplomacy* (New York: Cambridge University Press, 1984), 119–120; Warren I. Cohen, *Empire without Tears: America's Foreign Relations, 1921–1933* (New York: Alfred A. Knopf, 1987), 62; Frank Costigliola, *Awkward Dominion: American Political, Economic, and Cultural Relations with Europe, 1919–1933* (Ithaca: Cornell University Press, 1984), 190–192.

21. Quoted in Costigliola, *Awkward Dominion*, 188.

22. D. C. Watt analyzes the complexities of Anglo-American elite interaction in *Succeeding John Bull: America in Britain's Place, 1900–1975* (Cambridge: Cambridge University Press, 1984). For the post–World War I period, see 40–68.

London. The British expanded their propaganda activity with the creation of the Empire Marketing Board in 1926, the British Council in 1934, and the British Broadcasting Corporation's (BBC) Empire Service in 1932 and Foreign Language Service in 1938. The United States, however, was treated as an exception and declared off limits for the agencies whose task was "the projection of Britain."[23]

While British officials attempted to dispel the legacy of suspicion, wary American politicians, journalists, and academics investigated how and why wartime propaganda had influenced the U.S. public. Initially, the investigation had focused on German activities. In 1919, the Military Intelligence Branch of the U.S. Army published a study that defined propaganda as a "form of invisible, almost inaudible gas attack, either directly upon the trenches or far back of the line."[24] The study listed German attempts to exploit anti-British attitudes among Irish Americans and "Hindus" (the term commonly and inaccurately used by Americans at the time to refer to all the people of the Indian subcontinent), to make African Americans "resentful and disloyal," and to cause a feud between labor and capital "far back of the line" in the United States. The Senate conducted an investigation in 1918–1919 on "Brewing and Liquor Interests and German Bolshevik Propaganda," which neatly linked the perceived enemies of the United States as the war ended and the Red Scare and Prohibition began. These early postwar analyses described a form of propaganda that, in the tradition of the outside agitator, was responsible for social unrest.

In the twenties and thirties, analysts of World War I propaganda focused on Britain's success with the insiders rather than the outsiders of American society. In *Mein Kampf*, Adolf Hitler contributed to Britain's reputation for winning over the majority of American opinion by praising the ruthlessness and brilliance of its appeal to the "primitive sentiments of the masses."[25] On Capitol Hill, Senator Ger-

23. For instance, the Foreign Office requested that since Anglo-American relations were so important, the BBC should avoid any program that appeared to be aimed at the United States; Taylor, *The Projection of Britain*, 75. The development of a permanent public relations machinery in Whitehall is discussed in Mariel Grant, *Propaganda and the Role of the State in Inter-War Britain* (Oxford: Clarendon Press, 1994).

24. Military Intelligence Branch, Executive Division, General Staff, U.S. Army, *Propaganda in Its Military and Legal Aspects* (1919), 3.

25. Adolf Hitler, *Mein Kampf* (Boston: Houghton Mifflin, 1971), 183.

ald Nye of North Dakota investigated connections among arms manufacturers, J. P. Morgan, Jr. (the Wall Street financier who had served
as Britain's purchasing agent), and American entry into the war. The
Depression-era hearings concluded that the munitions interests fostered war, arms races, and imperialism in the quest for profits. American scholars, for the most part, viewed British propaganda as a
contributing but not the sole cause of American intervention in
World War I.[26]

The conclusion that propaganda could be used to manipulate the
American public raised concern over the role of citizen participation
in a democratic political system. In 1937 a group of academics organized the Institute for Propaganda Analysis, funded by the Boston
merchant-millionaire E. A. Filene. Evidently, Filene, fearful of the
power of propaganda, wanted Americans "to learn how to think."
The institute's monthly newsletter, circulated to educators, students,
publishers, journalists, businessmen, trade unionists, ministers, and
welfare workers, described how to recognize and evaluate propaganda. These scholars assumed that the American public could learn
to detect the devices of propaganda through rational and scientific
scrutiny.[27]

In contrast, Walter Lippmann argued in his 1922 book *Public
Opinion* that the American public was incapable of rational judgment. Lippmann, a young journalist for the progressive *New Republic*, had spent the war working first on President Wilson's secret

26. See Walter Millis, *Road to War: America, 1914–1917* (Boston: Houghton Mifflin, 1935); H. C. Peterson, *Propaganda for War: The Campaign against Neutrality,
1914–1917* (Norman: University of Oklahoma Press, 1939); James Duane Squires,
British Propaganda at Home and in the United States from 1914 to 1917 (Cambridge:
Harvard University Press, 1935). For an overview, see Warren I. Cohen, *The American Revisionists: The Lessons of Intervention in World War I* (Chicago: University
of Chicago Press, 1967).

27. Edward L. Bernays, *Biography of An Idea: Memoirs of a Public Relations
Counsel* (New York: Simon and Schuster, 1965), 443; the institute for Propaganda
Analysis board of directors and advisory board included Charles A. Beard, historian;
Hadley Cantril, professor of psychology, Princeton; Paul Douglas, economist, Chi-
cago; E. C. Lindeman, professor of social philosophy, New York School of Social
Work; Robert S. Lynd, sociologist, Columbia; Kirtley Mather, geologist, Harvard;
Ernest O. Melby, dean of education, Northwestern; Clyde R. Miller, professor of
education, Columbia Teachers' College; and James T. Shotwell, historian, Columbia.
Institute for Propaganda Analysis, *Propaganda Analysis: A Monthly Newsletter to
Help the Intelligent Citizen Detect and Analyze Propaganda* 1 no. 1 (New York,
October 1937).

committee planning American peace terms and then as a propagandist promoting those terms in Europe. His experience led him to reject Wilsonianism and offer a devastating critique of democracy. Lippmann observed that people did not have access to the information they needed to make decisions in the modern world and that the information they did have was distorted by the "pictures in their heads," or stereotypes. Because democratic governments could not follow the vagaries of public opinion, he concluded, they must direct and guide that opinion. Lippmann proposed that a specialized class of objective experts evaluate issues for news organizations, instead of allowing an unreliable press to interpret events. The public's role would be limited to approving or disapproving the recommended position. Lippmann neglected to consider the problem of locating a disinterested, objective specialized class, although he referred to them as "insiders."[28]

Advertisers and public relations agents carried the analysis of public opinion and propaganda by Lippmann and others to a logical and profitable conclusion. After fully capitalizing on its opportunity in World War I to demonstrate that anything from war bonds to enlistment could be sold successfully, the advertising industry burgeoned in the interwar years. Advertising experts warned against overrating the intelligence of the American public. James Davis Wolff, vice-president of one of the largest agencies, the J. Walter Thompson Company, based his advertising rules on the conviction that it was "nearly impossible for the nether nine-tenths to do critical thinking." Textbooks instructed advertisers to appeal to the customer's emotions, the irrational, and the subconscious. A 1940 book advised, "Don't sell the steak—sell the sizzle." Advertisers, unlike the worried democrats of the Institute for Propaganda Analysis, did not stress the rational approach to making choices. Given these criteria, the trade journal *Advertising and Selling* in 1948 rated the Nazis' propaganda chief, Joseph Goebbels, "the most successful advertising man of our time."[29]

28. Walter Lippmann, *Public Opinion* (New York: Free Press, 1965), 19. For a discussion of *Public Opinion* and its sequel, *The Phantom Public*, see Ronald Steel, *Walter Lippmann and the American Century* (Boston: Little, Brown, 1980), 171–185, 211–219.

29. Frederick Irion, *Public Opinion and Propaganda* (New York: Thomas Y. Crowell, 1952), 55, 190–193; Roland Marchand, *Advertising the American Dream:*

Closer to the style of propaganda to be practiced by the British in World War II was the new field of public relations. The legendary Edward L. Bernays, the nephew of Sigmund Freud and a veteran of the CPI, coined the term to replace the word "propaganda," which he believed had to be discarded after being tarnished by the kaiser and the communists. He was influenced by Walter Lippmann's analysis and others whose book titles speak for themselves: *Instincts of the Herd*, *Behavior of Crowds*, and *Man, the Puppet: The Art of Controlling Minds*. Publicity, as Bernays defined it, was a one-way street attracting public interest. Public relations, on the other hand, was a two-way street requiring business to adjust to popular demand and the public to be persuaded to purchase new products or services.[30] Public relations counsellors used opinion surveys to determine popular preferences and endorsements by "experts" or celebrities as well as favorable poll results to promote a product. Bernays echoed James Bryce's earlier observation on the curious manner of shaping opinion in the United States. According to Bryce, the statesman tested his views on the public. According to Bernays, the businessman tested his product on the public. Before the statesman and businessman took a position, their views or product had to pass the test of public approval.

These developments in the theory and practice of mass persuasion in the United States would both inspire and caution British propagandists in World War II. First, it was assumed that public opinion was powerful. In the 1937 debut issue of the journal *Public Opinion Quarterly*, the editors defined mass opinion as "the final determinant of political and economic action."[31] Second, politicians, academics, and the advertising industry agreed that public opinion could be manipulated. Advertisers and public relations counsellors who viewed

Making Way for Modernity, 1920–1940 (Berkeley: University of California Press, 1986), 9–13.

30. Bernays, *Biography of an Idea*, 287–291, 299.

31. The quotation is from: "Always the opinions of relatively small publics have been a prime force in political life, but now, for the first time in history, we are confronted nearly everywhere by mass opinion as the final determinant of political and economic action." *Public Opinion Quarterly*'s editor was DeWitt Clinton Poole; Harwood L. Childs was managing editor; the associate editors included Hadley Cantril of Princeton, Harold Lasswell of Chicago, E. Pendleton Herring of Harvard, and O. W. Riegel of Washington and Lee. "Editorial Foreword," *Public Opinion Quarterly* 1 (January 1937), 3.

people as consumers embraced the notion of public gullibility. The academics and politicians who saw people as citizens looked to education, investigation, and guidance as protection from propaganda. Political analysts noted the dangers to democracy of manipulative leaders and susceptible publics. Indeed, the apparent success with which the governments of fascist Italy, Nazi Germany, and Soviet Russia wielded propaganda as a tool of state power enhanced those apprehensions. Third, ideas about the effectiveness of appeals to reason and emotion would inform preferences for the discreet tradition of persuasion favored by the Foreign Office or the more aggressive propaganda advocated by the Ministry of Information. In his 1938 book *Propaganda in the Next War*, British writer Sidney Rogerson predicted correctly that his government would use the theme of "democracy versus dictatorship" to rouse support.[32] As propagandists were well aware, that theme would have to be delivered in a convincing manner, respectful of the traditions of democratic citizenship.

The apprehension with which Britain and the United States viewed the revisionist countries—Germany, Italy, and Japan—was not enough to unite the two. Prime Minister Neville Chamberlain tried to "do business" with Adolf Hitler through appeasement. President Franklin Roosevelt pressed for a stronger stand against the Nazi leader but offered no guarantee of assistance. To Chamberlain, American support meant American economic domination of the empire, and in any event, the United States could not be relied upon. His view seemed to be borne out by the neutrality legislation passed by Congress. Prompted by the munitions hearings, the Neutrality Acts, passed in 1935 and 1936, prohibited the export of arms and loans to any country at war.[33]

In the months following the Munich crisis of 1938, when British and French leaders attempted to appease Hitler by allowing Germany to seize part of Czechoslovakia, policymakers raised the question of whether a more extensive propaganda campaign should be intro-

---

32. Sidney Rogerson, *Propaganda in the Next War* (London: B. Bles, 1938). Rogerson's book had few fans in the Foreign Office, particularly after isolationist Senator Gerald Nye had a portion of it reprinted in the *Congressional Record*. See Lothian to FO, October 9, 1939, FO 371/22842 A7647/7631/45, and Minute by Cowell, February 12, 1940, FO371/24227 A1073/26/45, PRO.

33. C. A. MacDonald, *The United States, Britain, and Appeasement, 1936–1939* (New York: St. Martin's Press, 1981), 179–182; Wayne S. Cole, *Senator Gerald P. Nye and American Foreign Relations* (Minneapolis: University of Minnesota Press, 1962), 97–123.

duced in the United States. The British ambassador in Washington, Sir Ronald Lindsay, and the staff at the British Library argued that discretion should be maintained, especially when other foreign countries were increasing their propaganda. American opinion, they believed, would prefer the country that did the least. The British Library's Angus Fletcher recommended that personal friendships should be cultivated with American journalists, photographers, filmmakers, and such broadcasters as Edward R. Murrow of the Columbia Broadcasting System (CBS). American news organizations, Fletcher observed, were extremely jealous of their independence. The British should be aware of this and learn how American journalists worked, in order to be "ready to help."[34] The Foreign Office acted on these recommendations by enlarging the British Library and providing all possible assistance to American media representatives in London.

In the late thirties, British royalty captured American public attention. Probably the more sensational event for the American public, unplanned by propagandists, was the abdication crisis of Edward VIII in 1936. The love affair between the king and the twice-divorced American Wallis Simpson was one of the major news stories of the thirties and, according to David Culbert, "the first time radio listeners in large numbers paid attention to a foreign crisis as it happened." A Hearst newspaper's declaration that the royal marriage would lead to "beneficial cooperation between the English-speaking countries" did not move the British government to look with favor on the king's choice. His Majesty's government did plan two events in 1939 aimed at popular opinion, which it thought were highly successful. At the New York World's Fair, the British Pavilion exhibited the crown jewels, a film of George VI's coronation, the Magna Carta, and the English pedigree of George Washington. In the summer before the war, the first British monarch ever to visit the United States traveled to Washington and New York. It was reported widely that King George VI and Queen Elizabeth ate hot dogs and baked beans at the Roosevelt home in Hyde Park.[35] The attention to the affairs of kings

34. Angus Fletcher, "Report from the British Library of Information on British Propaganda in the United States," November 25, 1938, FO395/656 P368/151/150, PRO.
35. David Holbrook Culbert, *News for Everyman: Radio and Foreign Affairs in Thirties America* (Westport, Conn.: Greenwood Press, 1976), 18; Robert Hathaway, *Great Britain and the United States: Special Relations since World War II* (Boston:

and queens, the crown jewels, and George Washington's family tree celebrated the common heritage between the two countries. These events, however, focused on the past rather than on the present or the future. With the world again on the brink of war, following years of a debilitating economic depression, the British chose representative symbols of wealth and privilege that attracted attention but did not necessarily signify solidarity between Americans and Britons.

Robert Bruce Lockhart, a well-traveled British civil servant and writer, suggested that the Foreign Office might have to revise some of its assumptions about American opinion. Lockhart, who later headed the Political Warfare Executive, which was in charge of propaganda to enemy countries, toured the United States as a lecturer in the spring of 1939. The average American audience, he concluded, was better informed about Europe than the average British audience and would rather hear news from an American observer than from a European. Second, he warned London to beware of the misconception that the British understood the Americans because they spoke the same language.[36] Lockhart's conclusions were unusual. British officials seldom compared the general American public to the British public. They seemed to use some other standard that left the Americans with a rating of abysmal ignorance. He also gently hinted that His Majesty's government needed to educate itself about the United States, common language notwithstanding.

All in all, Anglo-American relations were not close at the outbreak of war. The economic nationalism of the Depression and the uncertainty over the policies of appeasement and neutrality intensified the two nations' differences rather than their common interests. Popular revulsion against the excesses of death and rhetoric during the First World War made both countries turn away from facing the possibility of a second. In the weeks before Hitler's armies invaded Poland, British officials hesitated to make overtures to the American public as they continued trying to live down the legacy of 1914–1918.

Twayne Publishers, 1990), 4; Dimbleby and Reynolds, *An Ocean Apart*, 114–115, 119.

36. R. B. Lockhart, April 15, 1939, FO371/22829 A3017/1292/45, PRO.

Before Pearl Harbor, the primary goal of British propagandists was to get the United States into the war but not at the cost of postwar cooperation. Fearful of accusations that they were conducting propaganda, Britain's policymakers adopted the "strategy of truth." They would rely on "information," the orchestrated presentation of news and events, to win U.S. support. It seemed unnecessary as well as unwise to recall too frequently the World War I theme of "civilization versus barbarism" as Nazi Germany's forces stormed through Europe. Although propagandists had carefully planned this strategy, they faced dilemma after dilemma in implementing it. Maintaining what was called the "no propaganda" policy, London officials turned, with the caution suitable to crossing a minefield, to the precedents established in World War I.

Lord Lothian, the British ambassador in Washington from August 1939 until his death in December 1940, expressed confidence that the Americans, who were ideologically opposed to Hitler, would eventually support Britain. An enthusiastic promoter of Anglo-American relations, he had been David Lloyd George's private secretary at the Versailles Peace Conference and later an experienced journalist and editor, with many connections in the United States. His optimism, however, did not lead him to conclude that influencing the Americans would be easy. American opinion must be monitored closely, Lothian reminded the Foreign Office, because under the U.S. Constitution, public opinion was the decisive factor in all major issues. He emphatically warned London not to enter U.S. political debates. Americans resented and feared foreign influence, especially that of Britain. The ambassador advocated a discreet method of persuasion, reminiscent of Gilbert Parker's cultivation of opinion leaders. Britain, he asserted, should use "intelligently directed publicity of the true facts."[37]

The Ministry of Information adopted the "strategy of truth" with the goal, as stated by the historian E. H. Carr, then working at the MOI, of creating a belief in Britain's military, economic, and moral strength. One of the flaws in Carr's strategy was the failure of the truth to illustrate strength. Very little could be done with such stark

---

37. David Reynolds, *Lord Lothian and Anglo-American Relations, 1939–1940* (Philadelphia: American Philosophical Society, 1982), 3–4; Lothian to Halifax, September 28, 1939, FO371/22839 A7053/7052/45, PRO.

events as the German blitzkrieg that swept through western Europe, the retreat of the Allies to Dunkirk, the fall of France in June 1940, and Britain's inability to defend its Pacific bases or purchase American supplies. Faced with facts like these, propagandists proffered a belief that Britain was strong enough to win the war with aid from the United States, that Britain and the United States had a common cause, and that a better world would emerge from the war. In June 1940 the new prime minister, Winston Churchill, declared that Britain would fight on "until, in God's good time, the New World, with all its power and might, steps forth to the rescue and the liberation of the Old."[38] Eloquence and declarations of faith embellished the "strategy of truth."

Among policymakers there was some question as to whether a low-key, factual approach would work in the United States. Sir Stafford Cripps, the socialist politician who, in May 1940, was about to become ambassador to Moscow, believed, like many of his compatriots, that Americans were essentially an emotional people. He advised that the main theme of British propaganda should be one of Anglo-American partnership in building a new world. Once Americans saw themselves in this light, Cripps assured Foreign Secretary Halifax, they would, "when the need arises, be easily led into the paths that are necessary for the implementation of common work." The view that Americans were emotional and easily led might have comforted Cripps, but it worried British officials, who feared that their quiet propaganda might be overwhelmed by ingenious German methods. Harold Nicolson, former diplomat, historian, and in 1940, parliamentary secretary to the Ministry of Information, hoped that, if patient and cautious, the British would win in the end. But Nicolson knew that some British observers of the United States were anxious that the methods of Hitler and Goebbels might succeed in exploiting the conflicting desires of the average American who wished to stay out of the war.[39]

38. E. H. Carr to Balfour, January 2, 1940, FO371/25174 W3839/3839/49; MOI report on joint meeting of the American Department (FO) and the American Division (MOI) on policy of publicity in the United States, April 24, 1941, FO371/26183 A2934/118/45, PRO; "Wars are not won by evacuation," June 4, 1940, Winston S. Churchill, *Winston S. Churchill: His Complete Speeches*, vol. 6, ed. Robert Rhodes James (New York: Chelsea House Publishers, 1974), 6231.
39. Cripps to Halifax, May 4, 1940, FO371/24229 3152/26/45, PRO; Nicolson

The U.S. government, which appeared to be unemotionally cal-culating Britain's ability to survive an invasion, responded slowly with an exchange of old destroyers for the use of British bases in September 1940. The deal took four months to negotiate. London tried generosity and blackmail, while Washington wondered how long it could wait and how much it could get.[40] Following President Roosevelt's election for a third term, Lord Lothian returned to the United States with bad news. The ambassador announced at a press conference at LaGuardia airport that Britain was "bust."[41] Churchill sent a long note detailing Britain's desperate need for planes and weapons. FDR declared that the United States must assist Britain by lending it supplies. In January 1941 the Lend-Lease bill was intro-duced in Congress as H.R. 1776, "An Act to Promote the Defense of the United States." The Americans drove a hard bargain over terms but provided loans and credits under the Lend-Lease agreement of March 1941. Opponents warned that Britain would again trick the Americans into fighting its war, but the United States had already abandoned neutrality.

As doubts about Britain's survival grew, the "no propaganda" pol-icy came under criticism in London by some who charged that not enough was being done to obtain American support. In response, Da-vid Scott, the Foreign Office undersecretary in charge of the American Department, described Britain's propaganda policy: "It is entirely wrong to define it as no propaganda whatever, or to think that a great deal of what is really propaganda (though we don't call it that openly) has not always been done in the United States. Lord Lothian and the Foreign Office have always advocated propaganda right up to the point where it begins to defeat its own object by making Americans

to Lippmann, January 20, 1940, Group 326, Series III, Box 93, Folder 1614, Walter Lippmann Papers, Manuscripts and Archives, Yale University Library, New Haven, Conn.

40. James R. Leutze, *Bargaining for Supremacy: Anglo-American Naval Cooper-ation, 1937–1941* (Chapel Hill: University of North Carolina, 1977), 72–73.

41. John Wheeler-Bennett wrote that Lothian told the American press, "Well, boys, Britain's broke, it's your money we want." According to David Reynolds, Aubrey Morgan of the British Press Service remembered that Lothian said Britain was bust, but he did not state quite so baldly that Britain wanted American money. The *New York Times* reported that Lothian asked for help: "England needs planes, munitions, ships and perhaps a little financial help"; see Reynolds, *Lord Lothian and Anglo-American Relations*, 48.

hostile or suspicious."[42] In other words, the British called their propaganda "no propaganda" and maintained what later would be called public "deniability." However much they were tempted to abandon the "strategy of truth," the British followed in the tradition of Gilbert Parker and William Wiseman by relying on the informational approach to support and influence the work of American opinion leaders who made and guided American public opinion.

American war correspondents had a high demand for news and information; London had some difficulty maintaining the supply. During the Battle of Britain, the ominous struggle between the Royal Air Force and the Luftwaffe, the "strategy of truth" ran into a roadblock—censorship. On one side was the Foreign Office and the MOI, which needed to provide their American clients with background information. On the other stood the military services, which argued that the publication of information risked lives, hurt operations, and aided the enemy. In August 1940, Lothian reported from Washington that German and British communiqués were so contradictory, Americans believed both sides were lying. He suggested showing American correspondents inside sources. Alexander Cadogan, the permanent undersecretary of the Foreign Office, noted that Britain's admissions of damage had not been completely honest nor did he think they should be. When Thomas North Whitehead of the Foreign Office asked A. V. Alexander, the First Lord of the Admiralty, for a more generous treatment of the American press, Alexander answered that he hoped he "would never live to see the Navy going in for cheap advertisement like the Air Force."[43] In addition to their concern about aiding the enemy, the services were reluctant to break with tradition. The propagandists saw their "strategy of truth" and openness being undermined.

The foreign secretary, Anthony Eden, tried to go over the heads of the services to the Cabinet by arguing that because Britain desperately needed American support, American correspondents should be allowed to tell Britain's story. At a meeting of the War Cabinet

42. Scott to R. A. Butler, March 24, 1941, FO371/26183 A2147/118/45, PRO.
43. Lothian to FO News Department and American Division (MOI), and minute by Cadogan, August 15, 1940, FO371/24231 A3799/26/45; Minute by North Whitehead, January 15, 1941, FO371/24232 A5006/26/45, PRO.

Defence Committee in May 1941, Eden and Lord Beaverbrook, the minister of state, urged that the Battle of the Atlantic should be dramatized in order to convince Americans of the seriousness of Britain's situation. They argued that restrictions on American journalists should be lifted. The prime minister and Alexander disagreed. They thought that Americans should not consider entering the war only when Britain was at its last gasp and that emphasizing the precariousness of Britain's position would depress their own people. The committee asked Eden, Beaverbrook, and Brendan Bracken, the minister of information, to produce a propaganda campaign to "influence American opinion to participate in the war." Beaverbrook, Lord Northcliffe's successor on Fleet Street and, as he had been in World War I, a believer in propaganda, arranged for American correspondents to be provided with background on the strategic situation. The foreign secretary and the service ministers would give weekly off-the-record press conferences. Beaverbrook reported to Eden that their arrangements for American journalists were as generous as the prime minister would allow.[44]

At the Ministry of Information, Sir Frederick Whyte, the head of the American Division in 1940, described his division's job as "working for the Americans here."[45] Those Americans included the top talent in the press and broadcasting. Murrow for CBS, Frederick Bate for the National Broadcasting Corporation (NBC), and John Steele for Mutual reached the hundreds of radio stations served by the three major networks. The regulars were assisted by a stream of war correspondents and visiting reporters from the United States, including Eric Sevareid and Larry Lesueur for CBS, and Frazier Hunt and James Reston of the *New York Times* for NBC. From its Washington embassy, London received advance notice of visiting dignitaries. For instance, on the eve of a visit by the dean of radio news, the NBC broadcaster H. V. (Hans von) Kaltenborn, Lothian entreated: "Be very good to him and do not mistake him for a German." Lothian was obeyed. Kaltenborn, a Milwaukee native, enjoyed a "wholly prof-

---

44. "War Cabinet Defence Committee Discussion of Propaganda in the United States," May 19, 1941, FO371/26184 A3893/118/45; Beaverbrook to Eden, May 27, 1941, FO371/26184 A4136/118/45, PRO.

45. Whyte to Lothian, January 1, 1940, FO371/24277 A709/26/45, PRO.

itable trip" because he gathered "a lot of extremely valuable information in a short time."[46]

The MOI and the Foreign Office News Department supplied news for American correspondents by arranging tours of war production facilities, areas hit by bombing raids, coastal defenses, and ports. The goal of the tours was to provide the Americans with stories showing Britain's determination and capacity to withstand invasion, thanks to material assistance from the United States. On one tour, for example, correspondents flew in American-built Lockheed planes stationed at the coastal command aerodrome in Norfolk. One of their young pilots praised his plane's ability to take punishment and still get home. On another tour, Americans visited the Third Division on the Sussex coast, where they saw the beach defenses, talked with Gen. Bernard Montgomery, rode in Bren gun carriers, and had tea with the Grenadier Guards. The head of the Foreign Office News Department reported that the resulting stories were "long and full of the right stuff." For Raymond Clapper, a syndicated columnist, the MOI's Tours Section arranged a trip to a Glasgow shipyard, a bomber station in York, a Birmingham factory, a fighter squadron, and the devastated town of Coventry. Clapper thought the MOI was "swell."[47]

The BBC's American Liaison Unit assisted American broadcasters in London by providing technical facilities in accordance with censorship restrictions. Scripts had to be written and checked in advance. During the broadcast, a British official sat with his finger on the "cut-out switch," which was to be used as a last resort. BBC personnel could hardly imagine any violation of the censor that would be more disastrous to British interests than deliberately cutting off an American broadcaster in the middle of a talk to the United States. They

---

46. Kaltenborn was the son of Baron Rudolph von Kaltenborn, a Hessian guards officer who came to America in protest against Prussia's absorption of Hesse, and a Wisconsin schoolteacher. His pioneering around-the-clock coverage of the Munich crisis in September 1938 won him acclaim and brought the radio prestige as a news medium. BBC monthly reports on broadcasts to the United States, FO371/24230 A3288/26/45; Lothian to Scott, April 16, 1940, FO371/24230 A3369/26/45, PRO; Hans von Kaltenborn Papers, U.S. Mss. 1AF, Box 217, State Historical Society of Wisconsin, Madison, Wis.

47. Minute by North Whitehead, June 18, 1940, and minute by Ridsdale, July 6, 1940, FO371/24230 A3464/26/45, PRO; Personal File Foreign Travel 1941, Raymond Clapper Papers, Library of Congress, Washington, D.C.

thought it embarrassing enough that at the New York end, all American broadcasts from London were identified as subject to censorship. Roger Eckersley, the head of the American Liaison Unit, asked John Steele, the London representative of Mutual, if the practice was really necessary, since it aroused suspicion about the content of the news broadcasts. Steele replied that the policy applied to all broadcasts from abroad and offered little hope that the network would change its rules.[48]

The Liaison Unit at times pressed the censors for looser restrictions on war correspondents. One of its most successful efforts was getting permission for Murrow to report each night from the roof of Broadcasting House during bombing raids on London. Murrow's terse narrative of destruction conveyed to American audiences the nature of the war being endured by the British people. The BBC took great care not to push the Americans to present the British case. They did not have to. In the months from June 1940 through the heavy bombing of September, American broadcasters shifted from neutrality to an ever-closer identification with the British.[49]

The MOI, the BBC, and the Americans were partners in getting out the story of Britain at war. The MOI worked ceaselessly behind the scenes to make tours possible despite air raids, blackouts, severe rationing, and limited transportation. The Americans in turn reported on the suffering and courage of the British people. Propagandists knew that the Blitz made sensational copy for American audiences; at the same time, they wondered if they or their country would survive it. Through the fall of 1940, they viewed with bewilderment and despair the United States's failure to take up the fight. Many of the Americans who lived through the Blitz with them sympathized. Almost as wary as the British were of being accused of propaganda, American journalists strove to maintain objectivity in their reporting.[50] They assured the British that reporting the news straight was the best way to reach the American audience. Their

48. Eckersley to Steele, November 18, 1940, and Steele to Eckersley, November 19, 1940, BBC WAC, R61/2 Censorship Procedure and American Liaison Unit, 1939–1944.

49. A. M. Sperber, *Murrow: His Life and Times* (New York: Freundlich Books, 1986), 174; Eckersley, BBC monthly reports on broadcasts to the United States, May to November 1940, FO371/24230 A3288/26/45, PRO.

50. Clapper to John Biggers, September 15, 1941, Container 9, Clapper Papers.

reports made the war vivid and immediate, the issues at stake clear and simple for the audience at home.

In contrast to their colleagues in London, British propagandists across the Atlantic found that the issues were not clear and simple and that many Americans were not sympathetic. The British viewed the "American front" as divided into three camps. At one extreme were the isolationists, and at the other were the interventionists. The British considered the first group enemies, the second group friends. In the middle was the majority of the population, who were neither. The British hoped to influence this middle group to shift to the interventionist position. At the beginning of the war, the American public showed overwhelming sympathy for Britain, France, and China, but a majority thought it was more important for the United States to stay out of the European war than to ensure the defeat of the Axis powers. During the Battle of Britain, opinion polls registered a shift. Americans thought it was more important to ensure Britain's victory than to stay out, and they approved aid to Britain. From the summer of 1940 on, a majority of Americans believed that it was more important for Germany to be defeated than for the United States to stay out of war. When asked directly, however, if the United States should declare war on the Axis powers, a consistent 80 percent answered no.[51] A majority of Americans supported the Allies against Hitler and approved of aid, but they did not want to go to war. These contradictory results provided ammunition for both isolationists and interventionists.

"Isolationist" was a label applied to people of all political persuasions who opposed U.S. involvement in the war. Isolationists supported the defense of the western hemisphere and argued that the United States was safe from European wars. Some isolationists feared that a war would bring an end to New Deal reforms. Others worried that in war the president, the military, and big business would acquire too much power. Isolationism tended to be stronger in the Midwest and weaker in the South, stronger in the Republican Party and weaker in the Democratic Party, stronger in rural areas than in

51. "The Need for Better Publicity in the United States," June 11, 1941, FO371/26184 A4063/118/45, PRO; Wayne S. Cole, *Roosevelt and the Isolationists, 1932–1945* (Lincoln: University of Nebraska Press, 1983), 11; Gallup, *Gallup Poll*, 133–257.

urban, stronger among women than men, stronger among those with less formal education, and stronger among German, Irish, Italian, and Scandinavian ethnic groups. The America First Committee, organized in September 1940, was a dominant voice of the isolationist movement. Under the chairmanship of Gen. Robert Wood of Sears and Roebuck, its most important speakers were Republican senator Gerald Nye of North Dakota, Democratic senator Burton K. Wheeler of Montana, and Charles Lindbergh, the aviator hero.[52] Both Republicans and Democrats carried nonintervention statements in their party platforms but for the 1940 election nominated internationalist candidates: Wendell Willkie, a Wall Street Republican, and Franklin Roosevelt, the incumbent and a Democrat.

The most important figure on the internationalist-interventionist side was President Roosevelt. Once re-elected for his third term, he set out to undercut the isolationists' position. Throughout 1941 the president moved the United States from a position of nonbelligerent ally to a state of undeclared war. At the ABC (American-British-Canadian) talks concluded in the spring of 1941, the future allies agreed to concentrate their forces on defeating Germany first. By the summer, the U.S. Navy had established a convoy and escort system across the Atlantic. American troops occupied Iceland. As the United States inched its way into war, German forces invaded the Soviet Union on June 22. The Germans made spectacular advances and within a month were 130 miles from Moscow. The Russians suffered tremendous losses but held on. Recognizing that the attack on Russia postponed Hitler's invasion of Britain, Churchill offered immediate assistance to the Soviet premier, Joseph Stalin. The United States, more reluctantly, extended Lend-Lease to the enemy of its enemy. In August, Roosevelt and Churchill reached a major agreement on war aims, known as the Atlantic Charter. Although the agreement was not the hoped-for declaration of war, Churchill and others viewed the charter as an implicit commitment of Anglo-American cooperation in the making of the war and the planning of the peace. The charter called for self-determination, freedom of the seas, and an open economic system. To the last point, the British added the clause "with due respect for existing obligations," to protect its imperial

---

52. Cole, *Roosevelt and the Isolationists*, 8, 379–381; Manfred Jonas, *Isolationism in America, 1935–1941* (Ithaca: Cornell University Press, 1966), 70–99.

preference system. This exception, along with Churchill's claim that self-determination applied only to territories under Axis domination and not to the British Empire, reminded observers that underneath the new closeness, old rivalries festered.[53]

FDR took an indirect approach to influencing opinion on foreign affairs. He shunned making statements that would tie him to specific policies. In the tradition of the New Deal "alphabet agencies," he set up a series of poorly funded, overlapping information offices.[54] Much of his energy went into working closely behind the scenes with private internationalist groups to influence opinion. Most likely, he expected the British to follow a similar tactic. Roosevelt sympathized with Britain, but he did not support a full-fledged foreign propaganda campaign in the United States. The president's closest aide, Harry Hopkins, apparently told the British on a visit to London in July 1941 that any propaganda by them was unnecessary because the president would take care of it.[55]

Roosevelt's benevolent lack of enthusiasm for Britain's propaganda efforts heightened British concern that their propaganda be unobjectionable. The president knew what the British were doing. John Wheeler-Bennett, a historian turned propagandist, recorded his exchange with Roosevelt, whose son was one of Wheeler-Bennett's students, at the University of Virginia commencement in June 1940: " 'What are you doing now?' he asked. 'Well sir,' I answered, 'I'm driving to Washington to try and catch a plane out to Norman, Oklahoma. I'm due to speak at the University there tomorrow morn-

53. Waldo Heinrichs, *Threshold of War: Franklin D. Roosevelt and American Entry into World War II* (New York: Oxford University Press, 1988), 206; Reynolds, *Creation of the Anglo-American Alliance*, 259.

54. Richard W. Steele, *Propaganda in an Open Society: The Roosevelt Administration and the Media, 1933–1941* (Westport, Conn.: Greenwood Press, 1985), 125. These agencies included the Office of Government Reports, headed by Lowell Mellett in September 1939; the Division of Information of the Office of Emergency Management, headed by Scripps-Howard editor Robert Horton in March 1941; the Office of Civilian Defense, headed by New York mayor Fiorello LaGuardia in the spring of 1941; and the Office of Facts and Figures, under Archibald MacLeish in October 1941. International agencies included Nelson Rockefeller's Coordination of Inter-American Affairs in August 1940; Col. William Donovan's Office of Coordinator of Information and its adjunct, the Foreign Information Services, under Robert Sherwood, in the summer of 1941. Winkler, *Politics of Propaganda*, 20–27.

55. G. Campbell to Radcliffe, January 10, 1942, FO371/30667 A446/399/45, PRO.

ing.' He smiled again. 'Propaganda, I suppose?' 'We call it information, Mr. President,' I answered and he laughed with that leonine backthrow of the head." Roosevelt limited his direct assistance to such small acts as ensuring that Wheeler-Bennett caught his plane to Oklahoma by inviting him to join the presidential motorcade from Charlottesville to the Washington airport.[56]

President Roosevelt's public position—all aid to Britain short of war—was promoted by the internationalists. The first major group, the Committee to Defend America by Aiding the Allies, also known as the White Committee in honor of its popular chair, the Kansas editor William Allen White, formed in the spring of 1940. The White Committee pressed for the passage of Lend-Lease in early 1941. The Century Group, closely connected to the Council on Foreign Relations, organized in the summer of 1940 to push for assistance to Britain and rearmament in the United States. Some of the group's leading members were Herbert Agar, editor of the *Louisville Courier-Journal*; Dr. Henry P. Van Dusen of Union Theological Seminary; and Henry Luce, the publisher of *Time*, *Life*, and *Fortune* magazines. The Fight for Freedom Committee, organized in April 1941, urged U.S. intervention in the war. Fight for Freedom had close ties to the White House through Harry Hopkins and Stephen Early, the press secretary.[57]

The American front was highly charged. Like America First, internationalist and interventionist groups organized local chapters, held rallies and parades, and lobbied American leaders and the public. Opinion leaders on both sides of the debate argued that democracy was in peril. The rest of the public continued to prefer to stay out of the war. At official levels in Washington, Anglo-American relations turned into a bustling enterprise of purchasing missions, military delegations, and diplomatic exchanges.[58] As for propaganda, the British improvised. They drew on existing organizations, created new ones, collected and discarded personnel.

The British expanded the capacity of the British Library of Information by setting up the British Press Service (BPS) in New York in

---

56. Wheeler-Bennett, *Special Relationships*, 97.
57. Mark Lincoln Chadwin, *The War Hawks of World War II* (Chapel Hill: University of North Carolina Press, 1968), 22, 44, 159; Cole, *Roosevelt and the Isolationists*, 469.
58. Heinrichs, *Threshold of War*, 19.

October 1940 to provide news and background to the American media. The staff included Aubrey Morgan, a Welsh Liberal and businessman, who surveyed the press. Morgan, married to Constance
Morrow, was the son-in-law of Dwight Morrow, a partner in the
Morgan bank and a former U.S. ambassador to Mexico, and the
brother-in-law of Charles and Anne Morrow Lindbergh. Apparently,
family relations suffered some strain, but as Anne Morrow Lindbergh
recorded in her diary, the bridges remained open. She respected Morgan's vibrant commitment to his cause. Her sister Constance put in
long hours at the British Press Service and found time to mother her
own children as well as three young Englishmen of Morgan's staff
who slept on her sofas and were in and out at all hours.[59] John
Wheeler-Bennett was in charge of the research section. Isaiah Berlin,
an Oxford professor, handled Jewish and labor issues. By April 1941
the BPS had a dedicated staff of eighty, with thirty volunteers. The
offices were open and accessible to American journalists twenty-four
hours a day, seven days a week.[60]

   While the overt propagandists praised Anglo-American accord,
covert propagandists took on the task of discrediting anti-British activity. The British Security Coordination (BSC), using the cover name
of British Passport Control at Rockefeller Center in New York, protected British shipping from sabotage, engaged in counterespionage,
and trained agents. In World War I, the British secret service had
targeted German, Irish, and Indian sympathizers as anti-British; from
1939 to 1941, the BSC identified prominent isolationists and America First leaders as anti-British activists. The BSC supplied J. Edgar
Hoover, the Federal Bureau of Investigation (FBI) chief, Col. William
Donovan, later head of the Office of Strategic Services, and the press
with reports, some accurate and some forged, of German fifth-
column activities and German funding of American isolationist organizations.[61] The BSC also made errors in judgment that were

---

59. Aubrey Morgan first had been married to Anne and Constance's sister Elisabeth, who died in 1934. Anne Morrow Lindbergh, *War Within and Without: Diaries
and Letters of Anne Morrow Lindbergh, 1939–1944* (New York: Harcourt Brace
Jovanovich, 1980), 105, 333–335.
   60. Memo by Peake, April–May 1941, FO371/26184 A3352/118/45, PRO; Isaiah
Berlin, interview with author, Washington, D.C., November 10, 1988. For a lively
account of British propaganda efforts in the United States prior to Pearl Harbor, see
Nicholas John Cull, *Selling War: The British Propaganda Campaign against American
Neutrality in World War II* (New York: Oxford University Press, 1995).
   61. H. Montgomery Hyde, *Room 3603: The Story of the British Intelligence Cen-*

harmful to the spirit of cooperation the MOI and BPS had toiled to create. For instance, the BSC wanted one of its critics, Assistant Secretary of State Adolf Berle, Jr., removed from the State Department. When the FBI discovered a BSC agent attempting to damage Berle's reputation, the bureau ordered him to leave the country. The extent and effectiveness of the BSC's covert propaganda is difficult to gauge, but certain attentions from the FBI were clearly undesirable.[62]

In July 1941 those who had been pressing for an expansion of the British propaganda network finally overcame the proponents of extreme caution. The New York–based BPS established branch offices in Washington, Chicago, and San Francisco. Its goal, stated privately by its head, Sir Gerald Campbell, the British consul general in New York, was to get the United States into the war. Given the limitations of not being able to do anything that looked like propaganda, on the one hand, and the vastness of the country they were supposed to influence on the other, it was more important than ever to use American channels. British propagandists strengthened contacts with the media, relied upon internationalist and interventionist groups, and tentatively approached other organized groups, such as civic clubs, labor unions, and churches.[63]

Propagandists also cultivated sympathetic American opinion leaders in the media. National radio broadcasters included Raymond Gram Swing of the Mutual Network, Kaltenborn of NBC, and Edwin C. Hill of CBS. Prominent journalists included Dorothy Thompson, an outspoken anti-Nazi who wrote for the *New York Herald Tribune* and did radio broadcasts, and Ernest Lindley, *Newsweek*'s Washington bureau chief and a favorite columnist of the White House. Walter Lippmann worked closely with the British embassy by fulfilling the

---

ter in New York during World War II (New York: Farrar, Strauss, 1963), 3, 73; This effort complemented reports on Nazi propaganda delivered by the British Press Service to journalists and the Fight for Freedom Committee. "Fifth Column Stuff," Diaries 1940–42, Clapper Papers; British Press Service File, Fight for Freedom Committee Papers, Box 11, Seeley G. Mudd Manuscript Library, Department of Rare Books and Special Collections, Princeton University, Princeton, N.J.

62. Adolf A. Berle, *Navigating the Rapids, 1918–1971: From the Papers of Adolf A. Berle*, ed. Beatrice Bishop Berle and Travis Beal Jacobs (New York: Harcourt Brace Jovanovich, 1973), 402; Francis MacDonnell argues that the BSC successfully exploited existing American fears of German espionage and fifth column activity; Francis MacDonnell, *Insidious Foes: The Axis Fifth Column and the American Home Front* (New York: Oxford University Press, 1995), 105.

63. "Points Made by Sir Gerald Campbell in His General Talk," July 7, 1941, FO371/26187 A6243/118/45, PRO.

role of the "insider" expert he had defined in *Public Opinion*. His syndicated column, "Today and Tomorrow," was estimated to have 8 million readers. In March 1941 Lippmann asked Lothian's successor, Lord Halifax, what he thought would be "the most useful direction in which to prepare public opinion for the next race now that the Lend-Lease bill was through." Halifax suggested that an important issue was convoys and the use of American air pilots; he urged that Lippmann "keep it up" on the promotion of cooperative financial relations. Thomas North Whitehead, the Foreign Office's American expert, called this circle of support a "well oiled '100% American' propaganda machine" and claimed it as a triumph of Britain's "no propaganda" policy.[64]

In the search for unobjectionable methods of reaching regional and local audiences, the BPS turned to civic organizations known to welcome free speakers. Along with universities, John Wheeler-Bennett listed women's clubs and other service clubs—Knights of Columbus, Rotary, Lions, Kiwanis, Elks, and Shriners—as "professional listeners." From September 1939 to December 1941, Wheeler-Bennett spoke on why Britain was at war to these audiences in thirty-seven out of the forty-eight states. He recalled vividly the standard luncheon menu of "fruit cocktail, chicken with a green salad topped off with a round of tinned pineapple with a ball of Philadelphia cream-cheese in the hole in the middle," ice cream, ice water, and very weak coffee. He also recalled friendly receptions. At some point, most of those employed in the British propaganda network spoke at an American club meeting. A midwestern Lions Club astonished Isaiah Berlin by roaring its applause. Roger Makins, a British diplomat and later ambassador to the United States, reported that the best he and his fellow speakers could do was to leave the audience "with the feeling that they heard a guy from the British Embassy who seemed a good sort of a guy and had a fine message."[65] Although they did not expect to achieve far-reaching results, British officials attempted to expand on the dinner-party rapport reached with social elites during the First World War by adding luncheons with the American middle class.

---

64. Halifax to Churchill, March 13, 1941, PREM 4 27/9; North Whitehead, June 3, 1940, FO371/24229 A3183/26/45, PRO.

65. Wheeler-Bennett, *Special Relationships*, 81–82; Graham Hutton, interview with author, August 17, 1988, London, Eng.; Roger Makins on his trip to the Middle West, April 3, 1945, FO371/44614 AN1171/152/45, PRO.

Ernest Bevin, the minister of labor and a member of the War Cabinet, urged that British foreign policy must change to stress a commitment to the well-being of working-class people if Britain wished to remain a world leader after the war. The former general secretary of the Transport and General Workers' Union provided the Foreign Office with a list of American union leaders to contact. In New York, Isaiah Berlin monitored labor organizations. He met with William Green, the president of the nation's premier union, the American Federation of Labor (AFL), but not with John L. Lewis of the Congress of Industrial Organizations (CIO). Berlin considered Lewis an enemy because the charismatic labor leader had taken an isolationist position and opposed Roosevelt for re-election in 1940. London sent over carefully selected representatives of British labor to court American workers. Sir Walter Citrine, the president of the International Federation of Trade Unions, was instructed to explain how democratic and unified the social structure of Britain had become. The Welsh miner and labor leader John Jones toured the United States with a message that would become a cornerstone of British propaganda. The war, Jones declared, was "a people's war against Hitler, not a war against capital."[66]

The major organized religions were the target of the MOI's message about the moral values at stake. Five hundred Protestant leaders and editors received a weekly bulletin on the spiritual issues of the war. The *Christian Newsletter* went to 350 Protestant leaders identified as sympathetic but not enthusiastic about the British cause. Dr. Van Dusen supplied the mailing lists. American Catholics and Jews were usually treated separately. According to a report by the British Library's Robert Wilberforce, American Catholics were mostly second- or third-generation Americans, and the Church hierarchy was dominated by the Irish. Though not actively anti-British, most were passively antagonistic and tended to be isolationist. As they had done in the First World War, the British circumspectly approached Irish Americans through the Catholic church. Almost thirty-five hundred

---

66. Bevin to Halifax, December 27, 1940, and Bevin, "Note on Diplomatic Service," January 4, 1941, Reel 1, 4.12, Halifax Papers, Churchill College Library, Cambridge, Eng.; interview with Berlin; North Whitehead, October 31, 1940, FO371/24232 A4695/26/45, PRO; Minutes of steering committee meetings, Papers of American Defense, Harvard Group, November 5, 1941, HUD 3139.600, Courtesy of the Harvard University Archives.

copies of the weekly *Catholic Newsletter* were sent to Catholic leaders and editors. The newsletters were not labeled as productions of
the MOI. At the BPS in New York, Isaiah Berlin worked with Jewish
leaders, who were mostly, he found, pro-Roosevelt and pro-war. Berlin hired an American to translate MOI material into Yiddish for the
Yiddish press.[67]

Propagandists approached American ethnic organizations with
caution and concern. London officials pictured the "native" American as white and of British origin with, as Lloyd George had put it,
"our breed on top"—a perspective familiar to many Americans.
Most of these officials knew very little about America's ethnic cultures. When the British consul in Baltimore, J. W. Taylor, presented
London with a detailed breakdown of ethnic populations by region,
income, reading habits, and literacy rates, the Foreign Office greeted
with high praise the first serious attempt at "market research" undertaken by a consular officer. Taylor reported on the number of
magazines and newspapers read by "native white families," "foreign
born white families," and "Negro families" in the southern states.
He reported that he discounted African Americans from consideration as a target audience because even though their opportunities for
education had improved, certain features of citizenship, such as voting, were not encouraged.[68]

In 1940 Taylor submitted an analysis of ethnic American groups.
Of the 33 million foreign-speaking people in the United States, 6
million lived on farms, generally on some of the more prosperous
farms. Taylor noted that unfortunately the poor sections of rural
America were inhabited largely by people of "Anglo-Celtic stock,"
which was a blow to the "our-breed-on-top" theory. Of the 6 million
German Americans, more than 1.5 million had been born in Germany. German societies and newspapers were concentrated in the
Midwest. "The German," Taylor observed, "is very slow to lose his
national feeling." The 5 million Italian Americans, of whom 1.75
million had been born in Italy, lived mostly on the East Coast and
on farms in California and Nevada. At the end of his report, he

67. Martin, "Report on the Work of the Religious Division," June 26, 1941,
FO371/26186 A5268/118/45; Wilberforce, August 16, 1939, FO395/657 P2679/151/
150, PRO; interview with Berlin.
68. Baltimore consul report, FO371/24229 A3188/26/45, PRO.

concluded that friendly foreign-born groups, such as the Poles, the Czechs, and the Finns at 1.9 million, outnumbered the enemy foreign-born population of Germans.

In London, propaganda policymakers discussed how and if ethnic groups should be used to stir up support for the Allied cause. North Whitehead insisted that it was a mistake to consider the use of ethnic groups as a question of friendly versus unfriendly foreign elements. The son of British philosopher Alfred North Whitehead and a former professor at Harvard Business School, North Whitehead was one of the few analysts in the American Department of the Foreign Office familiar with the United States. He felt it necessary to add such comments to Foreign Office minutes as "Poles in America are Americans." He noted that Americans were ashamed of the lack of integration of ethnic minorities and would resent any action by Britain to heighten non-American loyalties.[69]

The British did find a way to reach ethnic Americans when many foreign groups requested financial support for propaganda activities in the United States, especially representatives of Eastern European countries overrun by Germany or, in the case of Finland in 1940, by the Soviet Union. In accordance with the "no propaganda" policy, the Foreign Office did not want to be discovered covertly funding such groups, but it encouraged and assisted whenever possible. British propagandists did set up and largely fund the Inter-Allied Information Committee in New York in the summer of 1940. The committee organized rallies of ethnic groups in support of the war throughout the United States. The British themselves could not be caught spreading atrocity propaganda because of the lurid memories of World War I. They could, however, assist the "small Allies," such as Czechoslovakia and Poland, to tell atrocity stories on behalf of the Inter-Allied Information Committee.[70]

69. North Whitehead, November 1939, FO371/23131 A19272/27/55 and April 1940, FO371/24229 A3009/26/45, PRO. Thomas North Whitehead's investigation of American society was published in two works, *Leadership in a Free Society: A Study of Human Relations Based on an Analysis of Present-Day Industrial Civilization* (Cambridge: Harvard University Press, 1936), and *The Industrial Worker: A Statistical Study of Human Relations in a Group of Manual Workers*, vols. 1 and 2 (Cambridge: Harvard University Press, 1938).

70. Lothian to MOI, October 7, 1940, FO371/24231 A4025/26145; Donald Hall, "Propaganda among the Foreign Language Communities in the USA," February 4, 1941, FO371/26183 A609/118/45; Minute by N. Butler, September 27, 1941,

In the spring of 1940, the "no propaganda" campaign was critiqued by Rae Smith, an American advertising executive at the J. Walter Thompson Company. He described British propaganda as haphazard, with little "follow through" or "build up." The American said it failed to distinguish among groups and regions and therefore addressed no one in particular. The British were amateurish, he added, in their choice of medium, paying too much attention to the press and not enough to radio and film. Within a few weeks, Smith submitted an elaborate plan for propaganda in the United States, which he assured the Foreign Office would not alter the policy of telling the truth; it would "*emphasize* the truth" by eliminating "insignificant detail" that distorted "the deepest truth" of the present situation. He drew up a chart of the people to be interviewed on radio, such as "political names of all grades from P.M. down," "U.S.A. citizens here now," "glamourous war personalities," "prominent refugees," "ordinary refugees," "men on active service, wounded, etc.," and what they were to say. For instance, the script for the rear-gunner bomber began, "Thank God for my movable turret, I say." Smith's specific plan was never used, but he had exposed the Foreign Office to the format of a large-scale advertising campaign. He urged them to set specific goals, consider American attitudes, such as loathing of Nazism and distrust of Britain, recognize the importance of appealing to people's fears, and use timing, simplicity, imaginative artwork, and the new media, especially radio.[71]

To reach the public, the British began to turn to radio, the chief means of communication and entertainment in the daily lives of Americans. Propagandists recognized from the beginning of the war that the BBC's shortwave audience in the United States was small. Turning his marketing talents to radio, J. W. Taylor, the British consul in Baltimore, explored the options. He uncovered a survey conducted by NBC that put the shortwave audience at 1.8 percent of American homes with radios. Americans preferred the network stations, some of which rebroadcast BBC programs. Most stations

---

FO371/26288 A7635/118/45; Campbell to Monckton, June 7, 1941, FO371/26185 A4420/118/45, PRO.

71. "Different Applications of 'Plan U' of Propaganda in the United States," May 14, 1940, FO371/24228 A2033/26/45, PRO.

carrying BBC programs were in the southeastern region, where only 10 percent of American families with radios lived and where Britain already enjoyed strong support. In the "East North Central Region," including Chicago, where Britain faced the least support and which had 23 percent of the country's families with radios, only six stations carried BBC programs. Taylor concluded that even if the BBC's shortwave broadcasts could compete with the popular and expensive commercial programs on American radio, they should not try to do so. The British should promote goodwill and cooperation, not competition, with American networks.[72]

Although the BBC's shortwave audience was small, British propagandists considered it a valuable audience because it included a number of people, especially members of the media, who created and led opinion. Hoping for more rebroadcasts of BBC programs on American networks, the MOI in February 1940 urged the BBC to make its shows more attractive to Americans. They discussed replacing the Oxford accent disliked by Americans with a Canadian or Scottish accent. They thought the presence of more ordinary people on the radio, such as cab drivers, dockers, and housewives, would have more appeal. Both NBC and the Canadian Broadcasting Corporation carried the BBC's weekly "tear-compeller"—the program *Children Calling Home*, which featured evacuated children in the United States and Canada talking via radio to their families in England. In March 1941 the BBC defined its objective as getting "the most from the U.S. as quickly as possible with the exception of manpower." Its job was to describe the effects of the war on ordinary people in order to make Britain's needs seem real to American listeners. One of the BBC's techniques was a "thank-you broadcast." Graphic descriptions of the arrival of American donations of clothing for homeless families turned the thank-you into a request for more.[73]

The other wide-reaching medium was film. The British Press Ser-

---

72. J. W. Taylor to Fletcher, August 5, 1940, FO371/24230 A3762/26/45, PRO.
73. Lothian to Halifax, September 28, 1939, FO371/22839 A7053/7052/45, PRO; Asa Briggs, *The War of Words*, vol. 3 of *The History of Broadcasting in the United Kingdom* (London: Oxford University Press, 1970), 176; Frank Darvall (MOI), "Notes on Broadcasting," December 13, 1939, FO371/24277 A231/26/45, PRO; T. Rendall, "Broadcasting to North America," March 7, 1941, BBC WAC E2/19/1; Maurice Gorham, *Sound and Fury: Twenty-one Years in the BBC* (London: Percival Marshall, 1948), 117. The creation of the BBC's North American Service in May 1940 is discussed in Chapter 2.

vice disseminated MOI documentary shorts on Britain at war to
groups like the White Committee and Fight for Freedom, and to
universities and clubs. The MOI's film adviser, Sidney Bernstein,
owner of the Granada cinema chain, struck a deal with Warner
Brothers through Hollywood's Motion Picture Committee for National Defense. Warner Brothers agreed to show commercially two
MOI short films, *London Can Take It* (1940) and *Christmas under
Fire* (1941). Hollywood committed itself to pro-British films. Several
released in 1941 told the story of individual Americans fighting
alongside the British. Warner Brothers made *International Squadron*
with Ronald Reagan, and Twentieth Century-Fox produced *Yank in
the RAF*, starring Tyrone Power. In the film Power, as the cocky
young American, was supposed to die, but the MOI requested that
he be allowed to live, in the interests of Anglo-American relations.
Hollywood's sympathies for Britain were evident in such films made
before Pearl Harbor as *Mrs. Miniver* and *Journey for Margaret*, in
which five-year-old Margaret O'Brien played an evacuated child.[74]

Throughout the period of U.S. neutrality, British officials sought
evaluation from friendly Americans. At a dinner for London literati
in February 1941, Wendell Willkie, when asked if Britain had made
any propaganda mistakes, replied, "not a foot or toe placed wrong."
Other Americans were more candid. The Press Committee of the
Harvard Group of American Defense, advocates of U.S. intervention,
supplied North Whitehead with a "brutally frank" commentary. It
recommended that British organizations replace many of their personnel, who were ignorant of the United States and whose "intellectual inflexibility" would prevent them from learning. It complained
that Britain treated the United States as a homogenous culture and
urged that the propaganda consider regional, social, economic, and
political differences. The commentary contrasted Germany's image
of invincible efficiency with Britain's presentation of itself: "We do
not want to hear about mountain-climbing, or the beauty of certain

74. K. R. M. Short, "Cinematic Support for the Anglo-American Detente, 1939–
1943," *Britain and the Cinema in the Second World War*, ed. Philip M. Taylor (New
York: St. Martin's Press, 1988), 124, 129; Frederic James Krome, " 'A Weapon of
War Second to None': Anglo-American Film Propaganda during World War II"
(Ph.D. diss., University of Cincinnati, 1992), 47–92; Clayton R. Koppes and Gregory
D. Black, *Hollywood Goes to War: How Politics, Profits, and Propaganda Shaped
World War II Movies* (Berkeley: University of California Press, 1990), 45.

sections of Britain. We want stuff on sports, the R.A.F. and free speech. We want stories of Anglo-American cooperation. We want stories of how the war is bringing together the British classes. . . . We do not want stories about how Britain is fortified for crisis by the old school tie, or the existence of an aristocracy, or by the virtue of 'muddling through.' " The Harvard Group counseled British propagandists to see America the way Americans did (or at least as the Harvard Group writers did), as a country both diverse and unified. One of its members, Arthur Schlesinger, Jr., later recalled, "We wanted British propaganda to be effective."[75]

William Wiseman, the former British intelligence officer turned New York banker, delivered an evaluation that reflected his own lessons of World War I. He warned that it was a fundamental mistake to assume that President Roosevelt was on Britain's side and that the British could leave the shaping of opinion to him. "America is not on our side," Wiseman stated bluntly. "The people do not like us and never will." The British were deceived, he argued, by the support of a select social group and friendly sections of the press. He stressed that Anglo-American relations would not become easier or less vital if and when the United States entered the war. The British had to be prepared to put their case before the Americans for years to come.[76]

In November 1941 North Whitehead offered three major recommendations for the propaganda campaign. First, the British had to provide the Americans with "the broad picture," a framework for understanding the war, to be illustrated by facts and figures. He suggested that a suitable person for this job would be someone with the mentality of a historical novelist rather than a journalist. Second, London had to deliver the latest information and guidance on how to present that information to a more tightly knit propaganda network composed of the British Press Service, the embassy, and the consulates. Third, propagandists had to know what Americans were

75. Harold Nicolson, *The War Years: Diaries and Letters, 1939–1945*, ed. Nigel Nicolson (New York: Atheneum, 1967), 143; "Memorandum on British Publicity," October 30, 1941, FO371/26188 A9268/118/45, PRO; Arthur M. Schlesinger, Jr., interview with author, March 31, 1994, New York, N.Y.

76. William Wiseman, "The American Front," June 13, 1941, Sir William Wiseman Papers, Group 666, Series 2, Box 13, Manuscripts and Archives, Yale University Library, New Haven, Conn.

really thinking. North Whitehead noted that British observers tended to exaggerate the emotional swings of opinion; he advised that British representatives travel around the country to collect a more accurate analysis of American attitudes. "The single most vital factor in our post-war collaboration," declared North Whitehead, "will be the attitude which public opinion in America adopts towards us."[77]

North Whitehead's proposals coincided with the escalation of the war on many fronts. Preoccupied with the undeclared war against Germany in the Atlantic, the U.S. government tried to avoid a conflict in the Pacific with Japan. But Japan's expansion into China and French Indochina in July pushed Washington to react by establishing a trade embargo, cutting off shipments of oil and scrap iron, and freezing Japanese assets in the United States. The United States demanded that Japan withdraw from China; Japan refused and broke the deadlock by attacking Pearl Harbor on December 7. In response, the United States declared war on Japan. On December 11 Germany and Italy declared war on the United States. Roosevelt cabled Churchill, "All of us are in the same boat with you and the people of the Empire, and it is a ship which will not and can not be sunk."[78]

The Japanese had succeeded where Britain had failed to unite the Americans and bring the enormous power of the United States into the war. The British had achieved incremental measures of American support by working closely with the Roosevelt administration. Meanwhile, as one Foreign Office official put it, London had witnessed the "irritating spectacle" of the president held back by public opinion. The prime minister and the Foreign Office considered the U.S. Constitution a stumbling block. As Churchill had remarked with some exasperation, "The American Constitution was designed by the Founding Fathers to keep the United States clear of European entanglements—and by God it has stood the test of time."[79] The Consti-

77. North Whitehead, "British Publicity in the United States Based on a Visit in October 1941," November 15, 1941, FO371/26188 A9268/118/45, PRO.

78. Roosevelt to Churchill, December 8, 1941, in Warren Kimball, ed., *Churchill and Roosevelt: The Complete Correspondence*, vol. 1 (Princeton: Princeton University Press, 1984), 283.

79. Martin Gilbert, *Finest Hour, 1939–1941*, vol. 6 of *Winston S. Churchill* (Boston: Houghton Mifflin, 1986), 1259. On November 12, 1941, Churchill explained to the War Cabinet the "difficulties which faced President Roosevelt as a result of the slow development of American opinion and the peculiarities of the American Constitution."

tution gave Congress a check on foreign-policy powers, thereby intertwining American politics and public opinion into a process British officials felt was unnecessarily complicated. The nerve-wracking passage of Lend-Lease legislation confirmed London's preference for circumventing Congress by relying on such executive agreements as the Destroyers for Bases Deal or the president's commander-in-chief powers, which he had used to order the U.S. Navy into an undeclared war in the Atlantic.[80] The British knew, however, that even if constitutional restraints could be avoided, the American administration would still desire public support for its actions. David Scott of the Foreign Office concluded, "It follows, therefore, that public opinion in the United States is the point we must attack."[81]

This decision brought British propagandists up against the precedent and legacy of World War I. Lord Lothian had warned that obvious propaganda aroused a "cold fury" in the Americans; yet he and other British policymakers knew it was possible to influence American opinion. The resulting "no propaganda" policy had incorporated the discreet method of working through American opinion leaders and using an informational approach. "Events of course are the real propaganda," stated David Scott, "but in the long run these events can only be made to tell in the right way if they are seen in their proper perspective."[82] The mission of British propagandists, using the "strategy of truth," would be to provide the "proper perspective."

For the British, this mission would be motivated by the memory of the failed peace of World War I and the hesitation of the United States to join the fight against Nazi Germany, as well as by the prospect of constructing a lasting peace after World War II. The United States and Britain "will pull together adequately for the duration," North Whitehead predicted. "Whether they remain together after the armistice is another and very important question."[83] Once the United States became an ally, British propagandists concentrated on two parts of their campaign. They built a cohesive propaganda organization designed to present Americans with the facts and framework

80. Reynolds, *Creation of the Anglo-American Alliance*, 258.
81. Scott, April 15, 1941, FO371/26184 A3823/118/45, PRO.
82. Scott, May 20, 1941, FO371/26184 A3893/118/45, PRO.
83. North Whitehead, "British Publicity in the United States Based on a Visit in October 1941," November 15, 1941, FO371/26188 A9268/118/45, PRO.

of the British cause. They also conducted an extensive study of American opinion in order to influence it. They had learned that the sensational story of the Blitz got them attention but not adequate results. Although the cautious nature of the "no propaganda" campaign constrained the development of themes and methods, the policy did lay to rest some of the legacy of distrust left from World War I. British propagandists were now in a position to build the foundation for the partnership they sought to have in place by war's end.

2   The Battleground of American Opinion

> Public opinion in America is like a giant, conscious of his strength, often lunging and plunging irresponsibly at the sting of a midge, capable of taking fright at shadows, trampling down a forest to capture a butterfly, but, all the same, this child-like giant has the last word in American affairs, and is the being with whom we have to deal.
>
> —ROBIN CRUIKSHANK, 1943

British analysts often resorted to elemental metaphors to describe the United States. They wrote of forces moving in chaos and confusion, of scattered energies capable of unmatched production, and of cross-currents from distant regions of the continent clashing in a riptide at Washington.[1] In their eyes, the United States was a country of oceanic proportions that contained an empire of diverse races and regions. The British found the public opinion of the United States, like the country itself, difficult to define and explain. American attitudes appeared to be contradictory and changeable. Nevertheless, British propagandists pursued an understanding of American opinion because they believed that it played a decisive role in American foreign policy.

Propaganda policymakers had two major tasks after the United

1. See for instance, R. Campbell to Eden, August 31, 1943, FO371/34129 A8229/34/45, PRO.

States entered the war in December 1941. The first was to keep the wartime alliance running as smoothly as possible, given the inevitable tensions of collaboration.[2] The second was to create an acceptable political climate in the United States for postwar cooperation. To accomplish these tasks, British officials organized a transatlantic network of established government offices and temporary wartime agencies. Officials from the Foreign Office, the Ministry of Information, the British Broadcasting Corporation, the Washington embassy and the consulates, and the British Information Services conducted an in-depth analysis of American opinion in order to find ways of influencing it.

Propagandists surveyed the topography of the battleground of American opinion throughout the war. In 1942 they perceived isolationism to be the chief enemy of a postwar partnership. Although the Japanese attack on Pearl Harbor appeared to have demolished the isolationist position, the British feared a resurgence once the Allies won. They also sought to help the U.S. government protect the "Germany First" strategy from domestic pressure to concentrate on the Pacific. They planned to foster the internationalist attitudes of Americans who had favored aid to Britain before Pearl Harbor. Propagandists found, however, that the dichotomy between isolationists and internationalists had disappeared. The one policy the U.S. public agreed upon was that the enemy must be defeated. Beyond that singleminded goal, Americans were divided over how to win the peace. In an attempt to sketch the contours of American attitudes, British analysts drew up new categories to describe the isolationist-internationalist spectrum.[3]

---

2. The wartime collaboration is discussed in Robert Hathaway, *Ambiguous Partnership: Britain and America, 1944–1947* (New York: Columbia University Press, 1981), 10–15; David Reynolds, "Roosevelt, Churchill, and the Wartime Anglo-American Alliance, 1939–1945: Towards a New Synthesis," in *The "Special Relationship,"* eds. Louis and Bull, 17–41; Mark A. Stoler, *The Politics of the Second Front: American Military Planning and Diplomacy in Coalition Warfare, 1941–1943* (Westport, Conn.: Greenwood Press, 1977), 160–168; Watt, *Succeeding John Bull,* 90–105.

3. These categories are drawn from a number of British opinion analyses. See especially R. Campbell to Eden, "Annex to Report on Opinion in the United States," August 31, 1943, FO371/34129 A8229/34/45, PRO; H. G. Nicholas, ed., *Washington Despatches, 1941–1945: Weekly Political Reports from the British Embassy* (London: Weidenfeld and Nicolson, 1981), 38. For a discussion of U.S. opinion, see Barry D. Karl, *The Uneasy State: The United States from 1915 to 1945* (Chicago: University

On the extreme right they placed the "old isolationists," such as Senators Gerald Nye (R-N.D.) and Burton Wheeler (D-Mont.). The group included William Randolph Hearst's newspapers, Robert McCormick's *Chicago Tribune*, and Joseph M. Patterson's *New York Daily News*. Adopting the labels of war, the British regularly referred to these three as the Hearst-McCormick-Patterson Axis. They defined a second group as international imperialists, who favored U.S. involvement in world affairs in order to promote American economic interests. Those Americans, who seemed to be political internationalists and economic nationalists, included Wendell Willkie, the Republican presidential candidate of 1940, Senator Arthur Vandenberg (R-Mich.), and Eric Johnston, president of the U.S. Chamber of Commerce. The foremost proponent of international imperialism was Henry Luce, the conservative, interventionist publisher, whose 1941 essay "American Century" projected an activist role for the United States as the predominant world power in the postwar era. The British saw international imperialists as advocates of American nationalism on a global scale and therefore as unfriendly to British interests.

The remaining three categories supported some degree of cooperation with Britain. In the center of the spectrum the British placed Secretary of State Cordell Hull and Senators Tom Connally (D-Tex.), Harry Truman (D-Mo.), and Richard Russell (D-Ga.), who were friendly to Britain but dubious of global commitments. The fourth group on the spectrum favored U.S. involvement in international organizations and included those who advocated the idea of an Atlantic community as the foundation of postwar order. Many had been interventionists during the anxious months of 1940 and 1941, such as anglophile journalist Herbert Agar and members of the Fight for Freedom Committee. This group included the "friendly" Americans who would advise and assist the British propaganda campaign. On the left of the spectrum, the British placed the World New Dealers, who desired an American internationalism dedicated to social welfare and reform. This group's spokesman was Vice-President Henry Wallace. It also included the CIO, blacks, Jews, and poor farmers. The

of Chicago Press, 1983), 212–213; John M. Blum, *V Was for Victory: Politics and American Culture during World War II* (New York: Harcourt Brace Jovanovich, 1976), 272–287.

World New Dealers, the British noted, tended to be more supportive of the other members of the Big Four alliance—the Russians and the Chinese, and more suspicious of Britain's imperial tradition. These categories served as a rough map for British propagandists seeking a guide to the terrain of American opinion. Fully aware that these categories of isolationist and internationalist attitudes shifted according to issue, the war situation, and American politics, British analysts continually adjusted their charts.

After Pearl Harbor, propagandists planned a reorganization that would continue the information format of the "no propaganda" policy but would exploit the greater closeness in Anglo-American relations. They had begun to expand their target audience from national opinion leaders to include regional opinion leaders and organized groups such as churches and unions. In New York they had set up the Inter-Allied Information Committee, which encouraged American ethnic groups to support the Allies. These plans for expansion were interrupted on January 3, 1942, when the U.S. State Department presented the British ambassador, Lord Halifax, with a memorandum requesting that the British shut down their propaganda activities in the United States.

Throughout the negotiations that followed, the British claimed that, in the words of Sir Gerald Campbell, the head of the British Press Service, they did not do "propaganda in the sinister meaning of the word." An unconvinced Adolf Berle, the undersecretary of state and a major figure in the negotiations, duly noted this denial in his diary. The State Department memorandum diplomatically observed that, in the past two years, Britain had understandably sought active support in the United States for its war against Germany. The memorandum noted that since the United States was now an ally, it was important to avoid arousing any suspicion of British propaganda that might detract from American national unity and the determination to bring about common victory.[4]

The State Department listed its recommendations. First, there was no need for a British publicity service. News reporting should be left

4. Halifax to FO, February 25, 1942, FO371/30668 A2701/399/45, PRO; Berle, *Navigating the Rapids*, 397; "Memorandum," January 3, 1942, RG 59, Box 41, War History Branch Study, Working Source Material, Department of State, EU, Division of European Affairs, Folder: British Publicity in the United States, NA.

to American correspondents in Britain and to British correspondents in the United States. British press relations should be concentrated in the Washington embassy (not in New York), where the State Department could provide advice about American public relations. The British correctly read "provide advice" as "monitor activity." The State Department commended the New York–based British Library of Information and the British Press Service for presenting Britain's case with honesty and restraint; it did not want the British Press Service to be handled outside of the Embassy, however. In its investigation of British practices, the State Department had discovered that His Majesty's government conducted press work outside of diplomatic missions only in India, Burma, Singapore, and the United States. The U.S. government did not welcome being included in such imperial company. American officials, moreover, thought that press work should be left to American correspondents, who could do a better job of promoting the war effort. These correspondents had experience with "American psychology" and would not cause any domestic political complications.[5]

Second, the January 3 memorandum stated that because the United States had "long been proud of the loyalty of its citizens, whatever their ancestry or national origin," any activities that might cause differences of opinion among American ethnic groups could not be tolerated. This concern, which was at the heart of the U.S. government's objections, was directed against the Inter-Allied Information Committee's activities among American ethnic groups. The State Department preferred that foreign-born groups receive "uniform news designed for all people of the country."[6] Third, the raising of funds for British relief should cease. Such activities in the future would be the responsibility of the American Red Cross. The State Department wanted to establish American oversight of British activities in the United States. It did not object to British propaganda as long as it was done circumspectly, did not cause the administration any domestic political problems, and did not contradict President Roosevelt's promotion of national unity.

Making the best of the situation, Ambassador Halifax pointed out

5. T. C. Achilles, "Memorandum—Background," December 19, 1941, RG 59, Box 41, NA.
6. Ibid.

to London that the consolidation of British propaganda activity in Washington would facilitate the coordination of policy. He added that, in any event, the American government could prevent any publicity it disliked. Berle had assured Halifax that the U.S. government would take care of American opinion.[7] The Foreign Office did not object to the move from New York to Washington. It saw that the capital was becoming the center of interest as the administration exerted greater influence on public opinion. Brendan Bracken, the minister of information, disagreed. He consented to drop activity among American ethnic groups but not to close the British Press Service in New York, where the major news media organizations had their headquarters. He informed Foreign Secretary Eden that the State Department's request was based on the mistaken assumption that the British were doing propaganda when in fact they were not. The Foreign Office instructed the embassy to defend the British Press Service as merely "a service of facts and information."[8]

At the same time the State Department presented the British embassy with the memorandum on propaganda, the U.S. Congress was considering an amendment to the Foreign Agents Registration Act of 1938. Under the 1938 act, Angus Fletcher and Alan Dudley of the British Library of Information had been required as agents of a foreign country to register with the State Department.[9] The amended act would require that all political propaganda published by foreign agents be labeled as such. The act also allowed the Justice Department to inspect all propaganda material.[10]

Although the British had accepted the State Department memorandum with equanimity, they reacted angrily to the congressional

7. Berle repeated Harry Hopkins' message of the year before. Halifax to FO, January 11, 1942, FO371/30667 A399/399/45, PRO.

8. Bracken to Eden, January 13, 1942 and N. Butler to Washington, January 16, 1942, FO371/30667 A636/399/45, PRO.

9. "Foreign Propaganda Agencies in the United States," January 27, 1941, RG 59, 800.01B11, Registration/971, NA.

10. The act also applied to foreign agents using the United States as a base for disseminating propaganda to Latin America. F. E. Evans of the Foreign Office declared that this provision was "very sweeping and good-neighborly to an extreme degree." H. Freeman Matthews reported to Secretary Hull from the U.S. Embassy in London that more than half of the material disseminated by the British Overseas Press Service in New York went to Latin America. FO371/30667 A744/399/45; Evans, January 24, 1942, FO371/30667 A920/399/45, PRO; Matthews to Secretary of State, May 20, 1942, RG 59, 841.91211/13, NA.

legislation. Halifax wrote to Secretary of State Cordell Hull that Britain would cooperate in every way, but because of the "special relations between the two countries," Britain deserved special consideration. To London, Halifax wrote that he was concerned with the labeling requirement. From the beginning of the war, British policy had been to avoid any repetition of the charge that British propaganda manipulated the United States into the First World War. Therefore, Halifax insisted, material produced and distributed by the British must not be labeled propaganda. The ambassador warned that British government officials "could not afford, for the sake of the future, to be branded as political propagandists."[11]

The act's provisions for inspection, labeling, and registration caused a more serious problem for the covert activities of the British Security Coordination than for the overt activities of the British Press Service. Adolf Berle, who had found being the target of a BSC discrediting campaign "amusing, disturbing, and irritating," advised the president to sign the amended act. Berle wondered why the United States should allow any foreign spy system to operate within its borders, no matter whose it was. The president received the opposite advice from Col. William Donovan, head of the office of Coordinator of Information and later of its successor, the Office of Strategic Services, the American intelligence organization that had close ties to the British Security Coordination, and from Robert Sherwood, the playwright and presidential speechwriter who was working on American foreign propaganda. Both urged the president to veto the bill. He did so on February 9, 1942.[12]

In his veto message, Roosevelt announced that the Foreign Agents Registration Act had been designed properly when the United States was at peace to protect the country from foreign agents who fostered discord and weakened national unity. Now that the United States was at war in a partnership of twenty-five united nations, the president explained, the bill must be adjusted. The adjustments caused

---

11. Halifax to Hull, February 1, 1942 and Halifax to FO, February 25, 1942, FO371/30668 A2701/399/45, PRO.

12. Berle, *Navigating the Rapids*, 402; Berle argued that if British and American interests were the same, the Americans ought to be able to take care of covert activity themselves. If their interests were not the same, then the British were not welcome to run their operations on American soil. Berle to the president, February 5, 1942 and Sherwood to the president, February 4, 1942, OF 133, Immigration 1942, FDRL.

"no end of a row," according to Berle. The undersecretary of state seemed to have been referring to disputes over jurisdiction among the Americans, including Colonel Donovan's covert organization, the State Department, the FBI, and the Justice Department, rather than to a conflict between the British and the Americans. In meetings attended by Berle, Halifax, and Ronald Campbell of the embassy, the attorney general, Francis Biddle, and the FBI chief, J. Edgar Hoover (by phone), it was decided that the British Security Coordination would work only as a liaison in the United States, without conducting operations.[13]

The same people worked much more congenially to exempt Britain's overt propaganda organization from the requirements of the Foreign Agents Registration Act. A solution was reached by granting the attorney general the power to exempt agents of nations whose defense had been declared vital to the defense of the United States. The solution allowed the U.S. government to oversee the activities of its allies without requiring them to wear the label of propagandists before the American public. The revised act was signed April 30, 1942. The conditional exemptions required that the propaganda material not conflict with U.S. policy, that it be accurate and truthful, that the identity of the publisher be noted on all publications, and that a short description of the material be filed with the Justice Department.[14]

The British, pleased with the final legislation, acquiesced to most of the U.S. government's requests, with one major exception. They did not close down or curtail their propaganda activities but expanded them. The Inter-Allied Information Committee did discontinue its objectionable activity among American ethnic groups. The United States joined the committee in July 1942. Michael McDermott, head of the State Department's Division of Current Information, summed up the episode when asked whether there had been

13. February 10, 1942, FO371/30668 A2289/399/45, PRO; Berle, *Navigating the Rapids*, 400. When Halifax explained that the BSC should be acceptable because it worked with Colonel Donovan, Berle informed him that Donovan was only to do intelligence work *outside* the United States. March 10, 1942, RG 59, 841.20211/36, NA.

14. G. Campbell to MOI, May 1, 1942, FO371/30669 A4205/399/45, PRO. U.S. government officials viewed the material they received from the British as a mixture of propaganda and information. See, for instance, George Pettee to Elmer Davis, April 4, 1943, RG 44, Entry 171, 1850, OGR, Bureau of Intelligence, OWI, NA.

a plan to close down the British Press Service in New York. There had been such a plan, admitted McDermott, but all that happened was that the head of the British Press Service moved to Washington. The bulk of the work continued to be done in New York.[15]

The cooperative negotiations over the State Department memorandum and the Foreign Agents Registration Act set the tone for the type of teamwork that developed between the U. S. propaganda agencies and the British propaganda organization in the United States. The Roosevelt administration consolidated its propaganda activity into the Office of War Information (OWI) in June 1942. Its head, CBS broadcaster Elmer Davis, defined the office's role as putting the facts before the people.[16] Also in June, the newly organized British Information Services (BIS), combining the British Library of Information and the British Press Service, registered under the Foreign Agents Registration Act. At times, the policies of the propaganda agencies complemented each other. When they did not, the British usually pretended that they did. The brunt of this collaboration fell on British representatives in the United States, who carried out the propaganda policies devised in London.

One of their chief assets was Prime Minister Churchill's popularity in the United States; yet Churchill remained a somewhat distant presence in the development of Britain's propaganda campaign. The prime minister seemed to be more interested in censorship than propaganda as a tool for shaping opinion, although he was sensitive to its possibilities. Directing most of his attention to relations with President Roosevelt, he discussed with FDR such mechanics of influencing public opinion as coordinating the timing of press releases. British propagandists counted on Churchill's celebrity to get the attention of the American public when a bad impression needed to be revised or they wanted to get some special point across. He did not always accede to their wishes. For instance, in June 1944, when he was asked to speak on the British war effort, he replied, "Deeds not words." Or when asked to respond to criticism in the American press, he refused, noting, "we cannot afford to be rattled over every trashy

15. H. Butler to Bracken, July 17, 1942, FO371/30667 A1280/399/45, PRO; McDermott suggested that the matter might be taken up again, but no evidence has been found that it was. M. J. McDermott, April 13, 1942, RG 59, 841.9121/11, Box No. 4866, NA.
16. Winkler, *Politics of Propaganda*, 12.

press article in America." The prime minister did not always take his own advice. In June 1942, when *Time* magazine published an article describing Britain as weak and incompetent, Churchill asked Brendan Bracken, the minister of information: "Is *Time* Luce? This vicious rag should have no special facilities here." Churchill added that he himself "took some trouble" with Henry Luce and wanted some protest made.[17] Although he could not be depended upon to toe the propaganda line, especially on certain controversial issues, such as the future of the British Empire, Churchill took time to cultivate American opinion leaders and held sway as the best-known Englishman in the United States.

The Foreign Office, which oversaw propaganda policy, held paradoxical views on the possibilities of Anglo-American relations. A pessimistic attitude was expressed by the permanent undersecretary, Alexander Cadogan, who minuted one of Halifax's reports from Washington with the comment, "I don't know whether any American government can ever enter into an 'Alliance' in the proper and useful sense."[18] Policymakers could take dim comfort in maintaining Britain's prestige by planning to direct U.S. foreign policy indirectly. They would not be likely to think the United States worthy of inheriting Britain's role, even if they had admired the American political system and its leaders. At their most optimistic, members of the American Department hoped propaganda would "enlighten" Americans about their international responsibilities as defined by the British.

The department's American expert, Thomas North Whitehead, urged his colleagues to adjust their expectation that the United States learn to see the world from the British perspective. "Our aim must not be to understand why the Americans are so wrong about us," he advised, "but why from their standpoint the American attitudes are so natural and indeed so inevitable." The need to see the world from an American point of view, rather than being able to impose its own, was evidence of Britain's declining powers. Yet Foreign Sec-

---

17. Briggs, *War of Words*, 4; Kimball, ed., *Churchill and Roosevelt*, Vol. 2, 138; Halifax to Bracken, June 8, 1944, and Churchill to Eden, January 3, 1945, PREM 4 27/9; Churchill to Bracken regarding anti-British articles in the U.S. Press, June 5, 1942, PREM 4/26/8, PRO.

18. Cadogan, July 13, 1943, FO371/34138 A7147/57/45, PRO.

retary Eden wished to build a cooperative relationship, with Britain as the dominant partner. Since the impetus for creating the partnership in the first place was the recognition that Britain would be dependent upon the United States, the Foreign Office knew that this was an unlikely outcome. David Scott suggested that their dilemma might not be resolved until the Americans were able "to patronise us and we become a back number."[19] The available route out of the Foreign Office's quandary regarding Britain's future as the leading or subordinate partner was through persuasion and influence. It was a road the Foreign Office took with reluctance.

At times, the Foreign Office tradition of formality and deliberation was at odds with the characteristics of speed, flexibility, and creativity required for propagandists. Maurice Gorham, the energetic Irishman who headed the BBC's North American Service, claimed his dreariest memories of the war were the meetings held at the Foreign Office to plan policy relating to the United States. He explained why he asked to be to excused from attending: "There was an air of bloodlessness and unreality about them that depressed me terribly and made it all the harder to go back and go on doing my job. I used to look around that table and wonder whether if you stuck a knife into some of those people, anything but sawdust would come out."[20] Gorham refrained from naming the people he contemplated stabbing, but he did exclude North Whitehead, whom he considered the only congenial representative of the Foreign Office.

Along with the formal meetings described by Gorham, an informal group of Foreign Office and MOI Americanists met weekly. The group included North Whitehead and Frank Evans, who had served as consul general in New York, from the Foreign Office, Frank Darvall from the MOI, and occasionally Professor Nicholas Mansergh, an expert on Commonwealth affairs who ran the MOI's Empire Division.[21] They compared notes on how Foreign Office policies were translated into propaganda and took stock of the latest analysis of

19. North Whitehead, August 8, 1942, FO371/30670 A6581/399/45, PRO; Reynolds, *Creation of the Anglo-American Alliance*, 266; Scott, September 1, 1942, FO371/30670 A6581/399/45, PRO.

20. Gorham, *Sound and Fury*, 112.

21. Nicholas Cull, interview with H. G. Nicholas, March 3, 1988. I am grateful to Nick Cull for providing me with a copy of this interview.

American opinion. The American Department provided the long view for the MOI and the BBC, whose work was more immediate and responsive.

Staffed by an "irregular recruitment of available talent," the MOI had a rough start in the early years of the war, when it went through a series of ministers and earned a certain notoriety for incompetence. The ministry steadied in the summer of 1941 under the leadership of Brendan Bracken, publisher, financier, and loyal friend of Winston Churchill. The fiery minister excelled at press relations, cutting red tape, and defending the ministry to the Parliament, the services, and the Foreign Office. Perhaps his greatest asset was his closeness to the prime minister, who kept a room for Bracken at Number Ten Downing Street.[22] Bracken's highly public role was complemented by the administrative abilities of the director-general, Cyril Radcliffe. A brilliant barrister, Radcliffe was respected for his ability to reduce intricate problems to simple terms. A man of high principles and cool judgment, he oversaw the work of the MOI amateurs—the writers, artists, professors, and journalists who made up one of the liveliest bureaucracies in wartime London. Robert Bruce Lockhart, the head of the Political Warfare Executive, considered Radcliffe to be the ablest man he met during the war.[23]

Under the direction of the flamboyant political intriguer and the distinguished barrister, the MOI became the central clearinghouse for war news. It orchestrated the presentation of the news by delivering the official position, called "guidance," to the military services' press offices, other government ministries, and the BBC. The British government's determination to present a positive image of Anglo-American relations led it to revise its censorship policy in March 1942. It censored not only security-related information but also all matters likely to cause disharmony or ill feeling between the Allies and any criticism deemed undesirable or unfair.[24] The stricter cen-

22. McLaine, Ministry of Morale, 6–7.

23. Lockhart noted that Radcliffe despised the Foreign Office and that his one ambition concerning Whitehall was to get out of it as soon as the war was over. Radcliffe later served as Lord of Appeal from 1949 to 1964. Robert Bruce Lockhart, Comes the Reckoning (London: Putnam, 1947), 363; Robert Bruce Lockhart, The Diaries of Sir Robert Bruce Lockhart, ed. Kenneth Young, vol. 2 (London: Macmillan, 1980), 359.

24. "American Liaison Unit and Censorship Procedure," September 13, 1942, BBC WAC R61/2.

sorship policy clashed with the MOI's efforts to establish frank and open relations with the American media. After difficulties developed between the BBC and the American press as well as between the Foreign Office and the MOI, the censorship rules were quietly dropped in 1944.[25]

The MOI monitored broadcasts from all over the world. Using its news direction and production facilities, the ministry could respond with the British position quickly. Radio, newspapers, newsreels, and pamphlets carried a harmonious message to a large audience.[26] The MOI conducted propaganda for the British domestic audience under the home controller and, for Allied and neutral countries, under the controller of overseas publicity. The exception to this arrangement was propaganda to the United States. The American Division was considered so important that it was a separate entity, and its director had direct access to Brendan Bracken.

The American Division of the MOI was staffed by a group of talented wordsmiths with backgrounds in journalism, literature, and the university.[27] The chief, Robin Cruikshank, set the pace and temperament of the division. Cruikshank, who had been the American correspondent of the *News Chronicle* from 1928 to 1936, was wise, hard working, and warm-hearted. One colleague described him as

25. The British introduced political censorship in response to scathing criticism of British policy by Australian correspondents after the fall of Singapore. In a sharp letter to Eden in May 1944, Cyril Radcliffe (MOI) stated that the FO interfered with the duty of the censor by expecting it to stop leaks from Allied embassies. Radcliffe criticized the FO for trying to please the U.S. State Department by using censorship. The MOI's director general caustically noted that Secretary of State Hull's public denunciations of political censorship were hypocritical at best. The issues the FO wanted censored in the spring of 1944 were the work of the European Advisory Commission and negotiations about Polish-Soviet disputes. Radcliffe announced that the censor would limit its duties to security issues. Cyril Radcliffe, "Censorship of Outgoing Press Messages," February 16, 1944, and Radcliffe to Eden, May 18, 1944, INF 1/859, PRO; Robert Marett, *Through the Back Door: An Inside View of Britain's Overseas Information Services* (Oxford: Pergamon Press, 1968), 43.

26. Frances Thorpe and Nicholas Pronay, *British Official Films in the Second World War: A Descriptive Catalogue* (Oxford: Clio Press, 1980), 8–9.

27. The description of the American Division is drawn from Phyllis Bentley, "O Dream, O Destinations": An Autobiography (London: Victor Gollancz, 1962), 229–234; Mary Agnes Hamilton, *Uphill All the Way: A Third Cheer for Democracy* (London: Jonathan Cape, 1953), 109–124; Marett, *Through the Back Door,* 36–37, 71; Nicholas Cull, interview with H. G. Nicholas; Cruikshank, May 29, 1945, INF1/102, PRO; H. G. Nicholas, interview with author, August 16, 1991, Oxford, Eng.

"one of the most delightful men I ever met," and others confirmed that they and the MOI were extremely lucky to have him in the American Division. As deputy director of the British Information Services in New York from 1941 to 1942, Cruikshank was instrumental in the overhaul of the organization following the United States's entry into the war. By the time he returned to London in the summer of 1942 to head up the American Division, he was familiar with the needs and circumstances of British propagandists on the American front. Frank Darvall, Cruikshank's deputy director, was an efficient administrator who preserved what orderliness there was. Recruited for his background in the English-Speaking Union, Darvall's expertise in American and British history, constitutional practice, and law made him an indispensable resource.

The American Division's staff was divided into six sections. Section I handled the American journalists and broadcasters in London. Roger Machell of the *Daily Telegraph*, an army major who had been wounded in France in 1940, presided calmly over this largest and most chaotic section of the division. The MOI offices provided guidance, introductions, inspiration, and twenty-four-hour-a-day facilities for correspondents, where the typewriters and telephones were in continual use. Cruikshank believed there was no better way to influence American reporters "without appearing to be crudely propagandizing them." Section II took care of other American visitors to Britain, as well as Anglo-American societies. At its head was publisher Hamish Hamilton. Three years after rowing with the British team for a silver medal at the 1928 Olympics, Hamilton founded his own publishing company. He was transferred to the MOI in 1941, after serving with the army in Holland and France. Hamilton's contacts with American writers and journalists proved invaluable, as did his independent income, which enabled him to entertain American visitors. Section III covered labor and industrial relations and was headed by Lionel Elvin, a Cambridge professor with family connections to the trade unions. Section IV, which briefed British visitors to the United States, was under the direction of Herbert G. Nicholas, a professor of history who had been a Commonwealth scholar at Yale University.

Sections V and VI supplied the British Information Services in the United States. Section V, under Australian journalist Guy Innes, handled "hot news," the term for news of immediate interest. Section VI, under Yorkshire novelist Phyllis Bentley, distributed human-interest stories and feature articles to American magazines and the BIS monthly *Britain*. Bentley placed in American trade journals hundreds of articles describing the war-torn lives of British butchers, hairdressers, and other tradespeople, intended for their counterparts in the United States. In 1944, the tireless Mary Agnes (Molly) Hamilton, former Labour M.P., governor of the BBC, and biographer, joined the division as economic advisor.

The American Division personnel tended to be sympathetic to Liberal or Labour policies. They supported reform in Britain and the New Deal policies of the Roosevelt Democrats. Their origins and interests reflected the propaganda policy of correcting the aristocratic English Tory stereotype disliked by Americans. Most of the staff had lived in or visited the United States. Several had family connections there. Cruikshank, Darvall, and Nicholas' assistant, Lady Daphne Straight, were married to Americans. Daphne Straight's mother-in-law, Dorothy Whitney Straight Elmhirst, was, among other things, an old friend of Franklin Roosevelt. The Indianapolis-born Hamish Hamilton was half American. Elvin's assistant, Barbara Mercer Nairne, later Marchioness of Lansdowne, was an American. The American Division's kinship ties to the United States did not convince them of the inevitability of close Anglo-American relations. They did, however, feel committed to the reform spirit of the war and the promotion of the interests of the democracies.

Under the responsibility of the Ministry of Information during the war, the BBC, an independent corporation whose governors were appointed by the British government, was widely and correctly perceived in the United States as the voice of official London. The BBC attempted to downplay its official connection and win the trust of American listeners. Until August 1940, BBC broadcasts to the United States were under the jurisdiction of the Empire Service, whose world view located the United States somewhere between Canada and the British possessions in the Caribbean. On the eve of the Blitz, when the authorities recognized that the United States had become a crucial audience, the BBC created the North American Service.[28]

28. The MOI also oversaw the policies of the BBC's Overseas Services, except those

The BBC carried out the "strategy of truth" using a high standard of news reporting to commend itself to its international audience. Ernest Davies of the Talks Policy Committee set down the two objectives of the BBC's American policy. The first was to project Britain and Britain's war effort in the most favorable light to the United States. ("Subject, of course, to our usual standard of complete accuracy," Davies added.) The second was to remove and, when possible, to anticipate and forestall American criticism of Britain. The BBC saw its task as clearing up the misconceptions that stood in the way of maintaining the best possible Anglo-American relations.[29] Maurice Gorham, the head of the North American Service, was more direct: "Get Americans to listen to us and like us better."[30]

The BBC's version of the "special relationship" started out in 1942 with a strongly defined appeal to progressive American opinion. Davies announced that the BBC should project a vision of the postwar world in which the United States and Britain would have an "identity of interest" based on an international New Deal. Davies, who was married to an American, was a journalist and editor active in the Labour party and in 1940 was on the Fabian Socialist Executive. Although he knew that other views existed in the United States, Davies wanted the BBC to appeal to the "Century of the Common Man," as described by U.S. Vice-President Henry Wallace. To promote the theme of the Century of the Common Man, Davies suggested, the BBC should create a wider conception of international cooperation with other powers, especially the Soviet Union. It was important, however, not to appear to be interfering in American politics or lecturing to the listeners. "When it is our intention to remind Americans that they must share in responsibility for world peace which they failed to do last time," stated North American Service policy, "we should use some such general theme as 'the good citizen

to enemy or enemy-occupied countries, which were under the jurisdiction of Political Warfare Executive. "Organization of the MOI," RG 208, OWI Overseas Branch, Bureau of Overseas Intelligence, Great Britain, Entry 367, Box 318, NA; Briggs, *War of Words*, 403–405; Darvall, November 21, 1941, INF1/870, PRO.

29. Ernest Davies, Talks Policy Committee, June 2, 1942, BBC WAC E2/438/2.

30. Gorham, the former editor of *Radio Times*, is described in Roger Eckersley, *The BBC and All That* (London: Snapson, Low, Marston, 1946), 167, and Briggs, *War of Words*, 406.

of any country in the future must be a world citizen.' "[31] The BBC thought this general approach united the American and British people as good citizens of the world.

By 1943 the BBC expanded its appeal to include more of the isolationist-internationalist spectrum than the World New Dealers. One of its many American advisers, Morris Gilbert of the OWI, observed in a January 1943 memorandum that the newly elected U.S. Congress, with a stronger coalition of Republicans and conservative Democrats, threatened to dismantle the New Deal. He suggested that since the BBC could not convert people, it should strengthen the already converted by narrowing its target audience to New Dealers and organized labor. Denis Brogan, the BBC's intelligence expert on the United States, disagreed with Gilbert's advice. The Glasgow-born Brogan had studied history at Oxford and Harvard and had written on American politics. After brief stints at the MOI's American Division and at the Political Warfare Executive, Brogan, with his unbureaucratic manner and pungent wit, found a compatible place with the BBC. Brogan warned against neglecting friendly American conservatives. He argued that the BBC could not afford to suggest that the war was being fought for the New Deal. William MacAlpine, a Canadian who served as talks organizer, agreed with Brogan. He preferred what he called a policy of "crop rotation" to keep "all fields healthy."[32] Although the North American Service maintained a somewhat progressive line, BBC policymakers, recognizing that the United States was becoming increasingly conservative as the war went on, adapted to American trends.

According to American analysts of BBC programming, the North American Service had to adjust its broadcasting style as well as content. Daniel Katz, a Princeton professor and member of the editorial board of *Public Opinion Quarterly*, critiqued BBC's broadcasts to the United States in a 1942 study. First, Katz explained, BBC broadcasts had a high intellectual content and therefore a narrow audience appeal. For instance, when the BBC wanted a commentary on Britain's economic position they called in John Maynard Keynes, the

<hr />

31. Davies, June 2, 1942, BBC WAC E2/438/2; "North American Service Policy," undated (possibly 1943), BBC WAC E2/438/3.

32. Memorandum by Morris Gilbert with minutes by Brogan and MacAlpine, January 1943, BBC WAC E2/438/3.

foremost inventor of modern economics and principal adviser to the Treasury from 1940 to 1946. The rare exceptions to highbrow talks by academic, literary, and dramatic stars were broadcasts by a London taxi driver and a Yorkshire weaver turned writer. Second, the news bulletins lacked interest and immediacy, which Katz blamed in part on censorship. Third, Katz claimed that the BBC appealed to abstract ideas of humanity, decency, Christianity, and democracy in contrast to American propaganda, which, based on the direct stimulation of motives used by advertisers, appealed to security, materialistic gain, and egoism. American opinion leaders, who were the obvious intended listeners of the BBC, could deduce the logical actions demanded by Britain's abstract appeals. But if the BBC wanted the general American public to listen to the North American Service, Katz advised that it would have to drop the upper-class appeal and the university lecture style.[33]

The American radio broadcasters who advised the BBC elaborated on Katz's recommendations with on-the-spot demonstrations. The premier adviser was Edward R. Murrow, CBS's London correspondent. Murrow and the BBC had learned together how to report the war professionally. Murrow's London broadcasts had shown the power of being specific and concrete in news reporting, of avoiding the abstract, and of focusing on the everyday and the familiar. His BBC colleagues observed that through radio, Murrow spoke to ordinary people about ordinary people. For the BBC to speak to an American audience, it would have to adjust the tone of condescension inevitable in broadcasts delivered in the tradition of raising public standards. Whether Murrow thought the BBC could make such an adjustment was not clear. At a meeting with BBC officials, Murrow advised them to continue taking care of American correspondents as the best method of furthering Anglo-American relations.[34]

33. Daniel Katz, "Britain Speaks," in *Propaganda by Short Wave*, ed. Harwood L. Childs and John B. Whiton (Princeton: Princeton University Press, 1942), 114. *Propaganda by Short Wave* was the work of the Princeton Listening Center, a group of American scholars, linguists, and engineers who pioneered systematic monitoring of foreign broadcasts to the United States from the start of the European war. In the summer of 1941 the Princeton Listening Center was succeeded by the U.S. government's Foreign Broadcasting Intelligence Service or FBIS.

34. R. Franklin Smith, *Edward R. Murrow: The War Years* (Kalamazoo, Mich.: New Issues Press, 1978), 49, 85; Joseph E. Persico, *Edward R. Murrow: An American*

A second American, CBS newsman Wells (Ted) Church, told the BBC that it had to modernize the technical side of programming. He pointed out that American radio men were shocked by the BBC's lack of a production department. To illustrate his point, he noted that the BBC used one sound effects door for all door sounds, whereas Americans used dozens. Church insisted that timing and cues be dead accurate, especially if the BBC wished to rebroadcast its programs in the United States.[35]

Church also advised on the content of programming. For programs to the United States, Church instructed, the BBC must eliminate all words, such as "bastards," "hell," and "goddam," that were considered swearing in the American version of the King's English. This injunction was repeated by Maurice Gorham, who ordered a moratorium on profanity. The North American Service, he warned, must not jeopardize rebroadcasting by using words forbidden in the United States. With regard to the presence of U.S. troops in England, Gorham added that the BBC did not want American mothers to think that their sons were exposed to "godless, foul-mouthed people over here," no matter how the soldiers themselves talked. Other words forbidden in the interests of Anglo-American relations included "Tory," "Yankee" (always "Yank"), "Anglo-Saxon" (use "English-speaking"), and anti-German words, such as "Teutonic." To avoid offending German Americans, the BBC distinguished the enemy leaders from the German population by referring to them as "super bullies," "wolf pack," and "Nazi-Fascist gangsters."[36]

Church recommended changes in the BBC's presentation of contentious issues in Anglo-American relations. The American noted that in its reports, the BBC sparred with Americans, not the enemy. It countered praise of General Douglas MacArthur, commander-in-chief of the southwest Pacific area, with praise of General Sir Archibald Wavell, supreme commander of the southwest Pacific. It competed with reports on American production with old but previ-

---

Original (New York: McGraw Hill, 1988), 174; Briggs, War of Words, 293; May 5, 1942, BBC WAC R34/687.

35. Wells Church report, August 1942, BBC WAC E1/136.

36. Church, April 14, 1942, BBC WAC E2/438/2; Gorham, "Objectives of the North American Service," July 13, 1942, BBC WAC E2/438/2; Katz, "Britain Speaks," in Propaganda by Short Wave, ed. Harwood and Whiton, 145.

ously unreleased reports on British production. As an alternative, Church offered tributes to MacArthur and Wavell to balance the success of Field Marshal Erwin Rommel or reports on American and British production to counter German production.[37]

On the question of postwar economic policy, Church advised greater openness by Britain. For *Answering You*, a BBC program on which British experts answered questions sent in by American listeners, an American had posed the question "Will there be a change in the export policy of Great Britain to the United States?" Church had seen the Board of Trade's suggested response to the question. Unless the United States altered its demand for dollar payments, the Board of Trade replied, Britain would continue to need dollar-earning exports. The board recommended that the "delicate and difficult question" be carefully avoided. Church thought that policy ridiculous. Tell the Americans, he urged, that Britain had to earn money through exports because it had to spend money in the United States.[38] Like Murrow, Church advised the BBC to be straightforward.

With American advice and increased exposure to commercial radio, BBC policymakers learned about broadcasting to the American audience. After a trip to the United States, Gorham reported that the mental climate of listeners attuned to competitive commercial radio was entirely different from the broadcaster-audience relationship of a monopoly public service. Radio networks cajoled listeners with the latest song, comedian, serial hero, or gimmick. The war news reporting was sharp, incisive, and dramatic. Gorham decided that the BBC had been too sensitive to the possible diplomatic and political effect of its message, gearing it more toward the State Department than to the general American audience. The propaganda through news presented according to Foreign Office and MOI directives was too cautious and subtle for the American listener. He learned that Americans suspected the resulting uniformity of opinion presented on the North American Service. Gorham concluded, "Official London dulls our impact."[39]

The North American Service director called for more vigor and

37. Church, August 1942, BBC WAC E1/136.
38. Church, "Use by the British Government of One of Its Most Powerful Arms—the BBC," February 23, 1942, BBC WAC E1/136.
39. Gorham, September 14, 1942, BBC WAC E2/438/2.

candor in British broadcasting to attract American listeners. Gorham contrasted the American and British reporting style:

American: roaring across the Channel at mast-height, Flying Fortresses blasted the daylights out of two cargo ships

British: low-flying aircraft of Bomber Command attacked two cargo ships

The BBC could not and should not copy the American style, Gorham conceded, but it needed to become livelier. Gorham's motto became "British in content, American in appeal." He also insisted that the technical quality of the broadcast was itself a message of British expertise and efficiency to the U.S. listener. The broadcasts became more Americanized, meaning that they carried more entertainment, more stories about ordinary people, and more news commentary. The BBC shifted from an orientation toward the government as audience (both its own and that of the United States) to an orientation toward the American public as audience.[40]

Guided by London's coordinated policy, propagandists in the United States adapted and improvised in response to American opinion. The British embassy, as the Foreign Office counterpart, oversaw the propaganda network.[41] Its staff concentrated most of its energies on the cultivation of opinion leaders at the highest levels in both government and media. The British Information Services carried out guidance sent by the MOI American Division. Like the BIS, the BBC had its headquarters in New York, with branch offices in Washington, Chicago, and San Francisco. As in London, propagandists debated their analysis of U.S. political culture and the best way to influence it.

Lord Halifax, the British Ambassador, reflected many of the tra-

40. Ibid.; Gorham, *Sound and Fury*, 132; David Cardiff and Paddy Scannell, " 'Good Luck, War Workers!': Class, Politics, and Entertainment in Wartime Broadcasting," in *Popular Culture and Social Relations*, ed. Tony Bennett, Colin Mercer, and Janet Woollacott (Milton Keynes, Eng.: Open University Press, 1986), 110, 114–115.

41. Memoirs discussing the British embassy include Edward, Earl of Halifax, *Fullness of Days* (New York: Dodd, Mead, 1957), 241–309; Gerald Campbell, *Of True Experience* (New York: Dodd, Mead, 1947), 111–225; Paul Gore-Booth, *With Great Truth and Respect* (London: Constable, 1974), 119–147; Marett, *Through the Back Door*, 70.

ditional diplomat's views on propaganda. He recognized the importance of opinion in the American political system, thought it should
be fairly easy to influence, and had little idea about how to go about
it. Soon after taking up his post in Washington, Halifax wrote to
Eden in February 1941 that American politicians seemed to be as
afraid of public opinion as they were of the Germans.[42] Halifax, a
Conservative, caused propagandists some alarm. As former Prime
Minister Neville Chamberlain's foreign secretary, the ambassador
carried the stigma of appeasement. As a former viceroy of India, he
represented Britain's imperial tradition. And as an austere aristocrat,
he confirmed American suspicions of Britain's entrenched ruling
class. Sir Stewart Menzies, head of the British Secret Service, reported
to Alexander Cadogan that "Edward hadn't 'clicked' in the U.S."
Halifax's dignity eventually earned him enough respect in the capital
so that Isaiah Berlin could describe his popularity as moving from
zero to freezing.[43]

A second figure who received a mixed reception was the head of
the British Information Services, Harold Butler, the former director-
general of the International Labor Organization. The reorganization
negotiated with the State Department in the spring of 1942 required
that Butler be given the diplomatic rank of minister and work out of
the British embassy. An urbane man, Butler "hobnobbed with the
high and mighty." Some of his subordinates thought that he was
rather "stuffy," did not have a flair for his work, and failed to establish a rapport with American reporters.[44]

For their analysis of American opinion, the embassy and the BIS
drew on several sources, including polls, press surveys, BIS and consular reports, as well as impressions garnered by British representatives traveling around the United States. Close ties with Washington
agencies allowed access to their surveys of public opinion. The U.S.
government relied on opinion polls conducted by George Gallup, by

42. Halifax to Eden, February 4, 1941, Halifax Papers, Reel 2, 4.15.
43. The report from "C" (Menzies) was noted in Cadogan's handwritten diary
(not in typescript version). Cadogan added that there was not much that could be
done about it. Cadogan Diaries, May 6, 1941, Alexander Cadogan Papers, Churchill
College Library, Cambridge, Eng.; Lockhart, *Diaries*, 242.
44. Gore-Booth, *With Great Truth and Respect*, 170; Marett, *Through the Back
Door*, 79; N. Butler, January 26, 1943, FO371/34127 A2648/34/45, PRO; Sevareid
to Murrow, July 20, 1942, Reel 1, Eric Sevareid Papers, Library of Congress, Washington, D.C.

Elmo Roper for *Fortune*, and by the Denver-based National Opinion Research Center. Hadley Cantril and the Office of Public Opinion Research conducted private polls for President Roosevelt with the understanding that the president could more successfully educate opinion if he knew how much the public already knew on an issue and what they thought about it. The White House also was aware of the value of published polls in shaping opinion.[45]

British policymakers doubted the value of polls, however. Some objected to their measurement of volatile opinion. Prime Minister Churchill told the House of Commons in September 1941: "Nothing is more dangerous in wartime than to live in the temperamental atmosphere of a Gallup Poll, always feeling one's pulse and taking one's temperature. I see that a speaker at the weekend said that this was a time when leaders should keep their ears to the ground. All I can say is that the British nation will find it very hard to look up to leaders who are detected in that somewhat ungainly posture." Like Churchill, Foreign Office officials perceived something undignified about polls. In their view, polls violated the tradition of astute diplomacy. On a plan to undertake a detailed study of American opinion using polls and surveys, Gladwyn Jebb commented, "Generally speaking, the 'scientific' or Gallupian approach to problems of foreign policy fills me with dismay. What we want is insight based on intelligence and education and not 5 million facts about the habits and table manners of the inhabitants of South Dakota."[46]

To the Foreign Office, public opinion polls seemed a peculiarly American phenomenon. Where George Gallup saw poll-taking as a way to increase people's participation in their political system, the Foreign Office saw it as an opportunity for Americans to expose their ignorance. The Foreign Office's view was supported by Allardyce Nicoll, a British professor of Restoration drama at Yale University on leave of absence to the Washington embassy. "Americans indi-

---

45. Hadley Cantril, *The Human Dimension: Experiences in Policy Research* (New Brunswick, N.J.: Rutgers University Press, 1967), 55, 69; FDR to Lowell Mellett, August 12, 1940, PPF 4721, American Institute of Public Opinion, 1936–1940, FDRL; Oscar Cox to Harry Hopkins, February 13, 1943, PSF Subject File, Box 175, Public Opinion Polls, FDRL.

46. "The War Situation," September 30, 1941, Churchill, *His Complete Speeches*, vol. 6, 6495; minute by Gladwyn Jebb, July 8, 1943, FO371/34092 A6921/3/45, PRO.

vidually are essentially pollable," reported Nicoll, "anxious to reveal their thoughts on every conceivable subject and express their opinions even on subjects about which they know nothing."[47]

David Ogilvy disagreed. At age thirty-one, Ogilvy held the position of second secretary at the British embassy while working for British Security Coordination collecting intelligence on Latin American economies. After studying modern history at Oxford and training as an apprentice chef at the Hotel Majestic in Paris, Ogilvy had come to the United States in 1937 to study advertising. From 1939 to 1942 he worked closely with George Gallup, pioneering poll-taking techniques. At the embassy, he urged that analysts use polls to measure the "deep currents" of American opinion. He challenged the accuracy of Isaiah Berlin's famous political summaries that recounted the attitudes of Washington personalities. Although Ogilvy disapproved of Berlin's "readiness to embroider," he later admitted in a letter to his cousin, the writer Rebecca West, that Berlin's witty analysis probably attracted the attention of London officials, who would otherwise not have followed American developments as closely. Although aware of official London's preference for "insight based on intelligence and education," Ogilvy was disappointed that the BSC and the embassy disregarded his advice. After the war, he went on to prove that perhaps he knew what he was talking about when his New York advertising firm, Ogilvy and Mather, became a huge success.[48]

Propagandists, however reluctantly, did turn to polls to measure American attitudes and gauge trends over time. The British attended to poll results because they knew the Roosevelt administration considered them important.[49] British propagandists, who worked with

47. Allardyce Nicoll, June 26, 1943, FO371/34128 A6290/34/45, PRO. For an American view on polls, see George Gallup and Saul Forbes Rae, *The Pulse of Democracy: The Public Opinion Poll and How It Works* (New York: Simon and Schuster, 1940), 266.

48. David Ogilvy to Rebecca West (Mrs. Henry Andrews), August 18, 1955, David Ogilvy Papers, Box 29, Library of Congress, Washington, D.C. See also his autobiography: David Ogilvy, *Blood, Brains, and Beer* (New York: Atheneum, 1978).

49. Halifax to FO, June 26, 1943, FO371/34128 A6290/34/45; September 30, 1943, FO371/34129 A9195/34/45; Nicoll, "American Polls and Public Opinion," June 26, 1943, FO371/34128 A6290/34/45, PRO. The MOI used polls to analyze British opinion; see Marjorie Ogilvy-Webb, *The Government Explains: A Study of the Information Services* (London, George Allen and Unwin, 1965), 61–62. The shortcomings of 1940s polling techniques are discussed in John E. Mueller, *War, Presidents, and Public Opinion* (New York: John Wiley, 1973), 3–7.

their American counterparts on promoting Anglo-American relations, exchanged national public opinion surveys. London disapproved of the degree to which the BIS and the OWI shared confidential information, but British propagandists in Washington used this collaboration to gain U.S. government assistance in the presentation of their case.[50]

While the embassy staff pursued its analysis of American opinion and collaboration with the U.S. government and the OWI, the BIS in New York, known as "the factory," carried out the operations of the British propaganda effort. Aubrey Morgan, a Welsh businessman who had been the architect of the organization, ran it like an energetic shop manager. Under Morgan's charge were four sections or services. First, the Information Service, headed by D'Arcy Edmondson, included the old British Library of Information, a research section, and a section solely devoted to India. Second, the Press Service, under René MacColl, consisted of sections for news, radio, publications, military affairs, photographs, and commentators. Third, the Film Service, under Sidney Bernstein, included sections for theatrical and non-theatrical distribution of films. Fourth, the Cultural Services, headed by Professor W. J. Hinton, included sections for religions, exhibitions, women, and speakers.

Morgan patterned the BIS after a commercial organization rather than a government agency, because public relations was an accepted business in the United States. He demanded that the staff have the highest professional standards. The information produced by the BIS was its commodity. Radio networks, newspapers, clubs, and schools were its customers. Morgan made "the customer is always right" an unofficial slogan. The BIS approach was to let customers think they had discovered the truth by themselves.[51] In July 1942, CBS corre-

---

50. The MOI thought that three copies of its Weekly Home Intelligence Report went only to Harold Butler, to the BIS, and to General Beaumont-Nesbitt, adviser on publicity for the armed forces. Butler informed them that the report was edited and copied for distribution to the embassy, the BIS staff, the consuls, the heads of the British missions, and two or three members of the OWI who furnished the British with secret material in return. Radcliffe to H. Butler, May 18, 1943, and H. Butler to Radcliffe, May 28, 1943, FO371/34091 A4955/3/45, PRO.

51. Report on the BIS by H. Butler, Gerald Campbell, Michael Wright, P. Gore-Booth, and William Edwards, July 15, 1944, FO366/1392 XP4963/303/907; Morgan, May 26, 1942, FO371/30669 A4915/399/45, PRO; Hamilton, *Uphill All the Way*, 122; Marett, *Through the Back Door*, 82; Gore-Booth, *Great Truth and Respect*,

spondent Eric Sevareid reported to Murrow in London that the BIS went to great lengths to satisfy the requests of American journalists. He thought it was the best available source of detailed and accurate information about Europe as well as England.[52]

One way in which British propagandists confronted the enormity of their undertaking was to divide their mental map of the battleground of American opinion into sections. They thought of the Northeast as an internationally minded, Atlantic-oriented friend. The South was seen as friendly to Britain through cultural and social ties. The West was internationally minded but tended to be focused on the Pacific war and apathetic about Anglo-American relations. The Midwest was seen as the stronghold of anglophobia and isolationism.[53] Edward Gallienne, consul general in Chicago, expressed his frustration: "The majority of the people in the Middle West are ill-informed and ignorant; as they have little interest in anything outside America their opinions are valueless and unascertainable."[54] If ignorance explained anglophobia and isolationism, Gallienne and others concluded, propagandists must concentrate their educational efforts there.

Propagandists assumed their problem began with the presence of large populations of German Americans and other ethnic minorities such as Scandinavian Americans, who had supported neutrality. This premise prompted the minister of state, Richard Law, to wonder why Minnesota should have as its governor the internationalist Harold Stassen. D. J. Hall, the Foreign Office's expert on ethnic minorities, described Minnesota as "a slow-thinking but very sound area of the United States," not so likely to "blow hot and cold like the people of the East Coast." He explained, "I have seen a certain amount of the Scandinavians there and as an example of the slowness with which even the Norwegians change their attitude, it was not until

---

170–171. For discussion of MOI films, see Helen Forman, "The Non-Theatrical Distribution of Film by the MOI," 221–233, and Ian Dalrymple, "The Crown Film Unit, 1940–43," 209–220, in *Propaganda, Politics, and Film, 1918–1945*, ed. Nicholas Pronay and D. W. Spring (London: Macmillan, 1982).

52. Sevareid to Murrow, July 20, 1942, Reel 1, Sevareid Papers.

53. See, for instance, "Report of a Visit by Aubrey Niel Morgan to the West Coast of the United States," January 29, 1942, FO371/30667 A995/399/45, PRO.

54. Consul-General Gallienne (Chicago) to Halifax, November 19, 1943, FO371/34130 A11140/34/45, PRO.

1942 that they began to show their acceptance of the idea that they and their adopted country could no longer be immune from the effects of happenings elsewhere and must, therefore, play their part in the future."[55] Ethnic determinism was one way for the British to interpret midwestern attitudes.

Another more useful method was the extension of British representatives into an almost completely ignored region of the United States. As late as May 1943, Ambassador Halifax informed Brendan Bracken that "vast stretches of this country," particularly the Midwest and the mountains, were "untended by your faithful shepherds." Referring to the American people as "hungry sheep," Halifax urged Bracken to expand the MOI's efforts. "Thus when the winds of isolation blow from the mountains and the contagion of ignorance spreads from the great plains," wrote the ambassador, "the only antiseptic is more and more information."[56] Only Halifax, the devout Anglican and Yorkshire farmer, used the shepherd and sheep metaphor to describe Anglo-American relations. The ambassador's playful treatment of the subject went along with serious attempts by the Washington embassy and the MOI to increase the British presence in the United States. Into the Midwest they sent consuls, the BIS, and the BBC.

The British made inroads into the American interior by increasing the number of consulates from seventeen in the interwar years to thirty-three by 1942. Before the war, the only consulates between the Mississippi River and the Pacific states were in St. Louis, Missouri, and Galveston, Texas. The new consulates, staffed with information officers, filled in the neglected middle of the country in Cincinnati, Ohio; Houston, Texas; St. Paul, Minnesota; Kansas City, Missouri; and Denver, Colorado.[57] In October 1942, the *Denver Post* reported on the opening of the new British consulate by Roger Stevens, who would handle routine consulate matters, answer questions, and serve as an agent of the British Information Services in New York. Upon his arrival, Stevens announced that he thought Denver was "swell"

55. Minutes by R. Law and D. J. Hall, November 28, 1943, FO371/34130 A11243/34/45, PRO.
56. Halifax to Bracken, May 28, 1943, Reel 2, 4.20, Halifax Papers.
57. The British would have set up more consuls if they could have obtained more funding from the Treasury. Bracken to Halifax, June 21, 1943, FO371/34128 A6103/34/45, PRO; Wheeler-Bennett, *Special Relationships*, 78.

and reminisced about nights during the Blitz, when in a crowded air-raid shelter he slept with his head under an American-made refrigerator.[58]

The consuls kept the embassy and the BIS in Washington informed about regional opinion. They also helped shape it. To make the consuls valuable advocates of the British case, the embassy provided them with guidance from London and up-to-date information on British policy. Consuls distributed documentary films and advised the BBC on the local suitability of programming. The embassy staff, who imagined the consuls stationed in the wilderness, brought them to Washington periodically to meet wartime luminaries. The consuls could then return to their outposts with fresh news for the regional press.[59]

If the United States was a battleground, propagandists considered Chicago the front line. It was the home of General Wood, the chairman of America First, and Col. Robert McCormick, the proprietor of the *Chicago Tribune*. The Chicago branch of the BIS was staffed by D. Graham Hutton, a barrister and economist who had been the assistant editor of *The Economist*, and his assistant William Clark, a Commonwealth fellow and lecturer at the University of Chicago.[60] From his perspective in Chicago, Hutton viewed the propaganda organization with mixed feelings. He found the Washington embassy very supportive. Hutton dismissed the inhabitants of the Foreign Office. "Ignoramuses," he later called them, because they did not understand the vastness of the United States. The MOI, he thought, harbored patronizing attitudes toward Americans, although he considered Bracken, Radcliffe, and Cruikshank outstanding. The American Division, in turn, looked upon its man in Chicago as a "commander in an exposed position running on nerves and iron rations" and were under orders from Bracken to "give Hutton whatever he wants."[61] Although he too saw his job as a "formidable task," Hutton, who had first visited Chicago in 1937, loved the self-

58. Stevens to Scott, October 5, 1942, FO371/30672 A10338/399/45, PRO.

59. H. Butler to British consuls, July 22, 1942, FO371/30670 A7629/399/45; Malcolm, September 30, 1942, FO371/30671 A8528/399/45, PRO.

60. Clark was later the diplomatic correspondent of the *Observer* and vice-president for external affairs at the World Bank. William Clark, *From Three Worlds* (London: Sidgwick and Jackson, 1986), 11.

61. Interview with Hutton; interview with H. G. Nicholas.

sufficiency and self-confidence of the city. To him it was a worldwide crossroads of trade, transportation, and wartime communications from the European to the Pacific fronts.

Hutton developed close relations with Chicago media and civic organizations. In May 1942, for instance, Hutton noted that his office received about fifty requests a day for information on civil defense, mobilization, India, taxation and anti-inflation measures, shipping, the Royal Air Force, labor and production, health, and British personalities. He placed technical material in such publications as the American Medical Association's journal and *Pure Milk*. In March and April of 1942 alone, Hutton made thirty-six public addresses to groups including bankers, women's clubs, the state police, the Advertising Managers Club, university faculty, the Rotary Club, and the American Legion, all with appropriate press coverage.[62]

Hutton and Clark cultivated the local press of the region, where the small towns seemed insulated but friendly. The BIS distributed daily copies of the BBC's review of the British press to one hundred newspapers and radio stations in the Midwest, which Hutton and Clark followed up with personal contacts. Clark recalled that Bill Waymack, editor of the *Des Moines Register*, could be persuaded to write occasionally about Britain's war effort.[63]

In the evening, Hutton enjoyed friendly social meetings with Colonel McCormick at North Shore dinner parties, but during the day he sent caustic reports to the Foreign Office on the *Tribune*'s anti-British pronouncements. The most effective method Hutton discovered for challenging anti-British attitudes was to quote Berlin radio broadcasts to the United States about Britain and to Britain about the United States. German propaganda, which attempted to promote discord between the two allies, raised similar issues to those voiced in the *Tribune*. By comparing the anti-British sentiments of Berlin and the *Tribune*, the BIS deftly used the enemy abroad to deflect attacks on Britain.[64]

---

62. "Extract from Mr. D. G. Hutton's report," May 18, 1942, FO371/30669 A5140/399/45, PRO.
63. Clark, *From Three Worlds*, 17.
64. Hutton, December 31, 1943, FO371/38554 AN135/34/45, PRO. The *Chicago Tribune*, along with the Hearst and Patterson papers, used some of the same themes,

Hutton's goal was to prevent a repeat of 1919, when the United States rejected the peace treaty ending the First World War. He believed that American military and economic support was essential to Britain's future. His job was to inform London of American domestic political forces in the Midwest and to inform the American public of the importance of their commitment to maintaining the postwar order, even if they did not agree. Despite his efforts throughout the war and his affection for Chicago, most of Hutton's reports were not optimistic about the future of Anglo-American cooperation.[65]

Propagandists also hoped to infiltrate the Midwest by radio. The BBC debated the best way to reach American listeners. The direct route by shortwave reached a tiny but influential audience that included news reporters and analysts. American commercial programs required corporate sponsorship. The BBC considered adopting this practice in order to compete for the prime-time audience but ultimately rejected the option as being politically questionable at home and in the United States, as well as against its public service tradition. The solution was to convince American radio networks to rebroadcast BBC programs.[66]

High-level negotiations took place between the BBC and the presidents of CBS and NBC, William Paley and Niles Trammell. By February 1944, BBC programs were carried on 270 stations (30 percent of the total) for 130 hours of radio time weekly, with an estimated audience of 10 million. For example, the Blue Network (later ABC) carried the lively *Transatlantic Quiz*, an Americanized version of *Brains Trust*, with Lionel Hale and Alistair Cooke as questionmasters, and the erudite Christopher Morley and the audacious guesser John Mason Brown as the New York team. The knowledgeable Denis Brogan, who spoke "torrentially in a broad Scots accent," and a witty, irreverent young actor, David Niven, made up the London team.[67] To ensure the best possible coordination, Maurice Gor-

such as American suspicion of British war aims, employed by German propagandists; see the file on Axis propaganda in OF 4453, Propaganda, 1942–1945, FDRL.

65. Interview with Hutton; report from Hutton, August 16, 1943, FO371/34129 A7833/34/45, PRO.

66. R. A. Rendell, "Report on the Use of Radio in Anglo-American Relations," April 23, 1942, BBC WAC R34/687.

67. "BBC Rebroadcasting in the United States," February 3, 1944, BBC WAC E2/504/2; Gorham, *Sound and Fury*, 164.

ham spoke by telephone daily with his North American director, Lindsay Wellington, in New York. Both radio men were well aware that this was a wartime communication undertaken only at the highest priority, especially when it was clear from the telephone delays whether the prime minister was in or out of the country.[68]

The BBC prepared specially designed programs for the midwestern audience. It established close cooperation with station WLW in Cincinnati, Ohio, a 500,000-watt station that reached Michigan, Ohio, Indiana, Illinois, and West Virginia. On his program *Background in the News*, WLW broadcaster Gregor Ziemer featured the BBC's MacDonald Hastings. Hastings, who during one broadcast informed his American listeners that he did not wear a monocle and hoped that they would not hold his British accent against him, spoke on Britain's politics, newspapers, tax burden, and hospitality for the "American boys."[69] WLW broadcast programs featuring a Scottish housewife coping with the rationed feeding and clothing of her family, a clergyman from a blitzed church, and young men from Ohio and Indiana telling people back home what it was like to be a soldier waiting for D-Day.

With the assistance of the public relations office of the American armed forces, the BBC found farmers' sons from the WLW listening area, took them on visits to British farms, and recorded Anglo-American farm talk for rebroadcast over the Cincinnati station. During a 1943 visit to London by editor Herbert Plambeck from Iowa station WHO, the BBC collected guests for a London production of WHO's daily program *The Corn Belt Hour*. These included British farmers, a farmer's wife, a land girl (wartime agricultural worker) from a bombed area of Kent, a public relations officer from the Ministry of Agriculture, and two young farmer-soldiers from Iowa.[70] The resources spent by the BBC on an hour-long radio show indicated its eagerness to reach the Iowa audience. Following Maurice Gorham's instruction that it was necessary to get Americans to listen to the

68. Briggs, *War of Words*, 408; Wellington had a staff of seventy-three in the United States. The BBC's U.S. operation cost 100,000 pounds a year. The total cost of the North American Services was 300,000 pounds a year. "Broadcasting to and from the United States," February 6, 1945, BBC WAC R34/575.

69. WLW memoranda, August 1943–May 1944, Gregor Ziemer Papers, U.S. Mss. 47AF, Box 16, State Historical Society of Wisconsin, Madison, Wis.

70. "Broadcasting to North America," BBC WAC E2/438/3.

BBC, the special programs for the midwestern audience targeted farm families, families of soldiers, and women. Much of the sympathy the United States had for Britain, it was thought, originated with the admiration American women felt for British women. The BBC believed that women—a key radio audience—played an important role in influencing American opinion.[71]

When the BBC's North American Intelligence Section conducted a survey of 3,516 New York and Chicago radio owners in September 1944, it learned that more than 25 percent were not interested in hearing about Britain. One in ten asked for news of American soldiers. The BBC asked the 38 percent who desired more information about Britain for specific interests. The New York audience wanted to know about postwar problems and international relations; the most frequent questions concerned India and Palestine. New Yorkers desired information on broad political and economic questions, particularly labor issues, and more discussions of women and children's problems. The Chicago audience was more interested in life in wartime Britain, the air raids, the robot bombs, and the blackout. It preferred more entertainment and nonwar subjects. Chicagoans, more than New Yorkers, were curious about Britain's attitude toward America. One concern of the Chicago audience that was absent in New York revolved around Britain's help in the war against Japan.[72] According to this survey of the Chicago audience in particular, the BBC would find it hard to reconcile its objective of getting Americans to listen to them with its goal of discussing postwar issues.

The Foreign Office American Department reflected on the "rather gloomy picture" presented in reports from the United States in the spring of 1943. After a 10,000-mile trip across the United States in

71. March 3, 1942, BBC WAC E2/438/2. Another specific target audience was American children. The BBC wanted to correct anti-British attitudes through educational broadcasting to the schools. W. M. Newton, the BBC representative in Chicago, was stunned to discover that there was no federal or hardly even a state authority for education. The decentralization of the American education system made it difficult for the British to pursue this method. Newton noted that Michigan had a program for public instruction by radio. He recommended it for study to the BBC. W. M. Newton to North American Director (BBC-N.Y.), "Report on U.S. Educational Broadcasting with Reference to Prospects for BBC Cooperation," November 28, 1944, BBC WAC R34/575.

72. North American Intelligence, "Desired Information about Great Britain for U.S. Listeners," November 27, 1944, BBC WAC E1/205/1.

1943, Thomas North Whitehead reported that the isolationist-international spectrum of opinion was complicated by dangerously disruptive internal tension. Sectionalism as well as prejudice, directed particularly against blacks, Mexicans in the West, and Jews, were part of the "normal American pattern" and unlikely to weaken the U.S. war effort. But, North Whitehead pointed out, sectionalism and prejudice could gravely affect prospects for postwar collaboration. Frank Evans summarized the political significance of the situation. The year 1944 would see the election of a Republican Congress, probably nationalistic in color, which meant a uniting of the isolationists and international imperialists, both groups that were seen as threats to British interests. That year would probably also see the reelection of President Roosevelt, which would entail "complete executive paralysis at the time when it is most important that the Administration and legislature should be in harmony." In other words, the administration would cease to be capable of committing the country on any long-term basis, and a positive foreign policy was unlikely. According to Evans, the advantage of American wavering would be to give the British an opportunity to gain the leadership.[73]

The difficulty was, of course, to gain "leadership." Describing the United States as "sort of a cauldron," the Foreign Office's J. G. Donnelly explained: "In a country so constituted it is quite reasonable to do what in other countries would seem unjustifiable, and indeed it is the recognised thing for foreign countries to take their case [directly to the American publicist], if not to the actual public. No one questioned the right of the Poles . . . the Irish or Congress Indians. . . . We are the one country which . . . must proceed with great caution." Propaganda policymakers had to confront the type of anti-British attitudes discovered by John Price of the British consulate in Kansas City, Missouri, while on a nine-day tour of southwest Kansas. Kansans, he found, distrusted British policy and, although they paid close attention to Prime Minister Churchill's speeches, were ignorant of British affairs. Price reported that his audiences seemed prepared to revise their conclusions when given new facts, but they had a dangerous "habit of criticism." For explanation, Nevile Butler cited Herbert Agar, the liberal editor of the Louisville *Courier-*

---

73. North Whitehead, April 8, 1943, and minute by Evans, FO371/34127 A3360/34/45, PRO.

Journal, who was assigned to the U.S. embassy in London by the State Department. Agar described the anti-British attitudes of isolationists as the only logical escape for isolationist philosophy because its proponents needed an excuse for not cooperating with Britain to "keep the peace."[74]

Propaganda policymakers concluded that in order to persuade the American public to regard their British allies as partners, they had to attack anti-British attitudes in the United States. They must design propaganda that would appeal to a wide range of audiences across the country. One way to reach the "childlike giant" of American opinion was to tell it a story.

74. Minute by Donnelly, February 26, 1945, FO371/44556 AN929/22/45; report by John Price and minute by N. Butler, May 20, 1943, FO371/34138 A4962/34/45, PRO.

3 The Story of "Comrades in Arms"

The note we should strike should always be that of "Comrades in arms" rather than that of "Grateful poor relations."

—FRANK DARVALL, JUNE 13, 1942

"The uniting of our troops in battle and the intertwining of our military and economic systems in the persecution of the war, and we hope and seek, in the protection of the peace," stated Frank Evans of the Foreign Office, "will point the way to a lasting intimate relationship." The opportunity to establish that relationship, he urged in the summer of 1942, "is at hand." The important work of the propaganda organization was to be expanded and improved. But, Evans speculated, "Whether this organization can subsist on the practical but unstimulating diet of strict realism in Anglo-American relations remains to be seen."[1]

For propagandists, the "strategy of truth" had never depended upon "strict realism." As Walter Lippmann had explained in *Public Opinion*, the successful propagandist wants a true beginning and a happy ending: "The propagandist exhausts the interest in reality by a tolerably plausible beginning and then stokes up energy for a long voyage by brandishing a passport to heaven."[2] British policymakers

1. Minute by Evans, July 27, 1942, FO371/30670 A6403/399/45, PRO.
2. Lippmann, *Public Opinion*, 109.

offered the "special relationship" as a passport to the heaven of peace and security in the postwar world. They rooted this message in the wartime alliance, but they feared that American distrust of British policy might lead the United States to reject postwar collaboration. So they devised compelling narratives about the war with happy endings about the peace.

The MOI's American Division defined its goal as the establishment of an Anglo-American "partnership on equal terms" in its publicity plan of February 1942. As an alternative to Hitler's New Order, propagandists would promote the "establishment of a new world order," an international system led by the Western, democratic, and capitalist countries under the direction of the United States and Britain. The plan outlined two all-purpose propaganda themes. First, Americans must be convinced that Britain was conducting an all-out war effort on the home front and overseas. Britain's relentless dedication to defeating the enemy would show Americans that Britain was a tough adversary and a worthy partner. Second, Americans must be persuaded that out of the war a new, democratic Britain had been born. The second theme explained how, after the evacuation of Dunkirk, the British had thrown off the old, ineffective order of appeasers. The Blitz had broken down class structures, and the war had become a "people's war." The "new-Britain" theme, already in play at home and overseas, took on a postwar significance. The British were not just fighting all out against fascism but for a reborn, robust Britain.[3]

With a qualification, the Foreign Office approved the plan to counter Americans' view of Britain as aristocratic and worn out. From Washington, Ronald Campbell, who as minister at the embassy from 1941 to 1945 was on his third posting to the U.S. capital since starting out as a lowly third secretary in 1915, derided the new-Britain theme as "bunk." He advised against encouraging Americans to believe that a new Britain, one more like the United States, would emerge from the war. He thought evolutionary rather than revolutionary change should be stressed. Cecil King of the Foreign Office

3. "Plan of Publicity in the U.S.A.," February 21, 1942, FO371/30668 A2695/399/45, PRO. Angus Calder, who acknowledges the new-Britain theme's usefulness for propaganda at home and overseas, describes its importance in helping people cope with the fear and confusion of 1940; Calder, *The Myth of the Blitz* (London: Jonathan Cape, 1991), 17–18.

agreed that the evolutionary theme was the best reply to Americans "who think we are either Fascists or Bolsheviks under the skin." The Foreign Office endorsed the MOI plan, with the instruction to project a gradual rather than radical transformation of British society. The new-Britain theme was designed to appeal both to American liberals who disliked British social structure and to American conservatives who distrusted the British labor and social welfare movement. In addition, as Frank Darvall noted, the new-Britain theme was intended to have a preventive function: "We also had very much in mind . . . the danger that the United States might go imperialist after the war and accept collaboration with Britain only in terms of superiority. For this reason it was expressly stated in our list of aims that we seek to create a popular basis in both countries for collaboration between the United Kingdom and the United States during and after the war on *terms of equality*."[4] By establishing a democratic partnership of "comrades in arms," propagandists hoped to ward off American domination.

The Foreign Office and the MOI knew that the war-effort and new-Britain themes already had wide appeal in the United States. Edward R. Murrow was the most famous American voice of the new-Britain theme, for his salutes to the ordinary people of London during the Blitz. Eric Sevareid reinforced Murrow's portrayal of the British people when, ill and exhausted after covering the fall of France, he returned to the United States. The former pacifist from Minnesota explained to lecture audiences how the Battle of Britain had changed his belief that people could not fight a war without losing most of their democratic rights. He asserted that there was more democracy in Britain in 1941 than there had been two years earlier.[5]

The theme of a new Britain rising out of the rubble had a gripping quality, as illustrated by the 1942 Academy Award–winning film *Mrs. Miniver*. At the end of the film, the minister declared to his congregation seated in the bombed village church, "This is the people's war!"[6] Mrs. Miniver's minister preached the MOI's "Plan of

---

4. R. Campbell to N. Butler, May 8, 1942, minute by King and minute by N. Butler, May 27, 1942, FO371/30669 A4747/399/45; Darvall to N. Butler, June 13, 1942, FO371/30669 A5722/399/45, PRO.
5. "Excerpts from Talk by Eric Sevareid," 1941, E-1, Sevareid Papers.
6. "Although," according to Cruikshank, "it had the defect of perpetuating the

"This is the people's war," declared the minister in MGM's 1942 Academy Award-winning film *Mrs. Miniver*. (Wisconsin Center for Film and Theater Research)

Publicity." In August 1941, Sidney Bernstein met for three hours with producer Louis G. Mayer of Metro-Goldwyn-Mayer and later reviewed the script. The new-Britain and war-effort themes not only suited Hollywood. Propagandists also used the principles of commercial advertising—the appeal to emotions, repetition with variation, and a single message—to promote these themes in the press and on the radio.[7]

The way in which propagandists told the story of "comrades in arms" changed throughout the war. As always, the method of the "strategy of truth" was vulnerable to events. Military victories and defeats, developments in domestic politics, and the emergence of postwar problems affected the new-Britain and war-effort themes. Propagandists adjusted the themes to studies of public opinion and apparent shifts on the isolationist-internationalist spectrum of attitudes about the postwar role of the United States. Inevitably, elements in the plot of the story had to be reworked, but the ending remained the same.

In the spring of 1942, the state of Anglo-American relations worried British and U.S. officials.[8] The fall of Singapore, the reverses in Libya, and the escape of the German battle cruisers, the *Scharnhorst* and the *Gneisenau*, from the English Channel had aroused American criticism. The isolationist newspapers shifted their stance against entering the war to attacks on British incompetence and imperialism. A survey conducted by Hadley Cantril for the U.S. government drew a thumbnail sketch of typical attitudes held by American critics of Britain:

The British are rather arrogant and seem to think they are superior to most people. They have not infrequently milked their colonies

---

legend that this is a semi-feudal society, wrapped round in the lace and lavender of charm," *Mrs. Miniver* was a hit in both the United States and Britain; Cruikshank, "Publicity and Policy in the United States," December 3, 1943, FO371/38505 AN430/6/45, PRO. For discussion see Koppes and Black, *Hollywood Goes to War*, 225–230.

7. Short, "Cinematic Support for the Anglo-American Detente," in *Britain and the Cinema*, ed. Taylor, 128; North Whitehead, "British Publicity in the United States," July 20, 1942, FO371/30670 A6845/399/45, PRO.

8. OWI Intelligence Report, February 23, 1942, PSF Subject File, Box 172, FDRL; discussed at meeting of Conyers Read, Ulric Bell, and R. H. Tawney, Labour Attaché to the British embassy. Conyers Read to William Langer, February 25, 1942, OSS R & A #822, NA.

for their own benefit and it is hard not to believe that we got into the last war because they tricked us into it.

Now we're all in a common fight and it is to our self-interest to help them, even though they probably won't pay their debts and will be sharp competitors when the war is over. But why can't the British government seem to work out a better military strategy and not constantly be losing?[9]

Opinion studies reported that approximately one-quarter of the American population was antagonistic toward Britain. An assistant to Archibald MacLeish, the head of OWI's forerunner, the Office of Facts and Figures, concluded, "The American public does need a good selling job on the English."[10]

Surveys also contained some good news. Although more than half of those surveyed considered the British to be snobbish and aristocratic, over half regarded the British as courageous and loyal. A majority of the public preferred Britain to any other country, but only a minute percentage favored an exclusive Anglo-American alliance.[11] Propagandists recognized that winning wartime popularity polls was a far cry from obtaining U.S. economic and military support in the postwar period. The BIS's head, Harold Butler, stated that the main purpose of his organization was "to create the right emotional attitude in the United States towards Great Britain"; it was not necessary for Britain to be loved, but to be respected.[12] Propagandists wanted the image of courageous and loyal comrades to deflect charges that Britain was fighting for empire, draining American resources through Lend-Lease, and not pulling its weight in the war effort.

9. More than half of those interviewed disapproved of British colonial policy. Four in ten believed that the British had gotten the United States into the First World War. See Hadley Cantril, "What the Americans Think of the British and Why," July 3, 1942, RG 44, OGR, Bureau of Intelligence, OWI, Reports and Special Memoranda, 1942–43, Sources Division Reports, NA; Survey of Intelligence, July 16, 1942, PSF Subject File, Box 173, FDRL.

10. John C. Baker, April 15, 1942, RG 208, OWI, Records of OFF, Decimal File of the Director, 1941–1942, Box 11, Entry 5, Folder 303.1 Allied Propaganda 1942, NA.

11. See, for instance, the OWI's "Anti-British Feeling by U.S. Citizens and British Reactions Thereto," December 16, 1942, RG 44, Entry 171, Box 1850, OGR, Bureau of Intelligence, OWI, Reports and Special Memoranda, 1942–43, NA.

12. H. Butler, "Postwar Organization of the BIS," July 26, 1944, FO366/1392 XP4963/303/907, PRO.

British officials relied on collaboration with U.S. government agencies to assist them in promoting a positive image of Britain to the public. From London, Nevile Butler observed that such collaboration carried with it potential drawbacks when, for instance, British policy diverged from American ideas; he thought, however, that His Majesty's government would gain a tremendous advantage if it could enlist the U.S. government in its effort to combat the charge that Britain would "fight to the last Australian." His wish was granted by the Office of Facts and Figures publication *Divide and Conquer.* The pamphlet described "what Hitler wants us to believe" and outlined Nazi attempts to foment disunity in the United States and among the Allies. *Divide and Conquer* attributed this story to German propagandists: "The Englishman, Dutchman, Frenchman, and Greek . . . were flying toward England in a crippled plane. To lighten the load and save the plane, advised the pilot, some people would have to jump. Both the Frenchman and Dutchman promptly dove out the door. 'For our countries!' they cried. The plane still faltered, and the pilot called for one more man to sacrifice his life. The Englishman arose, his face grave. 'For England!' he said solemnly—pushing the Greek overboard."[13]

The pamphlet went on to explain how people innocently had repeated this story, unaware of the enemy's intention to create "contempt for our ally and leave the impression that other people fight his battles." This point was supplemented by MOI statistics showing that as of December 31, 1941, more than 70 percent of British Commonwealth casualties were U.K. troops, with the rest from the Dominions of Australia, Canada, New Zealand, and South Africa, and from India and the colonies. *Divide and Conquer* enjoyed a distribution of 1 million copies and a reprinting in the *Saturday Evening Post,* with a circulation of 10 million. It might have been considered a drawback for the British to have this memorable story distributed to millions of people who had perhaps not yet heard it and who might now retell it with or without the label of enemy propaganda. Britain nonetheless had the assistance of Washington agencies in promoting allied unity. Robin Cruikshank reported that because the U.S. government had influence over hundreds of journals and radio sta-

13. N. Butler, February 16, 1942, FO371/30667 A1690/399/45, PRO; *Divide and Conquer,* April 1942, Box 53, Archibald MacLeish Papers, Library of Congress, Washington, D.C.

tions, collaboration was a "priceless opportunity" for "telling our story through this media."[14]

The OWI and the British embassy set up the Joint Committee on Information Policy in August 1942. Archibald MacLeish, OWI deputy director, Robert Sherwood, OWI overseas director, and Gardner Cowles, OWI domestic operations, met with David Bowes-Lyon of the Political Warfare Executive and with Harold Butler and Aubrey Morgan to discuss policies regarding the enemy and the allies, as well as the need for a "propaganda offensive" on postwar cooperation directed at the American and British people. In response to Morgan's contribution of the new-Britain theme, Sherwood suggested a "popular demonstration" of American and British war veterans and labor leaders meeting in Coventry to show "how the world of tomorrow will rise out of the ruins of today." A more practical outcome was the study of Anglo-American friction undertaken by Tom Wenner and Keith Kane of the OWI's Bureau of Intelligence and Isaiah Berlin, Robert Marett, and Paul Scott-Rankine of the BIS and the embassy's press department. Although the British genuinely were concerned with anti-American opinion in Britain, they placed greater emphasis on anti-British opinion in America. They presented the OWI with statistics and quotations about the war effort and progressive social measures to be used to rebut frequent criticisms. British officials knew that if they offered an exchange of propaganda the Americans would be more eager to cooperate.[15]

Both British and American officials considered American journalists and broadcasters as collaborators in the shaping of U.S. opinion. Averell Harriman, in London from 1941 to 1943 as President Roosevelt's special liaison with Prime Minister Churchill, took advantage of his extensive business ties, which included being a board member of Weekly Publications, publishers of *Newsweek*. In March 1942, Harriman informed Malcolm Muir, president and chairman of *Newsweek*'s editorial board, that he wanted *Newsweek* to "have an aggressive United Nations policy" and hoped that Muir agreed. Har-

14. Cruikshank to Darvall, June 2, 1942, FO371/30669 A4915/399/45, PRO.
15. Minutes of the Joint Committee on Information Policy, August 18, 1942, RG 208, Entry 1, Box 5, OWI; Isaiah Berlin and Thomas Wenner, "Report to the Joint Consultative Committee, February 2, 1943, RG 44, Entry 171, Box 1853, OGR; Thomas Wenner to Keith Kane, March 2, 1943, RG 44, Entry 171, Box 1856, OGR, NA.

riman added, "And don't forget the cornerstone of this is joint action by the United States and Britain." The U.S. military reinforced the expectation that reporters had a role to play in winning the war. The Supreme Allied Commander, Gen. Dwight D. Eisenhower, told a group of American newspaper editors, "Public opinion wins wars. I have always considered as quasi-staff officers, correspondents accredited to my headquarters." Many war correspondents who had seen fascism up close accepted these constraints as part of their own war effort. They agreed with Paul White, the head of CBS World News, who instructed all of his correspondents to remember that "winning the war is a hell of a lot more important than reporting it."[16] Propagandists counted on this attitude to convince American reporters to tone down any disapproval of their British ally.

The design and delivery of the new-Britain and war-effort themes corroborated the message of partnership. One of the advantages of the MOI's "strategy of truth" method was the sense of teamwork it inspired. Self-effacing MOI officials and peripatetic American correspondents worked together to get out the story of the war. For instance, Maj. C. B. (Bill) Omerod, an affable ex-soldier on the New York BIS staff, was a master at arranging interviews, providing letters of introduction to traveling correspondents, offering background material, and maintaining connections with a wide range of media figures, from H. V. Kaltenborn to Gregor Ziemer to Joseph C. Harsch of the *Christian Science Monitor*. To praise from Harsch, Omerod responded, "Unsolicited testimonials to our work, such as yours, are vastly encouraging to all of us here who are doing our utmost to achieve, through the production of accurate and factual information, a better American understanding of Britain and the British Commonwealth of Nations."[17] The MOI and the BIS were committed to establishing on a personal level the kind of Anglo-American cooperation they wished to foster at a national level.

16. W. Averell Harriman to Malcolm Muir, May 10, 1942, Container 162, W. Averell Harriman Papers, Library of Congress, Washington, D.C.; Eisenhower quoted by Reuters, April 25, 1944, in Knightley, *First Casualty*, 315; Edward Bliss, Jr., *Now the News: The Story of Broadcast Journalism* (New York: Columbia University Press, 1991), 152.

17. C. B. Omerod to Joseph C. Harsch, November 1, 1943, U.S. Mss. 2AF, Box 1, Joseph C. Harsch Papers, State Historical Society of Wisconsin, Madison, Wis. Kaltenborn met regularly with Omerod at the Harvard Club; U.S. Mss. 1AF, Box 218 and Box 209, Kaltenborn Papers; interview with Berlin.

Walter Lippmann, one of Britain's most influential American friends, disdained British propaganda efforts. In April 1942, Lippmann aired his views to Nevile Butler at the Foreign Office and to his old friend John Maynard Keynes, with whom he had shared disillusionment over the outcome of the 1919 peace conference. First, Lippmann admonished the British for not confiding their policies to American friends, who Lippmann thought were the most effective mouthpiece for getting their case accepted in the United States. He and the late Lord Lothian had agreed that cooperation between the two Atlantic powers must be the cornerstone of the postwar order. They believed that common security interests had dictated the necessity for the Destroyers for Bases Deal (September 1940) and the Lend-Lease agreement (March 1941). Now, Lippmann told Keynes, he was unsure about the British government's position on the changing nature of Anglo-American relations. Second, as a substitute for any serious effort to convey British policy to American editors, Lippmann observed that a campaign seemed to be underway to advertise Britain directly to the American people. He suspected that the embassy had become infected with one of the United States's worst diseases—confidence in publicity experts. Lippmann told Keynes that this was "stupid" and could only do harm. The correct way to explain Anglo-American relations to the public, according to Lippmann, was through Americans who understood both American opinion and the United States's vital interest in the British cause. Lippmann suggested that Keynes show his letter to Brendan Bracken.[18]

Officials in London responded rapidly to Lippmann's first complaint. Bracken cabled that he hoped Lippmann would meet with his director-general, Cyril Radcliffe, who was visiting New York. Nevile Butler wrote to Ronald Campbell at the embassy to make sure Lippmann met Field Marshal Sir John Dill, the highly regarded head of the British Joint Staff Mission. He asked the embassy staff to give Lord Halifax a hint of what was expected of him and directed other British officials Lippmann's way. Several weeks later, Lippmann reported to Butler that the much closer contact he had enjoyed recently

18. Lippmann to Keynes, April 2, 1942, FO371/30655 A4574/60/45; minute by N. Butler, April 24, 1942, FO371/30655 A4574/60/45; Lippmann to Keynes, April 18, 1942, FO371/30656 A8566/60/45, PRO.

with British representatives in the United States had been helpful to him. The Foreign Office sympathized with Lippmann's second objection and hoped the new reorganization of the British Information Services would improve British propaganda in the United States. The MOI learned to treat Lippmann as a "head of state," and the BIS dubbed him "the illustrious client." Isaiah Berlin, head of the BIS survey section at the embassy, met monthly with the prominent columnist to exchange analysis of American opinion and U.S.-Britain relations.[19] As one of the foremost American spokesmen for Anglo-American cooperation, Lippmann was highly valued by British propagandists.

Not all prominent American supporters of Anglo-American relations agreed with Lippmann's views on influencing public opinion. Supreme Court Justice Felix Frankfurter thought Lippmann too contemptuous of the American public or, in the case of one incident, American congressmen. At a dinner given by the Halifaxes for Foreign Secretary Eden, Halifax asked Lippmann's and Frankfurter's advice about Eden's off-the-record meeting with the congressional foreign relations committees. Since the committees included Senator Nye and other leading isolationists, the British were cautious about what Eden should say and how he should say it. Lippmann suggested that the foreign secretary tell the senators and representatives a "story," one which would make the congressmen feel as though they were in on things but would not tell them anything new or important.

Frankfurter dismissed the notion of treating Eden's remarks as a problem in evasion. He described the senators as mostly men of good will who remained ignorant about the role of the United States in international relations. Frankfurter, who privately noted his disgust with Lippmann's suggestion that the congressmen be treated like children and told a story, described Eden's problem as being a "question of teaching calculus to people who are not firmly rooted in the multiplication table." Frankfurter advised Eden to meet concerns about the British Empire and postwar policy with an assurance that the British people wanted the same things the American people wanted.

19. Bracken to Lippmann, April 17, 1942, Box 58, Lippmann Papers; minute by N. Butler, April 24, 1942, FO371/30655 A4574/60/45; Lippmann to N. Butler, May 27, 1942, FO371/30656 A8566/60/45, PRO; interview with Berlin; interview with H. G. Nicholas; Gore-Booth, *Great Truth and Respect*, 177.

In his version of the new-Britain theme, the British were not fighting to maintain an old system of privilege and imperialism but rather for social and economic democracy.[20]

Both Lippmann and Frankfurter wanted to improve Anglo-American relations, but they presented Halifax and Eden with different views of shaping American opinion. A cynical Lippmann viewed opinion as something to be manipulated by experts. His low estimation of the public coupled with his interest in strategic issues made him less likely to value the new-Britain and war-effort themes. Frankfurter, on the other hand, thought American opinion could and should be educated and was interested in social and political issues. British propagandists certainly thought American opinion should be educated with whatever method worked.

"Everything in this country requires to be a drama, or a 'story,' " reported one high-ranking British official in Washington to London. The voices of the BBC resounded with some of the strengths and weaknesses of the presentation of the new-Britain theme. Maurice Gorham noted the difficulty of conveying British virility with English accents that, to American ears, sounded silly and conceited. He thought RAF pilots sounded effeminate. His other challenge was the British habit of understatement. The BBC would find a commando or paratrooper "with a most desperate record . . . an enormous athlete with a face like Victor McLaglen—and then over the microphone would come 'Oh, it was nothing really,' in a little piping voice." Gorham's concern seemed to be a particular problem for radio, because British visitors to the United States found that the Americans professed to enjoy the English accent when heard in person.[21] Over radio, however, the voice alone had to carry the desired message.

The predominant voice of Britain was Winston Churchill's. The prime minister embodied a revitalized old Britain. As Murrow noted, Churchill "mobilized the English language and made it fight." He violated MOI rules by referring to the Germans as "Huns" and "ferocious pagan barbarians." He pronounced the Anglo-American

20. Felix Frankfurter, *From the Diaries of Felix Frankfurter* (New York: W. W. Norton, 1975), 218; Frankfurter to Cripps, July 9, 1942, Reel 77, Felix Frankfurter Papers, Library of Congress, Washington, D.C.

21. R. H. Brand to Sir John Anderson, August 23, 1944, File 197, Robert H. Brand Papers, Bodleian Library, Oxford University, Oxford, Eng.; Gorham, *Sound and Fury*, 114; Wheeler-Bennett, *Special Relationships*, 81.

partnership a "fraternal association" based on "blood and history." In an introduction to the U.S. Army's *Why We Fight* series of indoctrination films directed by Frank Capra, the prime minister thanked the U.S. government's generous treatment of Britain's war effort: "We feel honoured that our kith and kin across the Atlantic Ocean should teach their fighting men to regard us with so much respect and with so much goodwill. And we will make this good by comradeship in the field with the Armies of the United States as long as this struggle shall last and, if possible, after it is over (at least) for a long enough time to prevent it ever happening again." Churchill's rejoicing in ties of "kith and kin" was at odds with the MOI's attempts to move away from overt Anglo-Saxonism in order not to exclude large groups of Americans who had no British ancestry. He nevertheless used his heritage to great effect. Speaking before a joint session of Congress in late December 1941, he delighted his audience with the observation that if his father, instead of his mother, had been an American, he might have gotten to Congress on his own.[22] In person, over the radio, and on newsreels, Churchill's humor offered high entertainment, and his sweeping speech suited the drama of the times. He was the man of the "finest hour."

A second well-known voice in America was that of the actor Leslie Howard, who would have preferred to be recognized for his leading role as writer, director, and star of the 1941 film *Pimpernel Smith* rather than for his portrayal of the southern aristocrat Ashley Wilkes in Hollywood's 1939 blockbuster *Gone with the Wind*. Howard played Horatio Smith, the absentminded professor who outwitted the Nazis to rescue artists and intellectuals—representatives of western culture and tradition—from Germany. While assisting in a futile dig for proof of an early Aryan civilization, his archeology students discover their professor's secret mission and rally to his cause. Most significant was the wholehearted conversion of the skeptical, wisecracking American student, who then became indispensable to the

22. Smith, *Edward R. Murrow*, 114; Anthony Aldgate and Jeffrey Richards, *Britain Can Take It: The British Cinema in the Second World War* (Edinburgh: Edinburgh University Press, 1994), 47–48; "Anglo-American Unity," September 6, 1943 in Churchill, *His Complete Speeches*, vol. 7, 6823–6827; introduction by prime minister for the Capra films recorded at No. 10, September 29, 1943, PREM 4 99/5, PRO; "A Long and Hard War," December 26, 1941, Churchill, *His Complete Speeches*, vol. 6, 6536.

rescue plot. Released by United Artists in the United States as *Mister V.* in 1942, the film was described in the *New York Times* as "absurd derring-do," with Howard as "a gallant figure to capture the imagination and stir the blood."[23]

Howard carried on a version of this role for the BBC's North American Service from 1940 to early 1943. One of his last appearances before he was killed in June, when German fighters shot down his plane, was to host the BBC's celebration of President Roosevelt's birthday, on January 30, 1943. In his broadcasts, he claimed an Anglo-American identity, that he was a born and raised Englishman who lived and worked in the United States. He appealed to American values, quoted the Declaration of Independence, and called for unity of the English-speaking peoples "when the world goes mad." Howard projected the English civilization of Shakespeare, Rupert Brooke, and Henry Higgins, his role in the 1938 film *Pygmalian*. His persona of the "thinking man as hero"—quiet, ironic, brave—was considered a great success with the small audience of shortwave listeners in the United States.[24] It is possible, however, that for many Americans, he would still represent Ashley Wilkes, chivalrous, thoughtful, paternalistic, a man of the past ill-equipped for a world transformed by war.

The "ace of the BBC," according to Princeton analyst David Katz, was novelist J. B. Priestley, champion of the new-Britain theme. Priestley attacked the Christmas-card picture of quaint England and genteel country houses. In one broadcast, the novelist explained that the war was fought by the workers of industrial England, the people with bad teeth who lived on long dreary streets in dark towns. Katz suggested that Priestley's gritty version of the war contrasted favorably with the sentimental appeals of other BBC broadcasters, who referred to the bombing of "our cultural ancestors" rather than to ordinary people. Whereas Churchill glorified the unconquerable valor of Dunkirk, Priestley honored the little ships that went to rescue the evacuating troops. Priestley captured the popular attitude in Britain—that the people were fighting a hated enemy but also believed that they were fighting for a better life after the war, for decent

23. For a fuller analysis of *Pimpernel Smith*, see Aldgate and Richards, *Britain Can Take It*, 56–64.
24. Ibid., 66–73.

homes and improvements in health and education. Churchill's crusade, Howard's literary and intellectual civilization, and Priestley's "people's war" were good stories, admirably told. It was Priestley's speech, according to Gorham, which was "as good for an American audience as for a British."[25]

The BBC's sometimes heavy-handed delivery of propaganda themes in its news programs was analyzed by the Foreign Broadcasting Intelligence Service (FBIS). American social scientists applied qualitative and quantitative techniques to the analysis of the BBC and other foreign broadcasts. FBIS distributed its analysis of the BBC to the State Department, the OWI, the military services, the OSS, the Justice Department, the Bureau of Economic Warfare, and the Lend-Lease Administration. As a measure of Anglo-American cooperation, FBIS sent its weekly analysis of British propaganda to the British embassy, to the British Raw Materials Mission, and to the BBC in New York.[26]

In March 1942, a time of rampant criticism of Britain in the United States, FBIS noted that British commentators highlighted Britain's contribution to Allied victory: "Sacrifice is viewed as a price which Englishmen are happy to pay for freedom. One of the results of this spirit, according to the BBC, is that Britain is passing through a beneficent revolution in social structure and political outlook. . . . The BBC plays up Britain's uninterrupted aid to Russia, and her tendency to give all credit for successes to her allies rather than herself, as evidence of her modesty and good will, which do not merit suspicion."[27] To American analysts, the BBC's tone of nobility and graciousness seemed detached from the real war and strikingly at odds with the shocking string of Allied losses.

Evidence of the new-Britain theme appeared in full force with the

25. Katz, "Britain Speaks," in *Propaganda by Short Wave*, ed. Childs and Whiton, 117, 143; Aldgate and Richards, *Britain Can Take It*, 49–51; Gorham, *Sound and Fury*, 115.

26. FBIS analysts included Lloyd Free, Bernard Berelson, Hans Speier, and Alexander George. Analysts of British propaganda included Eric Estorick, David Truman, and Edward A. Shils. FBIS RG 262, Records of Analysis Division, Entry 73, General Records (Series I), 1941–44, Box 31, 33, and Entry 74, Box 36, NA. On the U.S. government's interest in communications research, see Daniel J. Czitrom, *Media and the American Mind: From Morse to McLuhan* (Chapel Hill: University of North Carolina Press, 1982), 133.

27. FBIS, "Weekly Review of Official Foreign Broadcasts" (hereafter "Weekly Review"), March 21, 1942, RG 262, Entry 33, Box 1, NA.

announcement of the Beveridge Plan, a social welfare program widely publicized in the winter of 1942–43. Allardyce Nicoll reported from the British embassy that according to the OWI, the Beveridge Plan was "the best piece of propaganda we have produced since the Battle of Britain." In a December 5, 1942 analysis, the FBIS reported that the BBC treated the Beveridge Plan as a fulfillment of progress promised by the Atlantic Charter. The BBC emphasized that the reform was not revolutionary and would not take Britain down "the road to Moscow." For Cincinnati's WLW, MacDonald Hastings plugged the plan by noting that Berlin radio had lambasted his earlier announcement of it. Hastings went on to say that Mr. Beveridge believed that the United States would eventually adopt a similar program, an indication that Beveridge and the BBC had not yet observed the political shift away from the New Deal.[28]

The turnaround in the war and at home in 1943 forced some adjustments to propaganda policy. Although the war returned prosperity to the United States after years of depression, it also brought mobility, dislocation, and protest. It inspired African Americans, who believed that democracy and freedom should be fought for at home as well as abroad, to organize against racial discrimination. In the words of the civil rights leader A. Philip Randolph, they planned to "shake up white America." The last groups to benefit from wartime full employment—blacks and Latinos—met with prejudice and violence as they moved to war production centers. Accepted and encouraged as temporary, women workers flooded the defense industry, challenging traditional notions of feminine roles. Gains toward gender and racial equality were tolerated only if they furthered the war effort. For minorities, these inadequate improvements inspired the desire for more. Such demands caused anxiety to mount among those who believed that the social order should "return to normalcy" once the national emergency was over. The trend away from social change, the economic recovery, and the priority Washington put on mobilization all weakened liberalism. In Congress, the Republicans, who gained seats in the 1942 election, joined with

28. Nicoll, "American Reactions to the Beveridge Report," January 19, 1943, FO371/34127 A1005/34/45, PRO; OWI Intelligence Report, February 5, 1943, PSF Subject Files, Box 174, FDRL; FBIS "Weekly Review," December 5, 1942, RG 262, Entry 32, Box 3, NA; WLW Memo, August 31, 1943, Box 16, Ziemer Papers.

southern Democrats, whose position was strengthened by their own party's losses elsewhere, to attack long-resented New Deal programs.

The growth of conservatism in the United States disappointed those British propagandists who, as Liberals, Labour Party supporters, and socialists, endorsed the message of the new-Britain theme avidly. At the MOI and the BBC, they highlighted the role of symbolic ordinary farmers, hairdressers, and cab drivers in the war effort, partly to demonstrate solidarity with ordinary Americans and also to show greater equality in British society. Like their liberal American counterparts in the OWI, they had viewed the war as an opportunity for engineering social change at home.[29] The Republicans and conservative Democrats in the U.S. Congress, who opposed social engineering, especially in any form that prominently featured Franklin Roosevelt, squeezed the New Deal element out of the OWI. The subject of social reform acquired a sharper partisan edge in the United States that took it out of the orbit of the Atlantic Charter's war aims and brought it closer to the forbidden territory of American politics. Whatever their personal politics, British propagandists began to play down the topic of social welfare reform and made sure that when it had to be mentioned, it was with a reassuring tone of moderation.

An invaluable way to attract a wide audience without controversy was to spotlight soldiers, especially as the Allied forces began to turn back the Axis. The BBC interviewed as many GIs as possible. One of its most successful shows, rebroadcast on the Mutual Network, was *American Eagle in Britain*, which featured talks with American soldiers at the Red Cross Rainbow Club in London. British military men, who were the embodiment of the war-effort theme, made tours of the United States, telling of their exploits. Raymond Clapper attended a Washington luncheon for Wing Commander Guy Penrose Gibson, whose two hundred bomber missions included the blowing

---

29. Kenneth O. Morgan describes the themes of common endeavor and classless sacrifice as part of "the facade of unity"; Kenneth O. Morgan, *The People's Peace: British History, 1945–1989* (Oxford: Oxford University Press, 1990), 3–28. For social and political histories of wartime Britain, see also Paul Addison, *The Road to 1945: British Politics and the Second World War* (London: Jonathan Cape, 1975); Angus Calder, *The People's War: Britain, 1939–1945* (New York: Pantheon Books, 1969); Arthur Marwick, *The British and the Second World War* (London: Thames and Hudson, 1976).

This photograph introduced the 1943 *Saturday Evening Post* article "Can Americans and Britons Be Friends?" with the caption "Many Americans still actively dislike George III, but a fun-loving British WAAF makes this soldier from Milwaukee forget his history lessons during an afternoon at Hampstead Heath." (UPI/Corbis-Bettman)

up of the Moehne and Eder dams.[30] The BIS arranged for servicemen to accompany exhibits demonstrating British technology and expertise. For example, two RAF officers acted as interpreters for a traveling exhibit of aerial reconnaissance photographs showing the results of air raids over enemy territory. The photographs, some as large as several yards, included before and after scenes of the bombing of Berlin.

In Cincinnati, Arthur Tandy, the British consul, made a news event out of the photography exhibit when it arrived at the Taft Museum. A museum curator, Katherine Hanna, announced that other special exhibits that year had included "Drawing and Paintings by Evacuated Children," "Red Cross Poster Designs," "This England," and "Blitzed Architecture of London." After the exhibit opening, Tandy's guests, including the RAF officers, U.S. Army Air Force personnel, and the mayor of Cincinnati, as well as Tandy himself were available for interviews.[31] The British consul's arrangements allowed local dignitaries, the press, and the public to experience the war effort vicariously and mingle with the warriors. According to Robin Cruikshank, servicemen were selected to serve as "living examples of the vigor and freshness of our people." The American Division's chief especially wanted those "still young enough to stand as pledges for our future," even if they were ill-spared.[32]

Soldiers, sailors, and airmen most literally embodied "comrades in arms," but others told the story as well. From 1940 to 1943, the American Division concentrated on sending British speakers to the United States when travel across the Atlantic was dangerous and restricted. In the first years of the war, the British had a story to tell of the new Britain and its will to fight. By 1943, though still sending speakers across to the United States, propagandists preferred that Americans to come to Britain. They now had a story to show. American visitors saw the scars of the Blitz and life under full mobilization. The shift in emphasis from telling to showing followed the 1943

---

30. Gorham, *Sound and Fury*, 164; Memoranda, October 6, 1943, Container 23, Clapper Papers.

31. The RAF exhibit was shown in New York, Washington, Chicago, St. Louis, Louisville, Cincinnati, Detroit, Cleveland, Boston, and Philadelphia. Memo from Graham, July 26, 1943 and Hanna to [Ziemer], July 28, 1943, Box 16, Ziemer Papers.

32. Cruikshank, "British Speakers in the United States," December 3, 1943, FO371/34102 A11195/15/45, PRO.

visit by five American senators who became so notorious in British official circles that it was only necessary to refer to them as "The Five." As members of the body that had rejected the League of Nations and had failed to ratify the peace treaty following World War I, senators figured prominently on the isolationist-internationalist spectrum. The 1943 visitors, representing Senator Truman's committee on the conduct of the war and the Military Affairs Committee, made a global tour to investigate the war effort. James M. Mead (D-N.Y.), Richard B. Russell (D-Ga.), Henry Cabot Lodge Jr. (R-Mass., identified in British notes as the grandson of "Treaty Lodge"), Ralph Owen Brewster (R-Me.), and Albert "Happy" Chandler (D-Ky.), received red-carpet treatment. Churchill met with them. Foreign Secretary Eden hosted a luncheon at the Savoy Hotel. The speaker of the House of Commons held a tea. After they left London they visited Egypt, India, and China. The minister of state at Cairo reported to London that apart from observing the U.S. military, the senators were most interested in oil. When the senators visited Ceylon, the British governor took them on a tour of the rubber estates and paddy fields surrounding Colombo. Senator Chandler reportedly complimented the governor with the observation, "Gee, Governor, I can see you are a good governor; the folks are sure glad to see you."[33]

The British were satisfied with their efforts until the senators returned to the United States in late September and set off a flak attack. They accused the British of violating the Lend-Lease agreement, of conducting a lethargic war effort in India, and of letting the United States do most of the fighting while the British acquired territory. The senators' findings were reported by the business-oriented *Kiplinger Washington Letter*, in its October 9, 1943, issue. The war effort was on a good footing, the newsletter announced, but "the British are out-slicking us, both now and for the postwar."[34] These charges

33. Minute by Malcolm, July 18, 1943, FO371/34092 A6722/3/45; "Visit to Ceylon of 5 United States Senators," September 3–5, 1943, FO371/38522 AN1326/16/45, PRO.

34. NBC interview with five senators, September 29, 1943; speech by Richard Russell to the U.S. Senate, October 28, 1943; and *Kiplinger Washington Letter*, October 9, 1943; Richard B. Russell Papers, Series 5, Subseries 10, Richard B. Russell Library for Political Research and Studies, University of Georgia Libraries, Athens, Ga.

The Five Senators, who harshly criticized Britain's war effort on their return home, pose here with workers in Abadan, Iran, during their 1943 world tour. *From left to right:* Henry Cabot Lodge Jr., Richard B. Russell, James M. Mead, Ralph Owen Brewster, and Albert B. ("Happy") Chandler. Major General Donald H. Connolly stands at the far right. (Richard B. Russell Library for Political Research and Studies)

struck raw nerves in Britain. They reinforced the negative stereotypes propagandists had labored to transform.

An affronted Churchill wrote to the president asking if Roosevelt had any objections to a rebuttal of the senators' charges. FDR privately told the columnist Raymond Clapper that the senators had attracted more attention abroad than they had at home, where people knew how to judge the remarks of someone like "Happy" Chandler. Senator Russell informed the president that despite press coverage to the contrary, 85 percent of their report was favorable. As often happened when flare-ups occurred, Harry Hopkins responded to Churchill for FDR. He acknowledged that the senators had caused friction but suggested that since many Americans agreed with some of the senators' views, the prime minister should wait until he could make a corrective statement in the context of some event. Churchill accepted Hopkins' advice. The Cabinet decided that the prime minister would give too much weight to the allegations if he answered them directly.[35]

The British government's lack of response dismayed America-watchers in the Foreign Office and the MOI. Richard Law, the minister of state, objected to dignified silence. Dignity might be admired, Law argued, by a minority of Americans. The majority, however, would only remember what the senators said in the headlines and that the British had no reply. He wanted to counter American accusations with the British side.[36] The desire of Law and the American Division of the MOI to tackle directly American criticism led to a consideration of the "Answering Back" campaign. British representatives in Washington argued that the only worthwhile direct rejoinder must come from the top, even though it would run against the practice of "saving" the prime minister for important statements. The embassy preferred using the indirect approach of getting U.S. correspondents to correct American criticisms for them, even though it

35. Cox to Hopkins, October 11, 1943, Harry Hopkins Papers, Container 314, Sherwood Collection, FDRL; Kimball, ed., *Churchill and Roosevelt*, vol. 2, 527–532; "2nd Roosevelt Private Conference," October 20, 1943, Memoranda 1942–43, Container 23, Clapper Papers; FO371/34221 A/9654/6274/45, PRO.

36. Law noted: "As things are we shall be immensely dignified. We shall become increasingly despised. And everything will have gone by default—though we won't even begin to suspect it." Law, November 24, 1943, FO371/34130 A10935/34/45, PRO.

had been observed that their usual friends Walter Lippmann and Raymond Clapper had failed to rebuke the senators. The "Answering Back" campaign did not satisfy those who wanted American accusations confronted.[37]

For Cruikshank, the affair of the five senators had shown "how easy it is for British interests to be made a football in the American party scrum." He warned of politicians and newsmen lying in wait to pounce on any indiscretions of a British visitor. When possible, Americans should do the talking, but certain subjects, Cruikshank observed, required British speakers who should be chosen "in accordance with the urgency of our propaganda needs." Into this category fit British servicemen; vindicators of the empire, a subject on which "friendly Americans" were ineffective because of lack of knowledge and inclination; and vocational speakers. The creation of goodwill was not enough. The MOI wanted a greater "publicity or propaganda yield" by targeting specific groups. For example, London would send agricultural spokesmen to publicize the development of British farming during the war, British workers to speak to American workers, and British professionals to speak to American professional organizations. The main message to be delivered over and over was that Britain was a vigorous, progressive, forward-looking nation, a "worthy partner and an equal, needed by America for her own safety and well-being, in war and peace." Speakers should never mention "Britain's plight or poverty," because that would destroy the argument.[38]

The MOI censored the choice of speakers. The government preferred that some citizens, such as one of its most outspoken critics, Labour M.P. Aneurin Bevan, not be allowed to speak in the United States. The MOI also desired that certain British visitors, such as a group of bankers and industrialists attending a foreign trade convention in the United States, be protected from publicity. The American

---

37. For his part, Clapper thought there was not much of an issue, since on the whole the senators had been pleased by their findings. Clapper to Harrison Salisbury, October 21, 1943, Correspondence, Box 51, Clapper Papers; Cruikshank to N. Butler, October 25, 1943, FO371/34222 A10055/6274/45; report by H. G. Nicholas, November 6, 1943, FO371/34222 A/10369/6274/45, PRO. See FO371/38555 and 38556 for discussion of the "Answering Back" campaign.

38. Cruikshank, "British Speakers in the United States," December 3, 1943, FO371/34102 A11195/15/45; minute by Graham Spry, December 23, 1943, FO371/34102 A11338/15/45, PRO.

Division concluded that although the U.S. public was ignorant of "simple economic truths," its education should be left to "those Americans who are familiar with our thinking." Those speakers allowed to go were briefed by the MOI before they left and by the British Information Services when they arrived.[39]

To assist in the briefing, a booklet drawn up in mid-1943, *Notes for Guidance of United Kingdom Officials Visiting the United States*, was distributed to forty government departments. In his introduction to the booklet, Alexander Cadogan, the permanent undersecretary of the Foreign Office, announced that Foreign Secretary Eden requested that all British representatives make a "serious attempt to understand the kind of people with whom they will have to work." *Notes for Guidance*, Cadogan warned, was unsuitable for American eyes. The booklet urged British representatives to show enthusiasm and confidence in Britain's future and asked its readers to "try to like Americans and *show* that you like them" by avoiding "British reserve." Comparisons between American and British ways of life were dangerous, cautioned *Notes for Guidance*, "since it is not easy to avoid offence." This warning applied in particular to the American form and method of government. Other pointers included:

It is polite to be expansive when business is being done. Accessibility, even to bores, is often essential.

An American's knowledge and interests are often wider than appears at first. Remember this.[40]

Visitors were urged to adopt American conversational practices. The booklet suggested that since personal questions were an accepted form, British representatives should ask them to collect useful information. For instance, a man might be asked where he came from, his state and city, his business, and the name of his firm. A woman should be asked about her cultural interest. Repeating names in conversation in order to learn them was common practice. The British government had produced its own version of a crash course in Dale

39. Halifax to FO, January 22, 1943, FO371/34098 A1593/A1660/15/43; Cruikshank to Butler, December 14, 1943, FO371/34102 A11338/15/45, PRO.

40. *Notes for Guidance of United Kingdom Officials Visiting the United States*, June 1943, FO371/34088 A2994/3/45, PRO.

Carnegie methods for winning friends and influencing "the kind of people with whom we will have to work."

Notes for Guidance advised on subject matter as well as form. British visitors were reminded not to take sides in the 1944 election. The booklet stated the official position on the Allies. On Russia, representatives were to say that no peace would be possible without the collaboration of the Soviets. For example, Cadogan briefed a delegation to the Foreign Trade Convention on the Soviet issue. In discussions with Republican businessmen, to whom ending the New Deal sometimes seemed "to rival winning the war in urgency," he advised the British businessmen to take the line that a fair trial must be given to Big Three cooperation.[41] The booklet noted that the United States had endowed the Chinese "with a degree of virtue few Chinese would claim." Unless the speaker had firsthand knowledge of the Far East, however, he or she should not attempt to correct this view. In addition to advice on manners, conversation, and subject matter, the booklet recommended a list of books on the United States, many of them written by the staff of the MOI's American Division, for British representatives to read on their ocean voyage.[42]

The Americans invited to Britain were chosen for their ability to reach a variety of audiences at home. Under an exchange program with the OWI, American visitors included theologian Reinhold Niebuhr, newspaper publisher Frank Gannett, the educational director of the International Ladies Garment Workers' Union, Mark Starr, and anthropologist Margaret Mead.[43] Mead attempted to explain the two societies to each other in numerous articles. For the Americans, she wrote "Ferment in British Education," "A G.I. View of Great Britain," and "As Johnny Thinks of Home: He Learns Little of England." For the British, she wrote "American Troops and the British Community," "Why We Americans 'Talk Big,' " and "What Is a Date?" directed especially at young British women.

41. N. Butler, September 28, 1943, FO371/34102 A9452/15/45, PRO.

42. The list included D. W. Brogan, *U.S.A.: An Outline of the Country* (1941) and *Politics and Law in the United States* (1941); Lionel Elvin, *Men of America* (1941); Phyllis Bentley, *Here Is America* (1942); Frank Darvall, *American Political Scenes* (1939); and by American historian Allan Nevins, *Brief History of the United States* (1942) and *America: Story of a Free People* (1942). *Notes for Guidance*, June 1943, FO371/34088 A2994/A11250/3/45, PRO.

43. Gallienne, January 5, 1944, FO371/38577 AN373/78/45; A. R. K. Mackenzie, April 6, 1944, FO371/38579 AN550/78/45, PRO.

This last topic might have provided propagandists with another variation of the "comrades-in-arms" story, but the issue of relations between American troops and British women was too delicate and controversial in both countries for any major build-up by government officials. Although at the end of the war, forty thousand British war brides would return home with U.S. servicemen, during the war propagandists promoted family life as occurring specifically among British men, British women, and British children, or among American men, American women, and American children. An ideal illustration of the type of preferred story resulted from Margaret Mead's visit to a residential nursery school located in the country, away from the heavy bombing. Upon her return, she wrote a moving account entitled "One Mother Goes a Long Way." The children, whose fathers— if living—were away in the armed forces and whose mothers worked in war factories, greeted every woman who came in from the outside as "mother." Mead watched one such mother be mobbed by forty children, who had to be embraced and fussed over, until at the end of an hour, she was able to sit quietly with her own child.[44]

Another success for the MOI's policy of inviting fifty U.S. opinion leaders a year was the 1943 trip of *Harper's* editor, Frederick Lewis Allen. The MOI Tours Section, which Allen thought remarkably thorough and attentive, arranged for the American editor to visit the coastal town of Plymouth, which the Germans had hammered in the spring of 1941. Allen rewarded MOI's attentions with "Notes on an English Visit," which appeared in *Harper's* January 1944 issue. Allen described life in Britain where, during the long blackout, a small child was overheard asking her mother what a lamp-pole was for. He detailed the effects of bombing he had seen, the deprivations of food and clothing, and contrasted the difference with the United States.[45]

44. "One Mother Goes a Long Way," January 4, 1944, written for the Harriet Johnson Nursery School by parent Margaret Mead; Margaret Mead Papers, I 26, Folder 1943, Library of Congress, Washington, D.C.; Other articles published respectively in *Journal of the American Association of University Women* 37, no. 3 (Spring 1944); *New York Times Magazine*, March 19, 1944; *Social Action* 10, no. 3 (March 15, 1944); *American Troops and the British Community* was published as a pamphlet in Britain; *The Listener* 30, no. 772 (October 28, 1943); and *Transatlantic*, no. 10 (June 1944); David Reynolds makes a fascinating and comprehensive study of the American presence in wartime Britain in *Rich Relations: The American Occupation of Britain, 1942–1945* (New York: Random House, 1995). He suggests the figure of forty thousand war brides on p. 422 and discusses "gals" on pp. 262–283.

45. Frederick Lewis Allen, "Notes on an English Visit," *Harper's*, January 1944,

Adopting both the new-Britain and the war-effort themes, Allen conveyed to his readers the endurance of the British people during the war.

Allen found Anglo-American relations to be one of the inevitable topics of conversation with Brendan Bracken, Robin Cruikshank, and Hamish Hamilton, his friend and host. American correspondents in London also showed concern over the state of the alliance. For example, the *New York Times* reporter James (Scotty) Reston was worried that the U.S. public was not aware of Britain's contribution to the war. He said that it was crucial to get Britain into the Pacific war once Germany was defeated. Otherwise, he thought, critics at home would accuse the British of "lying down on the job" and of getting ready to take over U.S. markets. Reston and Herbert Agar both expressed concern over the British people's admiration for the Russian war effort, although Reston felt that this admiration was in part determined by their ability to worship the Red Army from afar while coping with the build-up of American troops at close range. American correspondents heard and repeated the message that the United States and Britain must work together in order to get along with Russia.[46]

The MOI sought to correct the impression created by the five senators by courting Congress. Urged on by the Washington embassy, the American Division invited thirty-five congressmen to Britain between June 1944 and March 1945. The embassy sent London a brief on each visitor, including his or her interests, committee assignments, position on the isolationist-internationalist spectrum, and views on Anglo-American relations. For example, Walter H. Judd, a Republican from Minnesota, was described as "suspicious of British imperialism" and "a handful but worth tackling." James Richards of South Carolina was labeled "a progressive Southern Democrat, but shy of 'Big 4' stuff." Not all the visits were successful. Some congressmen returned to do imitations of the five senators. Overall, however, the embassy was pleased with the results. The congressmen addressed constituents and made broadcasts about the stark contrast between mobilized civilian life in Britain and the United States. Mi-

---

117–128; London Diary (1943), Box 1, Frederick Lewis Allen Papers, Library of Congress, Washington, D.C.

46. London Diary (1943), Box 1, Allen Papers.

chael Wright of the embassy wrote in January 1945 that the British were building a group of congressmen with a better understanding of Britain's position. By 1945, however, the Foreign Office and the MOI preferred to put their limited resources into visits by media figures, such as editors, journalists, and writers. London believed that these people were more intelligent, better educated, and more influential than congressmen.[47]

The MOI's speakers policy illustrated propagandists' attempts to coordinate the presentation of Britain. London sent British representatives to the United States with instructions on conduct and position statements. The MOI invited American opinion leaders over to show them Britain at war. It carried out the "strategy of truth" by selecting which sites would inspire American visitors to "see for themselves" the intensity of Britain's war effort. Propagandists hoped to make the American visitors into witnesses for Anglo-American cooperation. The propaganda themes would then be repeated by British visitors to the United States and reinforced by returning Americans.

By 1944 American military might and production capacity overshadowed Britain's, but the British hoped to remind the United States of their contribution through the war-effort theme. One of their greatest accomplishments was *Index to Invasion*, prepared for D-Day, June 6, 1944. To ensure that Britain received some of the credit for the long-awaited landing on the European continent, the American Division of the MOI put together forty pages of material for distribution by the BIS. Days ahead, the *Index* was flown across the Atlantic in a lead container guaranteed to sink if the plane happened to be shot down. On the morning of the invasion, the BIS staff rushed the *Index* out to the press and radio networks.[48]

Written in tough, journalistic language, the *Index to Invasion* opened with an account of Britain's war effort. The *Index* described the British island's role as the great western base for the invasion,

47. Halifax to FO, August 14, 1944, FO371/38581 AN3148/78/45; Halifax to FO, August 22, 1944, FO371/38581 AN3245/78/45; Wright to Broadmead and minute by Donnelly, January 29, 1945, FO371/44547 AN390/7/45; Judson, "Visits by US Congressmen to UK," March 16, 1945, FO371/44547 AN1040/7/45, PRO.
48. Bentley, *"O Dream, O Destinations,"* 234; "Report on British Publicity in the USA during the Early Stages of the Invasion of France," June 1944, FO371/38690 AN2783/2113/45, PRO.

thanks to the British people's stand in 1940. Readers were reminded that Allied attacks had relied on bases furnished by the British Commonwealth and Empire around the world. The first pages, entitled "Britain's Part," set up the context for the invasion. The bulk of the report contained statistics, background, and quotations from Churchill and U.S. general Omar Bradley, especially useful to broadcasters who were on the air all day with the biggest story of the war. The *Index* discussed the logistical problems of the invasion: weather, maps, beachheads, landing craft, training of paratroopers and commandos, air support, depots for supplies, salvage-rescue tugs, hospital ships, and mobile laundries. For comparison, sketches of other Allied landings in Tunisia, Sicily, and Italy were provided, as well as the specifications of every British and American aircraft known to be operating in the European theater. The *Index* allowed any commentator to speak authoritatively on the mechanics of the invasion while audiences awaited news of its success.[49]

Many Americans also turned to the BBC for news. Gorham and Lindsay Wellington, the North American director of the BBC, exulted in their accomplishment. Out of 914 radio stations in the United States, 725 carried BBC reports on the invasion. The *New York Times* radio editor praised the BBC for its outstanding coverage, especially the live broadcasts of the invasion. The BIS received similar tributes from the American media.[50]

Although the MOI, the BIS, and the BBC celebrated their success at claiming the attention of the American media during the early days of the invasion, other British officials complained about the increasing stridency of American nationalism. Halifax was dismayed by the lack of recognition given to the British by Americans. Isaiah Berlin disagreed. He believed that given every country's tendency to focus on its own troops, the Americans practiced great generosity in referring to Allied forces instead of American forces for the first three days of the invasion. An embassy analysis of the press coverage of the invasion concluded that headlines were the most nationalistic and editorials the most balanced. The analyst noted that, unfortunately,

49. Cruikshank to N. Butler, July 25, 1944, FO371/38690 AN3038/2113/45, PRO.

50. Gorham, *Sound and Fury*, 145; "Broadcasting to North America," BBC WAC E2/438/3; Morgan to Radcliffe, June 6, 1944, FO371/38690 AN2354/2113/45, PRO.

of the Americans who bought newspapers, only 25 percent read the editorials, whereas almost everyone read the headlines. Reports from the British consuls showed that local presses played down Britain's role; the most guilty cities included Boston, Chicago, and Kansas City.[51]

Propagandists' responses to the D-Day coverage reflected their views of their task and American opinion. The BIS and the BBC, aware of the competitive nature of the American media and the lack of interest most Americans had in non-American fighting, were pleased with their success. When the Joint Staff Mission complained to the MOI that the American press was not adequately covering the British war effort, Brendan Bracken retorted that Americans must be expected to write about American achievements. Otherwise, they might be transferred. As an example, he pointed out to them that London had recently lost "one of the best American journalists," James Reston, who had been recalled by the *New York Times* for being "too pro-British."[52] The Foreign Office and Lord Halifax tended to see in the Americans' nationalistic attitudes a portent of the future. If Americans were not solicitous of their allies while in the midst of a great joint effort, there could be little hope that they would be later, when Britain would have even less to offer.

Propagandists became more embattled as the United States increasingly dominated the war effort. Maurice Gorham predicted that the "dullest and most difficult period" for the North American Service would be when the war switched from the European to the Pacific theater. The BBC would be hard pressed to keep the attention of an American audience. Gorham set down the BBC's policy: keep at the forefront Britain's war effort in Europe and in the Pacific, recall the part played by the Soviet Union, ensure that the rehabilitation of Europe made the news, and keep alive the role of the Commonwealth

    51. Berlin to Malcolm, June 20, 1944, FO371/38557 AN2575/34/45; Mackenzie, August 1, 1944, FO371/38690 AN3238/2113/45, PRO.
    52. Bracken to H. Butler, June 13, 1944, INF 1/975. Isaiah Berlin wrote from Washington that Reston confirmed Bracken's explanation of his recall; Berlin to Malcolm, June 20, 1944, FO371/38557 AN2575/34/45, PRO. In his memoir, Reston said he replaced Ray Daniell in London for several months in 1943 until Daniell returned from a much-needed rest; James Reston, *Deadline: A Memoir* (New York: Random House, 1991), 126.

and Empire at the peace conference. The FBIS reported that the BBC had dropped references to ideals of reform and equality in order to concentrate on winning the war, with repeated assurances that Britain would finish the fight in the Pacific.[53]

The war-effort theme survived better than the new-Britain theme, which wound down because it became less convincing. With the smoke of the Blitz clearing, Americans observed that the British social structure appeared to have survived. In October 1944, several American correspondents in London agreed they had made a mistake in reporting that the war would produce a new Britain. Raymond Daniell of the *New York Times* used an anecdote from the United States to illustrate the persistence of inequality in both cultures. Daniell remembered "too well the Mississippi floods, when the local banker and little nigger boy together got out there and piled sand bags; but when it was over, he was still the banker and he still the little nigger boy."[54]

Edward R. Murrow also admitted that he had underestimated the resiliency of the Conservatives. The CBS correspondent had juggled his commitment to reporting the story of ordinary people with his role as an unofficial statesman welcome at the highest levels of the British and American government. He came to represent the quintessential American in London, sought out by the British and Americans alike for advice on Anglo-American relations. On the weekly North American Service show *Freedom Forum*, chaired by Sir Frederick Whyte, one-time head of the MOI's American Division, Murrow, as the American, engaged in wide-ranging political debates with the historian G. M. Young as the conservative and the political philosopher Harold Laski as the socialist.[55]

Respect for Murrow was high enough in London that in 1943, Bracken, with Churchill's agreement, asked the American correspondent if he would take over the program directorship of the BBC. Murrow considered it but declined. He had earned his reputation as a heroic pioneer of wartime broadcasting, but Murrow's advice to a BBC correspondent on his way to Washington revealed that his re-

53. Gorham, "The North American Service in the Post European War Period," June 5, 1944, BBC WAC E2/438/3; FBIS, "Weekly Review," February 5, 1944, RG 262, Entry 32, Box 4.
54. War Correspondent Notes, October 9, 1944, Container F-8, Sevareid Papers.
55. Gorham, *Sound and Fury*, 115–116; Sperber, *Murrow*, 175, 211, 237.

The BBC's dynamic weekly series *Freedom Forum* featured the Labour intellectual Harold Laski as the socialist, the historian G. M. Young as the conservative, Sir Frederick Whyte as the chair, and CBS correspondent Edward R. Murrow as the American spokesperson. (BBC)

porting experience had exposed him to manipulation and compromise. Murrow cautioned, "Beware of having your mouth shut for
you, of too much information too freely given." He continued,
"Don't get conned, don't bother about Anglo-American relations.
Just report on what's going on."[56] Murrow's advice outlined the pit-
falls for journalists exposed to the "strategy of truth."

As Maurice Gorham had foretold, it was difficult to maintain enthusiasm about a new spirit of Britain when Britain itself was no
longer the focus of attention in the fighting. Instead, what American
visitors saw, as arranged by the MOI, was evidence of wearing sacrifice and toil. "London is like the grimy anteroom to a great factory," described Eric Sevareid in the fall of 1944, "where people have
been working overtime on rush orders so long they are become a
little short with one another, less polite and formal; they are too busy
filling orders for great transactions which they control in the far corners of the earth; it is so different from the tight little situation of
1940."[57] During the Blitz, Britain had loomed large in Americans'
world view. With the exception of the great preparations for D-Day,
Britain appeared to have shrunk to the size of a small island once
the danger of invasion had passed, and Americans and Britons
looked to Allied ventures in the "far corners of the earth."

The last months of the war brought out both the successes and
limitations of the story of "comrades in arms." In April and May of
1945, the BIS was on hand to celebrate internationalism at the formation of the United Nations in San Francisco. Aubrey Morgan's
staff ran press conferences, radio broadcasts, informal meetings between the British delegates and the press, and provided the two thousand journalists attending with a daily press summary and
commentary. Erwin D. Canham, editor of the *Christian Science Monitor*, paid tribute to the "beautiful job" done by the "intelligent, affable, quick-witted and pleasant" people of the BIS. Said Canham,
"They know newspaper language [and] they are not too British; at
least they try not to be. . . . In all this service, there is extraordinarily
little propaganda, as such. Of course, you can say that it all propaganda. And in the best sense of the word, so it is. But it is helpful,

---

56. From interview with Leonard Miall quoted in Sperber, *Murrow*, 229; Frankfurter, *Diaries*, 256;
57. War correspondent notes, October 9, 1944, Container F-8, Sevareid Papers.

Major C. B. (Bill) Omerod of BIS-N.Y. (center) brought together H. V. Kaltenborn of NBC and Prime Minister Clement Attlee at the 1945 San Francisco conference. Omerod, traveling on the special California-bound train carrying hundreds of journalists, told a BIS colleague that there were only three people on the train "worth bothering about." Omerod, demonstrating his talents as the BIS's "star high-level contact" man, soon made himself and the three into an exclusive quartet. (State Historical Society of Wisconsin WH:[X3]50811)

it is straightforward, and it is as candid as you can expect under the circumstances. No alert newspaperman is going to be deceived or misled by such a system. He will utilize it, and that is what the British expect."[58] Aware that he was participating in a propaganda effort, Canham nevertheless qualified it as propaganda "in the best sense of the word." Years of planning, coordination, and hard work had culminated in the achievement of this picture of cooperation between "alert" newsmen and the "not-too-British" staff of the BIS.

At the same time, the new-Britain and war-effort themes had worn thin. The day after V-E Day, Ronald Campbell reported that Americans assumed "that the United States not only saved us by 'coming' in but that they alone saved us." The embassy's minister, who had in 1942 scoffed at the new-Britain theme, now pointed out the danger of a "myth" in which Britain was under obligation to the Americans and therefore would be forced to concede to any demands the United States might make.[59]

Neither ally liked to hear that the other had won the war. In London, Eric Sevareid shared Campbell's view that the Americans' "creeping superiority complex" made them difficult to bear. Britain seemed overrun by GIs, whose conversation consisted of "winning the war for you" and "the trouble with this country is. . . ." But he did not approve of the way the British disparaged Americans as a result of their "creeping inferiority complex." In March 1945, he noted that the British were "constantly reminding [the] public of 'when we stood alone in this island' kind of nostalgia for that period when they were the heroes of the world; *that* was the great achievement; all that states have done since all over the world doesn't quite count: 'oh well, those masses of men and machines.' As though not quite human, as though no human hearts and brains [were] involved; as though we were a nation of robots."[60] Part of the appeal of the new-Britain theme had been its respect for the sacrifices of ordinary people; Sevareid resented the lack of respect for the sacrifices of ordinary Americans. Exhaustion mixed with the longing of everyone for everyone to go home explained some of the strain in Allied re-

---

58. Morgan to Cruikshank, May 17, 1945, INF1/701, PRO; Canham quoted in Marett, *Through the Back Door*, 115–116.
59. R. I. Campbell, May 9, 1945, FO371/44575 AN1409/36/45, PRO.
60. "Notes . . . London, March 1945," Container F-8, Sevareid Papers.

lations in the spring of 1945. More troubling for propaganda policy was the way in which images that had symbolized cooperation—the new spirit of Britain during the Blitz and the U.S. embrace of internationalism following Pearl Harbor—were turning nationalistic.

The international themes had taken greater priority over domestic themes as the war went on. As they did, the notion of Anglo-American cooperation focused less on the "people's war" of ordinary Britons and Americans and more on the issue of global leadership and the role of national governments. For instance, British propagandists rallied their American friends to their defense on the issue of His Majesty's government's policies in Greece and Yugoslavia in the early weeks of 1945. Critics accused London of plotting to install reactionary monarchies in the two liberated Balkan countries. The U.S. government supported the return to Yugoslavia of its government-in-exile under King Peter, even though it recognized that the communist leader Tito and his partisans had more popular support. But it disapproved of British military intervention in the Greek civil war to suppress the more powerful left-wing faction. The Greek monarch, King George II, an extreme conservative known to have sympathized with Adolf Hitler, was held in disfavor by many Greeks. Washington refrained from official condemnation, but an outraged Roosevelt thundered in private, "How the British can dare such a thing! The lengths to which they will go to hang on to the past!"[61]

From the Washington embassy, Michael Wright explained to Philip Broadmead at the Foreign Office that "to convince a liberal that he is wrong, when he is in an emotional state and believes that he has more information than you is no easy task." Wright offered two arguments to shield British policy. The first denied that Britain sought to return kings to thrones around Europe, thereby defusing the Greek case. The second diverted attention from Britain by suggesting that the U.S. government had shirked its responsibility in this strategically vital region. Wright reported that Walter Lippmann was "consistently helpful and played as big a part as anyone." Joseph C. Harsch, James Reston, Raymond Gram Swing, and the *Newsweek* columnist Ernest Lindley also assisted. Bill Omerod of the BIS persuaded several news commentators, including Edward R. Murrow,

61. John O. Iatrides, *Revolt in Athens: The Greek Communist "Second Round,"* *1944–1946* (Princeton, N.J.: Princeton University Press, 1972), 213–214.

to respond on Britain's behalf. Wright enjoyed hearing a newspaper editor in Buffalo quote Murrow's broadcast back to him. "It is to [moderate liberals] to whom we must look to guide American policy on the sort of lines we want," concluded Wright. "When they join with America Firsters in attacking us, we are in about the worst possible position here. When they support us, and attack our traditional critics and opponents, we are in about the best position we can hope to achieve."[62]

Propagandists wanted their American friends and the British speakers touring the United States to confirm the public's "slight but growing appreciation" that the world was "not a very nice place." In a March 1943 interview with Raymond Clapper, Foreign Secretary Anthony Eden had done just that. Clapper noted that although Eden impressed him with his desire to bring the Big Four nations (Britain, the Soviet Union, China, and the United States) together, he also "left the feeling without actually having said it, that he is fearful of Russia and wants very much an Anglo-American front to put up against it."[63] Eden's implication offered a twist to the official British position that the United States and Britain must work together to get along with Russia but reinforced the fundamental message that Anglo-American cooperation was essential.

To keep alive the idea of equal partnership, propagandists sought to balance the United States's growing power with the British Commonwealth and Empire. The promotion of empire would not enhance the image of rebirth. It touched upon antique animosities in the United States, where the celebration of its severance from the British Empire was a beloved annual holiday. Propagandists considered projecting the reform spirit of the new Britain onto the Commonwealth and Empire as well as offering the empire as an economic and strategic advantage in an uncertain world. First, however, in 1942 they faced a crisis of immense proportions, for they could not portray the imperial crown as an asset if its jewel shone for independence.

---

62. Omerod (BIS-N.Y.) "induced Gabriel Heatter, Quincy Howe, Cecil Brown, and Frank Kingdon to take it up." Wright to Broadmead, February 26, 1945, FO371/44556 AN929/22/45, PRO.

63. Spry, December 3, 1943, FO371/34102 A11195/15/45, PRO; interview with Anthony Eden, March 18, 1943, Memoranda 1942–1943, Clapper Papers.

4 The Campaign for Empire, 1: Crisis in India

> I will put it like this: except for a few university professors who have had to study the question, American knowledge of India begins at 1939 or later. Before this, India is a hotchpotch of which the ingredients are missionaries' tales, Kipling . . . Bengal Lancers, Gandhi, Nehru, civil disobedience troubles, Sabhu, with some India League propaganda as seasoning, served up in a dish of British Empire china, period George III.
>
> —SIR FREDERICK PUCKLE, ADVISER ON INDIAN AFFAIRS, BRITISH EMBASSY, WASHINGTON, 1944

For many Americans, the term "British Empire" conjured up 1776, redcoats, and the Declaration of Independence. Although enemy forces occupied parts of it, the British Empire of World War II covered one-quarter of the globe and consisted of approximately 500 million people: the Commonwealth or self-governing dominions, including Canada, New Zealand, Australia, and South Africa; the mandated territories of Tanganyika, Cameroons, Togoland, and Palestine; the independent protected states of Tonga, Sarawak, Brunei, and Malaya; several colonies and territories, including Bermuda, Jamaica, British Guiana, the Falkland Islands, British Solomon Islands, North Borneo, Hong Kong, Kenya, Nigeria, Uganda, Somaliland, Malta, and Gibraltar; and the Indian Empire and Burma. Regardless of what Americans of the 1940s may have comprehended about the nations, colonies, and territories of the British Empire, most thought that independence from it was a natural and desirous objective. Americans believed that the British ruthlessly exploited their colonial peoples for profits, that they practiced "taxation without representation," and that they lazily and inefficiently ran the empire as an "upper-class racket."[1] Propagandists referred to this tradition of antagonism toward the British Empire as the "ancient grudge." The "ancient grudge" had smoldered over the years, ready to be rekindled during election seasons and whenever American economic interests in the imperial domain were at stake.[2]

British policymakers feared that American anticolonialism could obstruct the formation of a postwar partnership in at least two ways. The United States could reject any cooperation with the British Empire and retreat into isolationism, or it could pursue an independent, expansionist internationalism. Either way would be a disaster for the British, whose recovery depended on both American assistance and a restored empire. Propagandists faced a formidable dilemma. Britain's portrayal of itself as a strong and valuable partner of the United States in the postwar world depended upon the maintenance of its imperial power, one that the Americans threatened to declare obsolete.

During World War II, friction between the United States and Britain over the Empire affected military, economic, and political issues. Americans expressed their suspicions about the goal of Britain's military strategy by referring to Lord Louis Montbatten's Southeast Asian Command (SEAC) as "Save England's Asiatic Colonies." During Lend-Lease negotiations, the U.S. government pushed for an "open door" international economy by forcing Britain to promise to eliminate discriminatory practices. When Prime Minister Churchill dissociated the British Empire from the self-determination principle

---

1. Minute by King, June 26, 1942, FO371/30685 A5545/1684/45; extracts from memorandum by R. I. Campbell, October 14, 1942, FO371/30685 U1383/828/70, PRO.

2. Christopher Hitchens locates the origin of the phrase "ancient grudge," which appears repeatedly in British official documents, as the subtitle of Owen Wister's *The Straight Deal: The Ancient Grudge*. Wister, the author of *The Virginian* and a close friend of Theodore Roosevelt, attacked anglophobia in this and another book, *The Pentecost of Calamity*, published at the time of the First World War. See Christopher Hitchens, *Blood, Class, and Nostalgia: Anglo-American Ironies* (New York: Farrar, Straus and Giroux, 1990), 55.

of the Atlantic Charter, many Americans concluded that the United States and Britain did not share a common vision for the peace. American views of the empire—past, present, and future—did not bode well for the "special relationship."[3]

Nor did the propagandists find it easy to follow the preferred method of carrying out government policy by threading propaganda themes into their interpretation of news events. First, propagandists were attempting to arrange a harmony of British voices singing the cooperation anthem to the American audience, but they found policymakers to be out of tune with one another. In 1942 the national government had not yet forged a postwar imperial policy. The Conservative Party demanded the preservation of the empire. The Labour Party favored an international trusteeship system under which the European powers would continue to administer their colonies. The Colonial Office and the India Office tended to regard American opinion as a nuisance. The Foreign Office thought this attitude shortsighted given Britain's postwar dependence upon American assistance. The Ministry of Information and the BBC, sensitive to the attitudes of American opinion leaders, preferred to take a reformist position on the future of the empire. To their dismay, they discovered that the message of reform could be sabotaged by the prime minister. Propagandists, who were usually delighted with Churchill's popularity in the United States, discovered that his "we hold what we have" stance damaged their carefully disseminated theme of common interests and principles.[4] British policymakers all agreed their wartime imperial policy must be defended against American criticism, but the lack of a postwar policy gave propagandists little to go on.

Second, propagandists learned that the "strategy of truth" had severe limitations when bad news made it almost impossible to present events in a favorable light. Following Pearl Harbor, a series of military disasters highlighted debility and ineptitude. On December 10, 1941, Japanese bombers sunk the new battleship *Prince of Wales* and the famous battle cruiser *Repulse*; on Christmas Day, Hong

---

3. Thorne, *Allies of a Kind*, 337; Warren F. Kimball, "Lend-Lease and the Open Door: The Temptation of British Opulence, 1937–1942," *Political Science Quarterly* 86.2 (June 1971), 259.

4. Louis, *Imperialism at Bay*, 33–36; Frederick Puckle, Report on Tour of United States, July 1944, FO371/38611 AN2804/181/45, PRO.

Kong capitulated after a bitter seventeen-day siege; on February 15, the British defense of Malaya collapsed, ending with the surrender of 130,000 troops to a Japanese force half that size at Singapore. The U.S. losses of Wake, Guam, and the Philippines, as well as the frustrations of the first months of total mobilization, did not prevent the Americans from criticizing their war-weary ally. The "strategy of truth" broke down in front of Cecil Brown, the CBS correspondent in Singapore.

An Ohio State graduate and world traveler by freighter, Cecil Brown had reported for Hearst's International News Service in Rome for two years when he was recruited by CBS in February 1940. A year later, the Italian government expelled the thirty-four-year-old Brown for "hostile reporting." On his way to Singapore, he dodged bombs in Yugoslavia, saw Allied troops take Damascus, watched desert fighting in Egypt, and survived a plane crash in Malaya. On December 9, 1941, he was one of two lucky reporters invited to spend four days in the South China Sea with the Royal Navy. Disappointed not to be on the *Prince of Wales*, Brown collected notes for his story aboard the *Repulse*. When the Japanese sunk both ships, Brown was rescued from the oily, burning sea and returned to Singapore. In his broadcasts he spoke movingly about the courage of the Royal Navy officers and crew, and after six tries, he was permitted by the censors to say that the Japanese owed much of their success to the absence of British fighter aircraft.[5]

When Brown first arrived in Singapore in August 1941, he had enjoyed excellent cooperation from the British authorities as well as the flourishing social life at the Raffles Hotel. As the weeks went on, however, he became increasingly critical of British preparedness and frustrated with censorship restrictions. In his New Year's Eve script, Brown attempted to explain to his CBS audience the significance of Malaya as the world's most important source of tin, 70 percent of which went to the United States. The censor would not allow Brown to report that 50 percent of the tin-ore production was now in Japanese hands. The censor asked, "What do you want to make the picture so black for?" Brown replied, "What do you want to hide

---

5. Cecil Brown published his diaries of 1941 in *Suez to Singapore* (New York: Random House, 1942). The *Repulse* incident is covered on pp. 293–345.

the whole picture for?"[6] Brown went over the censor's head to Sir George Sansom, director of publicity for the Far East Command, who, in this case, approved the original script.

Brown complained about censorship to Robert Scott, the MOI head in Singapore, who was sympathetic and powerless. Scott agreed with Brown that it was better for the public to know the truth rather than believe the worst of the rumors. Scott blamed the high command, who, he said, "believed in propaganda in principle, but will do nothing to cooperate." Scott felt that the authorities' attempt to uphold morale by withholding the truth showed a serious underestimation of the local population. He remarked that the British in Singapore treated the Asians like children. Brown himself thought that the British might justifiably fear abandonment by the local population. It seemed to him that the Malays, the Chinese, and the Indians believed that they were fighting to maintain a system they no longer wanted; to them, this was not a people's war or a fight for freedom.[7]

Scott wasn't the only British authority in despair. Colonel Field, the deputy director of military intelligence who held daily press conferences, was asked by a British correspondent for some encouraging information in the first week of the new year. Field retorted, "I can't produce good encouraging propaganda in the situation we are in, and it is stupid to try." Unable to produce good news, the authorities distributed bland communiqués. Frequently prevented from reporting events as he saw them, Brown made private interpretations of the official news in his diary. For example, on December 18, the communiqué stated, "We have successfully disengaged the enemy," which Brown rewrote as "The British have evacuated Penang." Brown decoded the government newspaper's January 13 headline, "Singapore Beats Off 125 Raiders," to mean "what happened was Japs dropped bombs and went home."[8] Brown believed the official handling of the news coverage created a false impression of Singapore's predicament, damaging to the local war effort and the Allied cause.

6. Ibid., 382–383.
7. Ibid., 350–351, 387.
8. Ibid., 392; Cecil Brown Diary, December 18, 1941 and January 13, 1942, Cecil Brown Papers, U.S. Mss. 14AF, Box 3, State Historical Society of Wisconsin, Madison, Wis.

On January 8, 1942, the British authorities revoked Brown's accreditation as a war correspondent to prevent him from broadcasting, because, as they explained, his reporting harmed local morale. Two days earlier, Brown and the NBC correspondent, Martin Agronsky, had gone to Sir George Sansom to complain about censorship. Sansom told them that the War Council had decided that Brown's and Agronsky's broadcasts were to be censored as though they were local news reports and that "objective reporting and the local morale situation were irreconcilable." When the authorities canceled Brown's (but not Agronsky's) accreditation, Brown took up the case with Colonel Field, arguing that his CBS broadcasts were directed at the American public and were heard by only a few hundred people in Malaya. According to Brown's diary, the two men debated the role of facts in news reporting:

Brown: "Are you suggesting that any of my facts are wrong?"
Field: "No, I don't question any of the facts in your broadcasts, but it is the organization of them and the choice of words."
Brown: "As for example?"
Field: "You said our men were being 'dive-bombed and machine-gunned up at the front'."
Brown: "That's correct, isn't it?"
Field: "Yes, it is, yet I don't see why you have to say that."

Brown asserted that the best way to bring in American help was to convey how bad the situation was. Field confirmed that Brown's broadcasts were valuable in the United States but that they also depressed morale. Field said he thought Brown "should report the facts differently."[9]

Without success, Brown challenged this decision with the support of CBS and his fellow war correspondents. Further investigation revealed that the British had made him persona non grata because he had castigated the authorities. Sir George Sansom explained, "You praise our courage, but you criticize our minds and you know how the military react to that." Australian and American papers backed Brown with the argument that it was better to know the worst. In London, Brown's treatment prompted a question in the House of

9. January 8, 1942, Diary, Brown Papers; Brown, *Suez to Singapore*, 399, 400.

Commons. Brendan Bracken explained that the military authorities in Singapore decided that Brown's broadcasts "passed the bonds of fair criticism and were a source of danger."[10] On his journey home through Indonesia and Australia, Brown met with praise from individuals and polite hostility from Allied officials.

In 1942 Brown published his bestseller *Suez to Singapore*, made a lecture tour, won the Overseas Press Club's annual award for best radio reporting, and took over the news broadcasts of the popular Elmer Davis, who had been appointed head of the OWI.[11] Brown privately defined the wartime relationship between British authorities and American journalists. "There are two schools of journalism— those who play ball, take the official party line and hit it hard, are built up by the British, indulging in an occasional bit of mild criticism to give an aura of independence," he noted in his diary, "and those who try to tell what is actually going on."[12] Brown put his colleague in London, Murrow, in the first category and himself in the second. Ironically, Brown would have preferred to be like Murrow. He wanted to be able to work with the British the way Murrow did, with his riveting broadcasts of London's steadfastness during the Blitz. Murrow was able to describe the war as a "people's war"; Brown was not. In attempting to create a spirit of teamwork between American reporters and British government officials, propagandists had better success when the news was good or when they could, as in London during the Blitz, share common ground. They tried to avoid the kind of censorship used to ban Brown in Singapore because it destroyed the idea of partnership. They found, however, that their propaganda themes were challenged easily in imperial settings.

In 1942 British Empire propagandists had a rough task coping with the immediate war situation, divisions among policymakers, the resurgence of the "ancient grudge," and uncertainty over U.S. postwar economic and security interests. Although the British did not alter their fundamental goal of securing American assistance, they adapted their propaganda policy to changing circumstances: their

10. January 16, 1942, Diary, Brown Papers; Brown, *Suez to Singapore*, 435.

11. Brown continued to express his opinions on the air and parted ways with CBS in 1943. He then worked for the Mutual Broadcasting System, ABC, and NBC; Bliss, Jr., *Now the News*, 124.

12. January 29, 1942, Diary, Brown Papers.

own decline, the United States's predominance, and the increasing importance of the Soviet Union.

In order to present the empire under British rule as a thriving, invaluable asset to the United States, British propagandists worked to set the agenda of public discussion on imperialism and empire. From 1942 to 1945 the evolution of British propaganda policy on the empire took place in two phases, reflecting changing events and policy. The first phase encompassed 1942, when the British defended the empire from the harshest American criticism of the war. The key issue was the nationalist crisis in India. British propaganda contained the American debate over India by stressing the war effort and discrediting the nationalist movement. In the second phase, from 1943 to 1945, British propagandists turned from defending the empire to promoting it as they shifted their attention from war issues to postwar issues. They consequently developed a more sophisticated propaganda policy that used economic and strategic issues to place the British Empire within a global context of postwar problems. The evolution of British propaganda policy was not a steady march of progress. Propagandists had to assess the contradictions of and divisions within American opinion, including the Roosevelt administration, opinion leaders, and the general public. By mid-1943, British propagandists had become familiar with the terrain of American anticolonialism, but in 1942, when the empire was in crisis, they were still drawing the map.

One of the chief difficulties for the British as they developed a propaganda policy was the confusion surrounding the U.S. government's position on the future of the British Empire. President Roosevelt advocated the Atlantic Charter principles and suggested that colonial areas should be administered by international trusteeships. To a White House dinner guest during Churchill's visit in December 1941, FDR explained his version of American anticolonialism: "It's in the American tradition, this distrust, this dislike and even hatred of Britain—the Revolution, you know, and 1812; and India and the Boer War; and all that. There are many kinds of Americans of course, but as a people, a country, we're opposed to imperialism—we can't stomach it." The president explained that he had been urging the prime minister to take American attitudes into consideration. He disagreed strongly with Churchill's hardline stance against Indian independence, causing one of the major feuds in their relationship.[13] Roosevelt's concern was motivated by anti-imperialism and his desire to avoid any public antagonism that might disrupt the war effort.

His close friend and undersecretary of state, Sumner Welles, announced that the era of imperialism was over in a speech delivered in May 1942. Welles and the State Department promoted the gradual reform of imperial systems under international control, but excepted U.S. interests, such as Hawaii and the Panama Canal zone, from international supervision. The United States frequently held up its promise of independence to the Philippines as the model to be followed by its European allies.[14] Americans condemned Britain's imperial behavior and offered their own as a standard or an exception. British officials grappled with the contradictions between administration rhetoric, which was anti-imperialistic, and administration policy, which promoted gradual reform and the protection of the U.S. sphere of influence.

When confronting the blunter criticism of the empire by American opinion leaders outside the administration, British propagandists faced adversaries from across the political spectrum. They drew up an "enemies list," which bore some similarity to their categorization of isolationists and internationalists, to identify American groups and individuals who shaped American opinion regarding the British Empire.[15] At the top of the list were the "professional isolationist anglophobes," who included the Hearst, McCormick, and Patterson papers, Senators Burton Wheeler and Gerald Nye, and Representative Hamilton Fish. The second group, "professional liberals and left wing," included the *Nation*, the *New Republic*, Louis Fischer, a pro-Indian nationalist journalist, the New School of Social Research, and communists.

In the third category, "new internationalist-imperialist," the British placed former Republican presidential candidate Wendell Willkie and

13. Robert Dallek, *Franklin D. Roosevelt and American Foreign Policy, 1932–1945* (New York: Oxford University Press, 1979), 324; Robert Sherwood, *Roosevelt and Hopkins: An Intimate History* (New York: Harper Brothers, 1948), 512.

14. U.S. policy is discussed in detail by William Roger Louis and Christopher Thorne; see Louis, *Imperialism at Bay*, 147–150, and Thorne, *Allies of a Kind*, 209–218.

15. "Breakdown of Anti-British Groups and Individuals in U.S.A.," April 17, 1943, Graham Spry Papers, MG30, D297, Vol. 46–13, National Archives of Canada, Ottawa.

Henry and Clare Boothe Luce. It was time, Luce declared in *The American Century*, for the United States to "exert upon the world the full impact of our influence." As for the British Commonwealth, Luce added, "what we want will be okay with them."[16] Luce's vision of an American empire without boundaries and his dismissal of the British Empire, together with his ability to popularize these views in his widely read magazines, made him one of the most troublesome of American opinion leaders.

The remaining groups on the "enemies list" were just as outspoken but more narrow in appeal. The "professional pro-Asiatics" included the East and West Association, whose president, author Pearl Buck, advocated close American ties with Chinese and Indian nationalists. The Indian nationalist cause was promoted by the India League of America. The black press also strongly supported Indian independence. Churches and missionary groups monitored British colonial policy. Faced with critics from the left and right of American politics, the propagandists could not confront one group without offending another. The British instead responded with a defense of empire based on broad propaganda themes.

Americans generally relied on three examples to illustrate their distaste for the British Empire: Canada, Eire, and India. First, the British discovered that Americans believed that their neighbor to the north should be freed from the empire and that Canada should no longer have to pay taxes to London. When asked about these misconceptions, Ferdinand Kuhn of the OWI replied, "American knowledge of Canadian constitutional development stops at the War of 1812."[17] American interest in and ignorance about Canada, the British thought, provided an ideal opportunity to prove with facts the misguided nature of American attitudes about the empire. As usual, they turned to the tactic of getting others to make their case for them. But when they urged Canadian officials to explain to Americans their independent status within the empire, they found Ottawa to be uncooperative.

The Canadian government preferred to remain as aloof as possible from Anglo-American quarrels. When the Department of External

16. Henry Luce, *The American Century* (New York: Farrar and Rinehart, 1941), 19.
17. "Interview with F. Kuhn, OWI," July 7, 1943, Spry Papers, NAC.

Affairs discussed whether to assist British public relations, policy-makers decided they could best demonstrate their independence if given equal treatment on the Anglo-American Combined Boards, which was not what London had in mind. Instead of praising the empire for the British, the Canadian government established its own wartime information services in the United States, with the aim of showing that Canada was not "just a colony of England."[18] Sir George Sansom, now the British colonial expert at the Washington embassy, observed that at the 1942 Institute of Pacific Relations conference, the British delegation had almost as much trouble with the Canadians as they had with the Americans when the future of the empire was discussed.[19] Although individual Canadians participated in empire promotions, British attempts to recruit the Canadian government failed.

Like Canada, Eire had a long history as a source of contention in Anglo-American relations. American opinion over the most bitter imperial issue of the First World War had been mollified somewhat by Eire's neutrality during the Second World War. British propagandists decided to ignore the Irish Dominion as much as possible, although they welcomed any American or Commonwealth criticism of Eire's failure to fight on the side of the Allies. When, in 1944, Eire refused the United States's request that it send home Axis diplomats, the BBC reported that "Eire as a dominion of the British Commonwealth has an unquestionable legal right to do what she has done." The BBC reaffirmed Eire's independence while emphasizing its neutrality and isolating it from the Allies. When British speakers found it impossible to ignore questions about Eire, they answered as succinctly as possible. For instance, when asked whether Ireland was "completely independent," W. H. Gallienne, the British consul general in Detroit,

18. One Canadian official was not optimistic about influencing Americans: "I don't think it would pay to give any publicity to our disagreement with the British in the hope of impressing the Americans with our independence. . . . Even if we went to the length of issuing a declaration of independence and bombing London, I doubt if the Americans would really notice, and if they did they would forget about it next day"; "Anglo-American Antipathy," October 13, 1942, Department of External Affairs, Acc. 89–90/029, Box 30 31(s); Keenleyside on Charles Vinings' report on Canadian publicity in the U.S., July 28, 1942, RG25, Vol. 2924, File 2727-Z-1-40, NAC.

19. Minutes of meeting on American opinion and the British Empire (Sansom Committee), June 8, 1943, FO371/34091 A5904/3/45, PRO.

responded quickly, *"Very* independent."[20] Most British propagandists assumed there was little they could do to win over anti-British
opinion rooted in Irish sympathies, beyond working through the
Catholic church. The Irish issue did not symbolize the question of
British imperial integrity in American minds, as it had twenty years
earlier. The new symbol was India which, in the eyes of Americans,
had become the test case for Britain's intentions toward its Empire.

In 1942, India was in crisis without and within. Japan's advance
after the defeat of Singapore and Germany's success in North Africa
threatened a possible Axis meeting in India, thereby cutting off
China, the Soviet Union through Iran, and Persian Gulf oil. On February 22, Dwight D. Eisenhower at the War Department's planning
division concluded a bleak assessment of the Allied strategic situation
with "We've *got* to keep Russia in the war—and hold India!!!"[21] For
the British, holding India was also a political problem. The war had
demolished Britain's twenty-year-old policy of containing the independence movement.[22]

In 1784, a year after signing a peace treaty with the newly independent United States, in India the British government instituted dual
control with the East India Company trading corporation. Following
the mutiny of the Bengal army in 1857, the Government of India Act
transferred power over India to the crown. It created the cabinet post
of Secretary of State for India and the Government of India, headed
by a governor general or viceroy and administered by the Indian Civil
Service. Nine years after Queen Victoria was declared Empress of
India, a group of Indians who advocated self-government formed the
Indian National Congress in 1885. Following World War I, the Congress Party applauded Woodrow Wilson's Fourteen Points, which
included the principle of self-determination. Their representatives to
the Paris Peace Conference, however, were refused recognition, and

20. FBIS, "Weekly Review," March 18, 1944, RG 262, Entry 32, Box 4, NA;
Gallienne report, July 12, 1944, FO371/38577 AN2906/34/45, PRO.
21. Alfred D. Chandler, Jr., ed. *The Papers of Dwight David Eisenhower: The
War Years,* vol. 1 (Baltimore: John Hopkins University Press, 1970), 126.
22. The following discussion of British-Indian relations leading up to 1942 is
drawn from John Darwin, *Britain and Decolonisation: The Retreat from Empire in
the Post-war World* (New York: St. Martin's Press, 1988), 79–88; Gary Hess, *America Encounters India, 1942–1947* (Baltimore: Johns Hopkins University Press, 1971),
10–20.

India was represented by delegates selected by the British Government of India.

As a reform measure, the Government of India Act created a dyarchy in 1919, which allowed Indian self-government at a provincial level over such issues as education, public health, public works, and agriculture, while British authorities retained control over external, financial, and law and order matters. During the same year, at a peaceful mass rally against the extension of wartime emergency measures at Amritsar, troops led by Gen. Reginald Dyer opened fire on the protesters and killed hundreds. The Amritsar massacre turned millions of Indian moderates into nationalist revolutionaries. The Congress Party, under the leadership of Mohandas K. Gandhi or Mahatma, meaning "Great Soul," boycotted the 1920 elections to protest the limited self-government created by the new reforms.

Throughout the interwar period, the Congress Party launched campaigns of nonviolent civil disobedience in protest of British rule. The British responded with a combination of force and reform. They arrested and detained nationalist leaders. At about the same time Adolf Hitler was in prison dictating *Mein Kampf*, Gandhi was in prison dictating *The Story of My Experiments with Truth*. Jawaharlal Nehru, the aristocratic, Cambridge-educated lawyer who had served as the president of the Congress Party three times, spent nine years in prison between 1921 and 1947. The British hoped to weaken the movement for independence by instituting a process called "Indianization," which brought Indians into the officer corps and the senior civil service. The British intended that these Indians would loyally carry on British policy under self-government.

In 1935 Britain instituted constitutional reform under which Indians practiced full self-government on the provincial level and Britain controlled India's foreign policy, defense, and finance. Their policy of reform had been intended to weaken the Congress Party, but in the 1937 elections, the party gained control of seven out of eleven provinces. The process of constitutional reform and the integration of Indians into a parliamentary system was shattered when, in September 1939, the viceroy, Lord Linlithgow, without consulting the Indians, declared India to be at war.

The National Congress had long opposed fascism in Europe and Japanese aggression against China, but it protested being taken into war without any vote or show of consent. Congress leaders stated that a free India would fight willingly with the Allies. In August 1940 Lord Linlithgow and the Government of India offered to enlarge the viceroy's executive council of Indian representatives and set up a war advisory board as a consulting body without any real power. The British stated that at the end of the war, they would modify the 1935 reforms and move toward increased Indian self-government that ensured minority rights. The question of minority rights in an united India divided Indian nationalists. In 1940 the leader of the Muslim League, Mohammed Ali Jinnah, called for independent Muslim states. The Congress Party opposed the Muslim League's desire for separate status. To protest British policies, the Congress Party led a civil disobedience action that ended in October 1940 with the arrests of thousands, including Nehru. The Government of India released the protesters four days before Pearl Harbor, in part to mollify public opinion in Britain and the United States.

In early 1942, relations between the British and the nationalists were near the breaking point. As India mobilized for war, British authorities interfered in Indian lives and resources more than they ever had before. London became less conciliatory with Winston Churchill, who had vigorously fought the 1935 reforms, as prime minister. The British no longer tried to contain the Congress movement. By 1942 they moved to eradicate it. They dealt increasingly with parties opposed to the Congress, in particular the Muslim League. The Congress, the largest Indian party, responded by adopting open resistance to British authority.

In the United States, polls showed that a majority of Americans supported the independence movement. An OWI report of March 2, 1942, summarized the American press support for Indian independence. The press wanted the full mobilization of Indian manpower and resources in the war effort and genuinely desired Indian freedom. The report stated that much of the American press recognized that the status quo could never be restored in Asia and concluded that the liberation of colonial peoples should be a war aim. Some Americans believed that their prestige in postwar Asia rested upon their sponsorship of nationalist movements.[23] Although many of their reasons were rooted in self-interest, Americans' sympathies for India were understood by the British in terms of anticolonialism. The "an-

23. OWI intelligence report, March 2, 1942, PSF Subject File, Box 172, FDRL.

cient grudge" seemed to be in full force. Gandhi was referred to as India's George Washington; the 1930 Salt March, during which Gandhi made illegal salt to protest the salt tax, was compared to the Boston Tea Party; and students picketed the British embassy with signs stating that it was 1776 for India. The British feared that public pressure and the Roosevelt administration's own interest in India would lead to American intervention in the Indian crisis. If the United States were going to act on its anticolonial sentiments and interfere in the British Empire, India would be the most likely place. In the case of India, British propaganda policy was at its most defensive.

Propagandists attempted to manipulate American perceptions of events by controlling what the public did and did not learn about the crisis in India. One of their immediate problems was the sudden influx of American war correspondents who stopped in India on their way to the battlefronts and, finding a different kind of battle being waged, submitted damaging reports on the political situation. Propagandists tried to shape the impressions of reporters and broadcasters by arranging tours designed to "show what British rule has done" and by steering correspondents away from certain people and places. This tactic of guided tours did not work as well as it had in England. According to the MOI representative in New Delhi, Americans arrived with their opinions already formed. The correspondents, reflecting the views of the American public, he wrote to London, "have a pre-conceived conviction about the inherent right of free peoples to control their own destinies, and they apply this principle also to Asia."[24] Other British observers dismissed preconceptions as the cause of their bad press in India and instead blamed what they termed a "nationalist conspiracy." They accused the Congress Party of subjecting Americans to distorted views of the British role in India.

The Americans, in turn, suspected the activities of the Government of India's public relations personnel and found many of their stereotyped views of British colonial administrators confirmed by their travels.[25] After a grueling journey by Allied transport plane with var-

24. P. D. Butler (MOI, New Delhi) to Scott, November 3, 1942, FO371/34086 A192/3/45, PRO.
25. Noel Hall to Scott, October 10, 1942, FO371/30685 A9726/1684/45, PRO. See, for example, Cecil Brown's description of a young diplomat he met in Singapore who, he felt, represented all that Americans found "obnoxious in the British": "He was super-educated and super-academic—Eton, Oxford, the University of Berlin. He

ious military and government officials, war correspondents landed in New Delhi, to be welcomed by proper young officers who astonished them with the announcement that passengers would exit the aircraft in order of rank. On one occasion, Turner Catledge of the *New York Times* loudly announced, "I assume that means American taxpayers first," and stepped down.[26] Catledge's response expressed the American disregard for imperial hierarchy and suggested a new order to displace the old.

Unable to exert much influence on American correspondents, the authorities relied upon censorship. The major news source out of India was the Reuters News Service. In close collaboration with the Government of India, Reuters maintained a special service that transmitted Indian news to the United States through its London office, in cooperation with the India Office. Reuters' telegraph lines carried the reports of American correspondents, thereby subjecting them to the censorship authorities in New Delhi. Eric Sevareid recalled that it was impossible to send the truth out of India. Hoping to break Reuters' monopoly, the United Press Service (UP), through the American mission in Delhi, asked the Government of India to lease it telegraph lines. The request of the UP—a service, noted a British official, "free from such sense of responsibility and liability to Government influence as distinguishes the Reuter Service"—was denied.[27] By controlling the news, the British forced the American audience to rely largely upon Reuters, the North American Service of the BBC, and the BIS for information about wartime India.

Prominent spokespersons reinforced the British presentation of events in India. Several colonial experts targeted the foreign policy elite—government officials, academics, the media, and interested or-

---

was smug, priggish, aristocratic with no understanding of sex, poverty, misery or fervor. But worst of all, the way he talked, more daringly English-accented than Hollywood would attempt in caricature. . . . He was a Tory who was determined that his world of comfort and stodginess would never change, no matter how many wars might come"; Brown, *Suez to Singapore*, 153. See also Eric Sevareid, *Not So Wild a Dream* (New York: Atheneum, 1976), 238–243.

26. Sevareid, *Not So Wild A Dream*, 238.

27. "Publicity and Propaganda Function of the India Office Information Department: Appendix to Publicity and Propaganda in the USA," India Office memorandum, FO371/30685 A11702/1684/45, PRO; Sevareid, *Not So Wild a Dream*, 240; "Request by the United Press of America for Special Facilities in India," Spry Papers, Vol. 46–21, NAC.

ganizations. British ambassador Lord Halifax, who had been viceroy of India from 1926 to 1931, led the defense of Britain's imperial policy in the United States. He stated his opposition to Indian independence in more benevolent and paternalistic terms than those employed by Churchill.[28] The Government of India had its own representative in Washington, the Indian agent-general, Sir Girja Shankar Bajpai. Bajpai, a civil servant and member of the viceroy's executive council, arrived in Washington in the summer of 1941 as part of an exchange of ministers. His office was closely connected to the India Office in London and the Government of India in New Delhi. Supreme Court Justice Felix Frankfurter thought that the agent-general was in a difficult position as a symbol of British liberal policy toward India who had very little independent voice. The agent-general was allowed to deal only with Indian social and economic issues, whereas the BIS handled British constitutional policy and questions about India's foreign policy and security.[29]

Other experts included Lord Hailey, a former governor of the Punjab and the director of the African Research Survey; Sir Frederick Puckle, a veteran of the Indian Civil Service who became the adviser on Indian affairs to the British embassy in 1943; and Sir Frederick Whyte of the Royal Institute of International Affairs, who had served as president of the Indian legislative assembly. Both Puckle and Whyte had experience as propagandists, Puckle as secretary of the Department of Information and Broadcasting, and Whyte as head of the American Division of the MOI. Their training and status gave them access to the American audience they desired. Through personal contacts, speeches, and articles, they effectively put the key points of the British position before opinion leaders and the public. The British, however, tended to attribute greater success to their influence on American opinion than Americans did.

For example, at the international conference of the Institute of Pacific Relations, held at Mont Tremblant, Canada, in December 1942, the high-powered British delegation demonstrated its strengths and weaknesses as promoters of the British Empire. British, Cana-

28. Gary Hess discusses the activities of the India experts; see Hess, *America Encounters India,* 113–129.

29. Frankfurter, *Diaries,* 195; "Publicity and Propaganda in the USA; Its Organization and Control in Relation to India and Burma," India Office memorandum, FO371/30685 A11702/1684/45, PRO.

dian, and American observers agreed that the British had been under fire on the issues of the Atlantic Charter, India, and Hong Kong. The British delegation, including the left-wing Labour representative, unanimously defended British colonial policy. British participants reported to the Foreign Office that they had played their part very successfully.[30]

American officials at the conference agreed that the British delegation was well disciplined but noted several slips that tarnished the British position. The head of the British delegation, Lord Hailey, had referred to "the United Nations and the Dominions." The deputy head, Sir Frederick Whyte, at a full meeting of delegates from Australia, Canada, China, the Free French, India, the Netherlands East Indies, New Zealand, the Philippines, Thailand, the United Kingdom, and the United States, referred to the representatives of the "more civilized Western countries." Whyte chastised an Indian delegate publicly who spoke critically of the British.[31] American officials thought the conference informative but concluded that the British delegates' behavior was at odds with their position of progressive reform. At the same time as the experts educated American opinion leaders about the intricacies of colonial rule and the make-up of the empire, they confirmed American anticolonial attitudes.

Although the British considered opinion leaders their chief target audience, they attempted to defend the empire before the general public. American views of India were shaped in large part by popular films and literature. In his 1958 book *Scratches on Our Minds*, Harold Isaacs explored American stereotypes of Indian culture. His list included the fabulous India of maharajahs, the caste-ridden and impoverished India of the "very benighted heathen," the mystical India that had fascinated American transcendentalist writers of the 1840s, and Rudyard Kipling's India of Gunga Din and the "first class fightin' man."[32] Influential books about India included Katharine Mayo's

30. Report on the third meeting of the Law Committee, February 18, 1943, FO371/34067 A1914/3/45, PRO; Lester Pearson to Hugh Keenleyside, January 5, 1943, MG 26, N1, Vol. 68, Lester Pearson Papers, National Archives of Canada, Ottawa.

31. Lauchlin Currie, "Memorandum for the President," December 18, 1942, and Leo Pasvolsky and Stanley Hornbeck memoranda, January 1943, OF 669, Institute of Pacific Relations, 1933–1945, FDRL.

32. Harold Isaacs, *Scratches on Our Minds: American Images of China and India* (New York: John Day, 1958), 241–259.

Mother India (1927), a sensational discussion of the treatment of women in Indian society, and Bishop Frederick Fisher's *That Strange Little Brown Man, Gandhi* (1932), which, given the limitations indicated by the title, was at the time considered an admiring portrait. During the thirties, Hollywood produced several films glorifying the Raj, such as *Lives of a Bengal Lancer* (1936) and *Gunga Din* (1939).[33] British propagandists sorted through these images of India held by Americans and selected what they thought would be useful stereotypes to incorporate into their propaganda messages.[34]

Three primary propaganda themes emerged from the 1942 defense of British rule in India. Propagandists first turned to what might be called the theme of "complexity." They assumed that if Americans were ignorant about India, they could be educated by a parade of facts organized to justify British policy. Propaganda illustrated the complexity of the Indian situation by listing the diverse languages, religions, and cultures of the subcontinent. Pamphlets and speakers described the intricacies of the caste system, the delicate relations with the princes, and stressed that the Congress Party did not represent the entire country. The Hindu-Muslim split, which Churchill had pronounced "the bulwark of British rule in India," was a key element of the complexity theme.[35] The complexity theme implied that only the British understood the situation and, without their control, India would dissolve into chaos. Second, as unrest in India continued, the British employed the "war-effort" theme to portray the "Indian problem" as harmful to the Allied fight against the Axis powers. The war-effort theme reminded the American public that defeating the common enemy came first. No issue, including Indian independence, should be allowed to deflect energy and resources from the war effort. Third, in an effort to weaken American sympathies for Indian nationalists, the British initiated a campaign to

33. OWI asked RKO Studios to refrain from rereleasing *Gunga Din* (1939) during the war in the interests of Anglo-American relations; Koppes and Black, *Hollywood Goes to War*, 225.

34. British propagandists of course had their own stereotypes of India, which influenced their presentation of the country to Americans. In many instances their images and attitudes were similar to those held by Americans. For example, the expression "wog" (for wily oriental gentleman), used by the British to refer to Indians, was adopted rapidly by GIs in India during the war. Isaacs, *Scratches on Our Minds*, 317.

35. Churchill quoted in Thorne, *Allies of a Kind*, 235.

discredit the best-known leader of the National Congress Party, Mahatma Gandhi. All three themes were intended to explain why the
United States should not involve itself in the Indian crisis on the side
of the independence movement.

The complexity theme was used to explain the failure of the Cripps
Mission. In late March 1942, the War Cabinet sent Sir Stafford
Cripps to India. Cripps was to offer the Indians self-government at
the earliest possible date after the war as long as minority rights were
guaranteed. Under this proposal, the Muslim League, under Mohammed Ali Jinnah's leadership, would be allowed to create a separate
state of Pakistan. The Cripps proposals offered little change for the
duration of the war; defense would remain under British control. The
Congress Party thought the offer would lead to the division of India,
leave real power to the British, and differed little from earlier proposals.[36]

When Cripps tried to work out a compromise between London's
position and the Indians' demands, he moved toward granting executive powers to Indians. President Roosevelt's personal representative, Col. Louis Johnson, assisted Cripps in these negotiations.
Johnson's presence alarmed the British authorities, who feared American interference, but Johnson had no power. Although Johnson's
presence demonstrated FDR's sympathy for the nationalists, his lack
of authority showed that the president put Allied cooperation ahead
of anti-imperialism. The Congress Party welcomed the compromise
position. In London, the War Cabinet's India Committee was divided.[37] Clement Attlee and Ernest Bevin, the Labour Party leaders,
favored Cripps's compromise. Churchill and Leo Amery, the secretary for India, sided with the viceroy, who wanted control of executive powers to remain completely British. The India Committee
decided to withdraw Cripps's freedom to negotiate, in part because
the self-assured Cripps had kept the Government of India in the dark

36. R. J. Moore, *Endgames of Empire: Studies of Britain's India Problem* (Delhi:
Oxford University Press, 1988), 29–30; Hess, *America Encounters India*, 43–44, 50–
51.

37. Churchill had created the India Committee with Attlee as chair in response to
Labour criticism over India. The choice of Cripps to head the mission was intended
to defuse Labour protests. Churchill intended to defuse Cripps as well. Upon his
return from Moscow, Cripps's prestige was very high. Raymond A. Callahan, *Churchill: Retreat from Empire* (Wilmington, Del.: Scholarly Resources, 1984), 187.

about his actions, and Cripps was forced to withdraw his compromise offer. The Congress Party rejected the proposals, and the negotiations, conducted in confusion, ended.

Whatever outcome Churchill had intended, he clearly hoped that the mission would assuage critical American and British opinion. He wrote to the viceroy in March 1942 that the mission would "prove our honesty of purpose." The prime minister told Cripps that he had "proved how great was the British desire to reach a settlement" and that the "effect throughout Britain and in the United States has been wholly beneficial."[38] To Churchill, the failure was a success.

Initial British propaganda treatment of the Cripps mission reflected the confusion over the mission's accomplishments. To prepare its listeners for a successful settlement between London and the Indian nationalists, the North American Service of the BBC had temporarily dropped the complexity theme. An American analyst from the FBIS, mimicking the cheery tones employed by the BBC, observed that the mission was portrayed as the "happy culmination of a steady, evolutionary process" of British imperial policy. After the Cripps mission ended without a settlement, the BBC hastily resumed the complexity theme. It announced that the failure of the mission was inevitable given the extent of disagreement among the Indians. But to restore the required image of progressive reform, the BBC claimed that the failure of the Cripps mission was, after all, a success because the talks had brought home to Indians a greater sense of danger and need for cooperation. Without supportive evidence, the FBIS noted, broadcasters stated that the talks had paved the way for future agreement. They then turned to the war-effort theme. The more important, immediate problem of defense—the Indian Ocean had become "one of the most vital areas" of Allied war effort—deflected listeners' attention from the issue of independence.[39]

The British embassy's political report from Washington pronounced the Cripps mission a propaganda success. Although Amer-

38. Churchill to Linlithgow, March 10, 1942, in Nicholas Mansergh, ed., *The Transfer of Power, 1942–1947: Constitutional Relations between Britain and India*, Vol. 1, *The Cripps Mission, January–April 1942* (London: HMS, 1970), 394; P. J. Grigg, *Prejudice and Judgment* (London: Jonathan Cape, 1948), 327; Churchill to Cripps, April 11, 1942, in Mansergh, ed., *Transfer of Power*, Vol. 1, 739.

39. FBIS, "Weekly Review," April 4, 1942, Box 1 and April 18, 24–30 and 25, 1942, Box 2, RG 262, Entry 33, NA.

This offical MOI photograph came with the caption "Sir Stafford Cripps enjoying a joke with Mr. Gandhi on the steps of Birla House, Delhi." After the 1942 Cripps mission failed to halt deteriorating relations between Indian nationalists and British authorities, propagandists proceeded to discredit Gandhi. (Imperial War Museum IND.736)

icans were inclined to regard the negotiations as a show performed
for their approval, the report to London stated, they had been better
educated about India. There should be no more "glib generalizations
about the simplicity of the Indian problem." Opinion polls, however,
showed that Americans continued to support Indian independence.
A poll conducted during the Cripps negotiations showed that 78 percent of Americans were familiar with the plan to give India self-
government. Of that 78 percent, 41 percent thought India should be
given dominion status immediately, and 24 percent thought India
should be given dominion status after the war.[40] Not surprisingly,
the next embassy report stated that American criticism of British
policy in India had returned.

In order to assess the propaganda value of the Cripps mission,
Graham Spry, a Canadian journalist, former Rhodes scholar, London
executive for Standard Oil Company of California, and the personal
assistant of Sir Stafford Cripps, was sent to the United States immediately following his return from India in 1942. Spry announced
that he was authorized by Cripps to report on the mission to Ambassador Halifax, the BIS, and American officials, as well as judge
the role of the mission in American opinion on India.[41] His real goal
was to analyze the effect of the Cripps mission on American opinion
regarding Britain, the British Empire, and Anglo-American relations.
In New York, along with 150 press and camera people, he accompanied Lord Halifax to the Statue of Liberty for what would now be
called a photo opportunity. Halifax told Spry he believed that the
mission had won wide support in the United States. It had illustrated
the "difficulties of the problem" and had weakened support of the
Congress Party.

Spry's analysis of American opinion was more accurate than Halifax's. Before and after his walk to the Statue of Liberty, he visited
the offices of Time and Life. He learned that Henry Luce viewed the
mission favorably but suspected that London had interfered with the
negotiations. Although Cripps, and Spry after him, loyally denied
that London had cut off his negotiating powers, President Roosevelt

40. Nicholas, Washington Despatches, 31; Hadley Cantril and Mildred Strunk,
eds., Public Opinion, 1935–46 (Princeton: Princeton University Press, 1951), 327.
    41. Material relating to Spry's tour of the United States and Canada, April 1942,
Spry Papers, MG 30, D297, Vol. 45–20, NAC.

learned the truth from Colonel Johnson; American suspicions were well founded. Spry found the *Time* and *Life* staff he met, including C. D. Jackson, *Time*'s vice-president and wartime propaganda expert, to be well informed on India, defense, and British politics. They were sympathetic regarding the "difficulties" in India, but Spry noticed an underlying assumption that the British Empire was falling apart. He recognized the Lucian global view in the attitude that America would have to step in to rebuild the world. Spry talked with other American journalists and writers, including a group of radio broadcasters. NBC's H. V. Kaltenborn stated that Cripps had "whittled down the stick Americans used to beat the British lion."[42] In an interview with Spry, Wendell Willkie appreciated Britain's problem but said "it had to be cleared up." Spry found that American opinion leaders understood the British position in India but did not necessarily approve of it.

In addition to collecting opinion from Americans as he traveled around the country, Spry shaped opinion through press conferences and broadcasts. At a press conference on May 11, 1942, he was asked if all of India would follow the Gandhi philosophy of nonresistance if the Japanese invaded. Spry used the complexity theme to avoid a direct answer. He pointed out that broadcasting in India was done in twelve languages and explained that there were differences between the "fighting races" and the "non-fighting races." The advance arrangement of questions and answers in a draft script for a broadcast over the WOL Mutual Network of 210 stations demonstrated that Spry wanted to address publicly American skepticism regarding the outcome of the Cripps mission. Spry attributed its breakdown to the inability of the Indians to agree among themselves: "What the British Government offered to the Indian political leaders was the opportunity either to remain like Canada or Australia, part of the British commonwealth, or to draw up as the Americans did a declaration of independence. I can't see any way in which the British could have gone further than they did."[43] According to the script, the Mutual broadcaster did not question why, if the British had of-

---

42. Kenton J. Clymer, *Quest for Freedom: The United States and India's Independence* (New York: Columbia University Press, 1995), 68; material relating to Spry's tour of the United States and Canada, April 1942, Spry Papers, Vol. 45–20, NAC.

43. "Press Conference," British Press Service, May 11, 1942, Vol. 66–23 and "Broadcasts 1942," Vol. 66–20, Spry Papers, NAC.

fered the Americans an opportunity to draw up a declaration of independence, seven years of war followed. Apparently Spry got away
with this risky analogy.

Spry wrote an analysis of the role of India in Anglo-American
relations that was presented by Cripps to the War Cabinet in July
1942. Noting that the market for articles and speakers on India was
completely unsatisfied, the Canadian recommended active education
using the theme of complexity. He urged that no new development
in India should, if possible, be announced without "thorough prep-
aration of American opinion."[44] Although Spry advocated using the
complexity and war-effort themes, his analysis indicated the need for
a more aggressive propaganda strategy designed with a greater consideration for the American audience.

Although propagandists prepared for the next stage in the Indian
crisis, they did not have time to consider Spry's recommendation for
an in-depth study of U.S. opinion. On August 9, 1942, the Congress
Party voted for the "Quit India" resolutions that promised nonviolent resistance if Britain did not leave India. The Government of India
arrested Gandhi and thousands of Congress leaders the following
day. Demonstrations, mass strikes, and riots broke out. The British
broke the revolt by force by the end of August. As early as July 16,
two days after the Working Committee of the Congress Party had
resolved to demand Britain's withdrawal, the MOI produced a special issue of its guidance directives entitled "The Indian Situation."
The paper set down propaganda lines to be taken immediately regarding India and in the future if the Government of India should be
compelled to take "drastic action."[45]

First, propagandists increased their efforts to degrade the nationalists and expanded upon their argument that Gandhi and the Congress Party were to blame for the failure of the Cripps mission. The
MOI directive distinguished between what should be presented as
the official government position and an unofficial position to be disseminated through every available channel without attribution to the

44. "Conclusions to Notes for Memorandum on the Role of India in Anglo-
American Relations," Spry Papers, Vol. 45–20, NAC.
45. M. S. Venkataramani and B. K. Shrivastava, *Quit India: The American Response to the 1942 Struggle* (New Delhi: Vikas Publishing House, 1979), 266–267;
the following discussion is cited from "The Indian Situation," July 16, 1942, Overseas
Planning Committee, MOI, R34/693, BBC WAC.

British government. Official spokespersons, including BBC broadcasters, should refrain from attacking Gandhi and his colleagues directly. Direct attacks on Gandhi should be aired by quoting critical Indians, Americans, and Russians or by quoting approving Japanese or other enemy propaganda. The unofficial line should stress the Congress Party's responsibility for the breakdown of the Cripps mission and its unwillingness to accept any solution that did not give the party full power over minorities. Gandhi, directed the MOI, "should be gradually built up as a backward-looking pacifist and Petainist who has become a dangerous obstacle to the defence of India, and whose policies in fact if not in design play straight into Japanese hands." Other leaders, particularly Nehru, were to be presented as reluctantly loyal to Gandhi, to maintain the illusion of unity. Both the official and unofficial line held Gandhi and the Congress Party responsible for the failure to reach any resolution.

Second, the complexity theme was repeated. The MOI directive urged propagandists to argue that minorities such as the Muslim League, the Sikhs, and "the Depressed Classes" must be defended against the demands of the majority. The guidelines cautioned against using numerical comparisons of the Congress Party's members with other Indian parties. Contradicting previous instructions, the MOI warned that the truth should not "be strained" by suggesting that Congress was not a representative party. Statements by Indian leaders of other parties made in favor of the war effort should be highlighted. The conclusion the audience should draw from the complexity theme was that a British departure would result in chaos and civil war.

Third, the importance of winning the war was presented as "the indispensable condition of Indian freedom." British propagandists should explain that India could not be in complete control of its defense because of its strategic importance to the United Nations, in particular to China but also to the Soviet Union and, ultimately, the United States. The new angle to the war-effort theme was the inclusion of "the United Nations," the term for the Allies preferred by President Roosevelt and therefore adopted by the British. Not only Britain but the rest of the Big Four—China, the Soviet Union, and the United States—also had a stake in the defense of India. "We should," stated the guideline, "emphasize the heavy responsibility thus devolving upon us for the defence of India, which we intend to carry out in the interests of all the peoples of the United Nations including the great mass of the Indian people themselves." The three propaganda themes portrayed India as a nation in need of a strong hand without any political alternative to British rule and as a nation of vital strategic importance that the British were protecting for the benefit of all the Allies.

In the weeks leading up to the "Quit India" movement, the BBC followed MOI guidelines in preparing its audience for a crackdown in India by treating the situation with "increasing irritation." The BBC echoed the pledge of Leo Amery, the secretary of state for India, to defend India whatever happened. The broadcasts repeated frequently that the Indians alone failed to accept the Cripps mission's promise of postwar freedom. One FBIS analyst observed that the BBC portrayed Congress leaders as appeasers despite Nehru's stance against the Axis. Gandhi's position was presented as leading to the betrayal of the United Nations' cause and playing into the hands of the Japanese.[46]

BBC broadcasts somewhat blurred MOI's distinction between official and unofficial positions. News broadcasters described Gandhi as sincere and honest and attempted to "disabuse" their audience of any opinion that he was acting in a subversive manner. The FBIS report revealed that the supposedly unofficial line on Gandhi and the Congress Party was being delivered by a regular commentator, M. P. Vernon Bartlett, who quoted a friend recently returned from India as saying "the Working Committee of Congress had gone completely Fascist in their outlook."[47] By identifying Gandhi with appeasement, the reviled policy of accommodation with dictators, and with fascism, the propagandists appealed to potent labels associated with the enemy.

As they had seen following the Cripps mission, propagandists found that they could shape the American reaction to events for a short time. American official reaction was dominated by the demand for unity in the wartime alliance. Roosevelt expressed his exasperation with the British but declined to intervene. Although Sumner

46. FBIS, "Weekly Analysis of Propaganda Pressures on the U.S." (hereafter "Weekly Analysis"), August 1–7, 1942, RG 262, Entry 32, Box 4, NA.
47. FBIS, "Weekly Review," July 31–August 6, 1942, Box 2, and "Weekly Analysis," August 7–13, 1942, RG 262, Entry 32, Box 4, NA.

Welles defended the right of the United States to be outspoken about India, he cautioned privately, "We can't break with England on account of India. There are enough rifts in the lute already." The British embassy reported on August 16, 1942, that American officials continued to criticize British rule in India, but were convinced that Gandhi was a "bad man" from the point of view of the war effort.[48]

The British embassy was partially justified in claiming that the administration was sympathetic and the American public reaction satisfactory. An OWI analysis of August 1942 noted that the press editorials showed "great uneasiness" with the Congress Party's decision to attempt a nonviolent rebellion against British rule. It concluded that the American press was hostile to Gandhi and sympathetic to Britain. Indeed, individual columnists did draw on British propaganda themes. Walter Lippmann argued that the British in India were confronted with complex problems. Raymond Clapper said that Gandhi was "like a man jumping out of the hotel window to see whether it would kill him" and described Nehru as a Hamlet-like figure. Although the American public continued to believe that India should be granted independence, a poll taken in August showed a minuscule shift on the question of timing. Forty-three percent of the public continued to believe that India should receive its independence, but of that percentage, 47 percent thought it should happen after the war, and 46 percent thought it should happen immediately. The shift could easily be discounted by the margin for error, yet for the first time, it appeared that more people believed independence should be given after the war rather than immediately.[49]

Like the initial positive reaction and subsequent criticism following the Cripps mission, American support for Britain's policy in response to the "Quit India" movement was transitory. An OWI study of the American press showed that editorial and columnist comment in eighty newspapers in the month following the "Quit India" movement was 51 percent "anti-India," 40 percent neutral, and 9 percent

48. Hess, *America Encounters India*, 82; Louis Fischer, interview with Sumner Welles, September 25, 1942, Louis Fischer Papers, Seeley G. Mudd Manuscript Library, Department of Rare Books and Special Collections, Princeton University, Princeton, N.J.; Nicholas, *Washington Despatches*, 70.

49. OWI Intelligence Report No. 35, August 7, 1942, PSF Subject File, Box 174, FDRL; Hess, *America Encounters India*, 54, 82; Clapper Papers, Personal Files Memoranda 1942–1943, Box 23; Cantril and Strunk, eds., *Public Opinion*, 327.

"pro-India." The OWI indicated its own sentiments by categorizing support for the nationalists as "pro-India" and for the British as "anti-India."

Opinion shifted following Churchill's speech on September 10, 1942, in which he rejected further negotiations with the Indian nationalists. Churchill had reported to the House of Commons that the British authorities had repressed the unrest in India with "incredibly small loss of life," which he numbered at five hundred persons. The prime minister touched upon many propaganda themes in the conclusion of his speech:

> To sum up, the outstanding fact which has so far emerged from the violent action of the Congress Party has been their nonrepresentative character and their powerlessness to throw into confusion the normal peaceful life of India. It is the intention of His Majesty's Government to give all necessary support to the Viceroy and his Executive in the firm but tempered measures by which they are protecting the life of the Indian community and leaving the British and Indian armies to defend the soil of India against the Japanese.
>
> I may add that large reinforcements have reached India, and that the numbers of white soldiers now in that country, though very small compared with its size and population, are larger than at any time in the British connection.[50]

Churchill presented the British as calm and reasonable in the face of Indian violence, but his speech was not received well in the United States. "Winston's statement on India will not have done us much good here," complained Halifax to Foreign Secretary Eden. "Why must he talk about *white* troops, when 'the British Army in India' would have served his purpose just as well?" "The average person," reported the British consul in Detroit, "regards the stand of the British as completely stiff-necked and unreasonable." OWI found that comment was 35 percent "anti-India," 22 percent neutral, and 43 percent "pro-India," showing a significant shift in favor of the Indian independence movement. American officials at the OWI noted that American criticism of Gandhi was milder in the

50. Churchill, "The Situation in India," September 10, 1942, *His Complete Speeches*, vol. 6, 6677.

wake of Churchill's "no compromise" speech. They concluded that India was bad for Anglo-American unity. Moreover, Archibald MacLeish worried about the domestic implications. He thought that India "offered a ground for the isolationists to ride back into the picture."[51]

British propagandists regained support by employing the themes of complexity and the war effort against Gandhi. To protest the imprisonment of National Congress leaders, Gandhi began a twenty-one-day fast on February 10, 1943. British propagandists immediately perceived the danger of the fast both in India and for American opinion. The Government of India issued a statement deploring the use of fasting as a "political weapon." It blamed the Congress Party for the disorder of the fall of 1942, charging that the supposed nonviolent "Quit India" campaign had been marked by "sabotage and violence." A strict censorship policy enabled the British to link violence with Indians rather than with themselves. Gardner Cowles of the OWI, who accompanied Wendell Willkie on his worldwide tour, told Raymond Clapper that censors prevented American reporters from getting out their stories about machine-gunnings by British authorities.[52]

British observers monitored the American reaction to the announcement of Gandhi's fast. The Indian agent-general, Sir Girja Bajpai, reassured the viceroy that Americans were more interested in the war and domestic politics. Elmer Davis and Raymond Gram Swing told Bajpai they believed that American opinion would not be aroused unless there was an outbreak of civil disturbance or Gandhi's life was endangered. BIS analysts reported that the majority of the American press approved of the British position. Many newspaper editorials of February 1943 presented views of Gandhi long pro-

51. Halifax to Eden, September 14, 1942, Reel 2, 4.15, Halifax Papers; Halifax, "Review of Consular Reports from July to October, 1942," November 25, 1942, FO371/30672 A11418/399/45, PRO; "Comment on India in American Newspapers and Magazines," January 5, 1943, Special Memorandum No. 17, OGR, Bureau of Intelligence, OWI, Media Division Reports and Memoranda, RG 44, Entry 171, Box 1846; "Anti-British Feeling by U.S. Citizens and British Reactions Thereto," December 16, 1942, OGR, Bureau of Intelligence, OWI, Reports and Special Memoranda, 1942–1943, RG 44, Entry 177, Box 1850; "Minutes of the Joint Committee on Information Policy," September 10, 1942, RG 208, Entry 1, Box 5, OWI, NA.

52. FO to Washington, February 10, 1943, FO371/34144 A1575/93/45, PRO; Clapper Papers, Personal File Memoranda, Box 23.

moted by British propagandists. Angus Malcolm of the Foreign Office's American Department minuted the agent-general's report: "So far so good. If the Russians can go on filling the newslines until the fast is over we may get through all right."[53]

As the fast went on and Gandhi weakened, British propagandists began to prepare for his death. The MOI drew on established themes for its guideline "Mr. Gandhi's Fast and Possible Death." Using the past tense to discuss Gandhi, the guidance paper explained that setting him free unconditionally would have encouraged a revival of the serious unrest of the previous months. Such a revival would have had a disastrous effect upon the Indian army, the civil service and police, and the Muslim community, who would have regarded it as a British betrayal of their interests to the Congress Party. British authorities thought Gandhi's release would have a more disastrous effect on the Indian war effort than his death. They predicted that the "excitement" resulting from Gandhi's death would subside before India became a major base for important war operations.[54] The MOI wanted their propagandists to treat Gandhi's death in the context of war effort; their tone was to be regretful but tough.

The American Department of the Foreign Office analyzed the potential damage to Anglo-American relations. Nevile Butler hoped that the anticipated American casualty lists from Tunisia and American recognition of the value of Britain as a seasoned military ally would offset any outrage. "If Gandhi dies," Butler noted, "this will confirm Americans' feelings that we have an unfortunate knack of getting hated." He suggested that British references to Gandhi be phrased as "magnanimously as well as realistically as possible." "I agree entirely," David Scott responded. "We want to stick to the war effort theme and to Americans who say that we are wrong in our opinion about the effect of the war effort we can point to Cripps' proposals

53. BIS, "American Survey—India" February 15–19, 1943, FO371/34146 A2166/93/45; Bajpai to Viceroy, February 11, 1943, and minute by Malcolm, February 15, 1943, FO371/34114 A1663/93/45, PRO.

54. MOI and PWE Special Issues Committee Paper No. 22, "Publicity Treatment of Mr. Gandhi's Fast and Possible Death," February 23, 1943, FO371/34146 A2167/93/45, PRO. FDR's representative William Phillips reported to Washington from New Delhi that the British preferred Gandhi's death and resulting unrest to the appearance of weakness should they agree to Gandhi's position; Hess, *American Encounters India*, 101.

and to Gandhi's Jap appeasement line."[55] Gandhi in death was to be treated as an irresponsible saint. Any discussion of him was to made in the context of the importance of Britain and India as loyal allies in a common war effort.

The BBC prepared for Gandhi's death, reported the FBIS analyst; having "cast" Gandhi as the disobedient child, the British would now proceed to ignore him. He predicted that London would call Gandhi's death a suicide, while Tokyo would call it murder. The FBIS report concluded, "The resulting dismay and anger of the Indian people will be largely ignored on British broadcasts and highly exploited on Axis airwaves."[56] When not ignoring Gandhi, the BBC invalidated his beliefs as impractical and troublemaking. It avoided a discussion of the Indian people by referring to "the problem" only in terms of Allied interests.

For the most part, the British propaganda line on Gandhi was successful in the United States. When Secretary of State Hull stated that only the war mattered immediately, it was a gratifying echo of the war-effort theme. The secretary of state pleased the British further by responding to a group of American visitors who urged that the United States take some action about India with the remark, "Well, I am still waiting for one of you guys to tell me what Gandhi has done to help win the war." Surveys of the American press conducted by both American and British agencies showed that most of the press had adopted the British line stressing the priority of the war effort over Indian political movements, the need for the British to maintain order in India in time of war, and Gandhi's irresponsible role. By the time Gandhi ended the fast, he was widely discredited in the United States. American support for India's immediate independence had declined as well. A public opinion poll conducted in April 1943 showed that 19 percent of Americans opposed Indian independence. Of the 62 percent in favor of independence, 19 percent favored immediate independence, and 40 percent thought it should be granted after the war—a shift from months earlier, when most thought independence should be granted immediately.[57]

55. Minute by N. Butler, February 22, 1943, and minute by Scott, February 24, 1943, FO371/34146 A2166/93/45, PRO.

56. FBIS, "Weekly Review," February 20 and 27, 1943, RG 262, Entry 32, Box 4, NA.

57. Halifax to FO, February 16, 1943, FO371/34144 A1798/93/45, and Scott,

Although many Americans had accepted Britain's presentation of Gandhi's fast as a threat to military effectiveness, the British were disturbed to find that a persistent consensus of American opinion expected political progress toward independence. Along with relief that Gandhi had survived and that order in India had been maintained, members of the American media argued that democratic principles called for a return to negotiations for Indian independence. Cal Tinney, a commentator for the Mutual Network whose homespun delivery earned him the title "the Will Rogers of radio," remarked on the contradiction between Allied war aims and British rule in India. He noted that in looking beyond Gandhi's fast he could see "Indian people's cynical expressions now when you mention the Atlantic Charter and the Four Freedoms." Tinney connected events in India to Allied defeats in Singapore and Burma. "We lost those two places," Tinney stated, "because the native populace was fed up with the difference between the Four Freedoms as preached and the Four Freedoms as practiced." Tom Treanor of the *Los Angeles Times* thought that although the British had done a lot for India, they should "clear out," because as long as they remained in India, there would be trouble.[58]

George Sansom of the British embassy heard sentiments like Tinney's and Treanor's when he visited the West Coast in the spring of 1943. Sansom reported that "many educated and even thoughtful Americans" rejected the message of the complexity theme. They had little respect for the rights of minorities and thought colonial peoples should be left to work out their own problems even if the results were division and bloodshed. Civil war, Sansom had learned, was not un-American.[59]

The most famous warning to the British that the empire remained

---

FO371/34146 A3268/93/45, PRO; BIS to MOI, Survey Special—India, March 5–19, 1943, FO371/34146 A2975/93/45, PRO; Cantril and Strunk, eds., *Public Opinion,* 327.

58. "Media Comment on M. K. Gandhi's Fast," March 12, 1943, Special Memoranda No. 40, OGR, Bureau of Intelligence, OWI, Media Division Reports and Memoranda, RG 44, Entry 171, Box 1846, NA; BIS to MOI, Survey on India, April 9, 1943, FO371/34146 A2975/93/45, PRO.

59. Minute by Sansom, May 20, 1943, FO371/34091 A4901/3/45; minutes of a meeting of the members of Sir George Sansom's Committee, February 23, 1944, FO371/38522 A1062/16/45, PRO.

a serious source of friction in Anglo-American relations was *Life* magazine's "Open Letter to the British People," published in October 1942. The "Letter" accused Britain of selfish war aims and declared that "if you cling to the Empire at the expense of a United Nations victory you will lose the war because you will lose us." In reaction, the British put their defensive strategy into high gear. The Foreign Office arranged for Vernon Bartlett to write a rejoinder arguing that the empire had brought "law and security to vast areas of the globe until they have become politically adult." In broadcasts to their home audience, Edward R. Murrow and Robert Trout condemned the *Life* "Letter" as detrimental to Anglo-American cooperation.[60]

The BBC's North American Service, for the first time, singled out a specific American critique for extended treatment. One speaker admitted that much had to be done in the empire before anyone could feel satisfied with it but in an appeal to the progressive American audience, added: "One thing I think this war killed stone dead is the thing we used to call British imperialism. I know there are still some in this country who still think the old thoughts. But really, you know, they are now back numbers, just dodos. We, here, by and large, yes we really are, through with all that sort of nonsense." This view was refuted a few weeks later by the return of the dodo in Churchill's "First Minister" speech. Churchill declared to a London audience that he had "not become the King's First Minister in order to preside over the liquidation of the British Empire."[61]

When the BBC wanted to take a harder line in its treatment of the "Open Letter," it brought in an American, in this case, the *New York Herald Tribune's* Geoffrey Parsons. Like many American critics of the *Life* "Letter," Parsons accused the magazine of handing the Axis a propaganda weapon to split the Allies. He also derided *Life* for claiming to speak for the American people. To make his point, he quoted an American Flying Fortress pilot just returned from air raids over enemy territory, who, after reading the "Letter," asked, "Who

---

60. "An Open Letter from the Editors of LIFE to the People of England," *Life* 13 (October 12, 1942), 34; Ridsdale, October 13, 1942, FO371/30671 A9559/399/4; Ridsdale, October 11, 1942, FO371/30672 A9623/399/45, PRO.

61. Ewer quoted by FBIS, "Weekly Review," October 17, 1942, RG 262, Entry 32, Box 3, NA; "A New Experience—Victory," November 10, 1942, Churchill, *His Complete Speeches*, Vol. 6, 6695.

does publisher Henry Luce think he is, a nation?"[62] The British mobilized their resources to rebut *Life*'s slurs against their imperial policy but recognized the defensive strategy to be inadequate for any
long-term promotion of the empire.

Official U.S.-British relations in India reflected the tensions of temporary cooperation on a divisive issue. To distinguish the United
States from its British ally, the OWI had placed ads in Indian newspapers entitled "America Fights for Freedom," which told of the U.S.
promise of independence to the Philippines and its policy of "free
political and commercial association with all peoples of Asia." When
British authorities objected to these ads, the OWI canceled them in
favor of Anglo-American cooperation.[63] To make it clear to the Indians that American forces in India were there to fight the Japanese
and not to support British rule, U.S. military personnel under Gen.
J. W. Stilwell in the China-Burma-India (CBI) theater wore a special
Star of India patch.

Maj. Dean Rusk of Stilwell's staff recalled that American military
personnel were supposed to avoid contact with Indian nationalists in
order to maintain good working relations with the British. Rusk,
later U.S. secretary of state from 1961 to 1969, had been dean of
faculty at Mills College before being assigned to military intelligence
at the Pentagon in 1941. A former Rhodes scholar who won the Cecil
Peace Prize in 1933 with an essay comparing the British Commonwealth to the League of Nations, Rusk had heard Mahatma Gandhi
speak at Oxford University. Gandhi had explained that the secret of
his movement's power was that the British could not stay in India
without the Indians. In India during the war, Rusk could see for
himself that the goal of opening supply routes to China would be
stopped dead without Indian help. Contrary to British propaganda
themes, Gandhi and his followers were not irresponsible or appeasers
but instead cooperators with the war effort.

The Americans' desire to distance themselves from the Raj, however, did not prevent them from patronizing British clubs that ex-
cluded Indians. The practice of exclusion also affected Americans'

---

62. FBIS, "Weekly Review," October 17 and 31, 1942, RG 262, Entry 32, Box 3;
"Weekly Analysis," October 19, 1942, RG 262, Entry 33, Box 6, NA.
63. Malcolm, May 25, 1943, FO371/34091 A4735/3/45; Lumby (IO) to Dudley,
July 24, 1943, FO371/34092 A7063/3/45, PRO.

ability to work with their allies in the CBI theater. Rusk recalled that because the U.S. military treated African American GIs as second-class citizens, the Chinese and the Indians did not want to work with them. The CBI theater's low priority in the war meant that with the help of censorship, the awkwardness of Allied relations seldom reached the American audience.[64]

The exception to this managed calm was the visit of the five senators in August 1943. At home, the senators reported on the lethargy of the Indian theater. Senator Richard Russell returned with a widely circulated parody in which the U.S. military vented their frustration with the British way of warfare:

Listen my children, you need not fear
As they did in the days of Paul Revere
The British must have been more alive
Back in seventeen seventy five
Perhaps they doubted there'd be a fight
For history states they came that night
At the present time Paul Revere would say
"The British are coming but not right away"[65]

The parody went on to indicate that the British did most of their fighting over lunch, at tea, and with drinks at the club.

Senator Russell recognized that this exasperation had two sides. He believed the American general who said, "Our British allies, God bless them. I am sure that we irritate them nearly as much as they irritate us." Privately, he came away with exactly the point of view the British wanted. "My brief visit has certainly not given me any solution to the Indian problem, and I am perfectly willing to let the British work it out as best they can," he wrote to his mother from India. "From the little I have seen, I am convinced that anyone who tries to settle it, has an awful headache in store."[66] Unfortunately for

64. Dean Rusk, interview with author, June 26, 1991, Athens, Ga.
65. "1943 Trip Papers," Series 5, Subseries 10, Russell Papers.
66. RBR to Mother, August 31, 1943; first draft of report to Senate, 1943, Series S, Subseries 10, Russell Papers. Months later, Senator Russell announced: "I believe that the keystone of any lasting peace depends upon a complete understanding between the United States and the British Empire." Editorial, "The British Empire and the United States," *Fortune*, January 1944, 94–95.

propagandists, the five senators' public critique focused on the war effort in India. In 1943, with the nationalist crisis passed, Americans expected the British to do what they claimed and put all their energy against the enemy.

By defining the Indian crisis in terms of the immediate problem of the war effort, the British diverted temporarily the larger, more difficult question of American anticolonialism. By blaming the Indians for failing to agree on the Cripps offer and discrediting Gandhi, they had subdued American sympathies for the nationalist movement. American opinion leaders had accepted and used the war effort and complexity themes. Polls showed that the public had become more cautious on the question of Indian independence. Propagandists had successfully mollified American criticism of their India policy in 1942; yet anticolonialism persisted. The British turned from a defensive to an offensive strategy in their campaign for empire.

5 The Campaign for Empire, 2: "White Men in Tough Places"

> The American people do not like "empires" or "imperialism," though [they are] not unfamiliar with creating an empire and an imperialism of their own.
>
> —GRAHAM SPRY, 1944

The contradiction between Americans' anticolonial beliefs and their imperial behavior puzzled British propagandists. They viewed the United States as a continental empire, "with its subject negro and American Indian inhabitants, and its vast areas acquired from France, Spain and Mexico," to which was added Alaska, as well as overseas possessions in the Pacific and Caribbean.[1] To propagandists, the difference between British and American imperialism consisted of oceanic empire versus continental empire rather than ideology. But this perception did not seem to be shared by Americans, who believed that imperialism divided rather than united the two allies.

During 1942 the crisis in India had tested the Anglo-American alliance. Although most Americans, including President Roosevelt, had accepted the argument that the need for Allied unity outweighed the Indian demand for independence, Americans continued to equate progress with the break-up of the British Empire. Concern about the

---

1. Britain was not included in the list of countries from which the United States acquired territory. Subcommittee report, "Unfavorable American Opinions Regarding the British Empire," February 1943, FO371/34086 A1070/3/45, PRO.

persistence of American support for Indian independence drove British policymakers to gauge the attitudes of opinion leaders. While in Washington in March 1943, Foreign Secretary Eden went out of his way to cultivate Raymond Clapper. Eden asked Clapper what complaints he had, in particular about India. Clapper recorded his reply and the subsequent exchange: "I said you folks have won so I guess it doesn't matter much for awhile. Eden said, you mean Gandhi's fast. I said that and the whole situation. I said India [is] not in the danger now that it was a year ago when I was out there so that it did not matter so much now. I said I had been very critical of London's handling of India and that I didn't think it could go on that way in the long run."[2] Eden stated that there was little chance of a settlement while Gandhi lived, but eventually India would have a place in the Commonwealth. The British temporarily "had won" the propaganda battle of India by discrediting Gandhi and using the complexity and war-effort themes.

With the improving military situation, however, propagandists would be less able to contain the public debate over the empire within the context of the war effort. In March 1943, Graham Hutton, the BIS chief in Chicago, sent to London a report entitled "The Chicago Tribune's Anglophobia on a New Course." Hutton wrote that the *Tribune* editorials and news reporting had shifted from emphasizing British military reverses to attacking the Commonwealth and Empire. The effect, Hutton concluded, was to warn that the "postwar world will not be a safe, prosperous, or secure place for Americans as long as this British 'Empire' rambles all over the globe, immense, populous, like-minded, and permeated (allegedly) by un-American 'class-system,' monarchy rule, etc."[3] The *Tribune*'s anglophobia, as expected as mud in spring, had hit upon a vulnerable issue.

The worst attacks on the empire in the U.S. press, moreover, would not be balanced by a wholehearted defense from the U.S. government. The Roosevelt administration insisted that a peaceful postwar world must be based upon liberal principles. The Atlantic Charter

2. Clapper thought he had been granted an interview because Halifax had reported to Eden that Clapper was critical of Britain's India policy; interview with Anthony Eden, March 18, 1943, Personal File Memoranda 1942–1943, Box 23, Clapper Papers.

3. Cruikshank to FO, April 1943, FO371/34090 A3972/3/45, PRO.

called for self-determination and the open door. Article 7 of the Lend-Lease agreement committed Britain to ending discriminatory trade practices. Throughout 1943 and 1944, President Roosevelt and the State Department pushed for international control over colonial powers in the form of trusteeships. International trustees would schedule timetables for independence, establish an international police force, coordinate development, and open ports and territories to free trade. The British, who interpreted "free trade" to mean American trade and "international control" to mean predominately American control, opposed a U.S. invasion of their empire.[4]

Policymakers wanted to prevent American interference in the empire, but not at the expense of a resurgence of isolationism. The consul general in New York, Sir G. Haggard, urged the Foreign Office to take preventive measures or else "when peace terms come to be discussed realists in the American Government dealing with India and the British Empire are likely to be out-voted and disowned by the masses of the electorate unless the latter are instructed on such matters, and we shall be confronted with the same kind of disastrous decision as when America repudiated the Treaty of Versailles." This fear of isolationism explained the Foreign Office's dissatisfaction over Senator Robert Taft's statement in June 1943. The Ohio Republican remarked that India was not the business of the United States and should be left to Britain. Nevile Butler warned that Senator Taft's "traditional ulterior motive was to avoid his country being called upon to under-write the British Empire."[5]

Butler predicted that if the Americans could be persuaded to underwrite the empire, they would demand some say in imperial affairs as part of the price. "It will require knowledge of their mentality as well as firmness to keep them successfully within the proper limits," he concluded.[6] Butler's manner of expression perhaps indicated an unsuitability for personal contact with Americans, but he did identify the task at hand. Propagandists had to study American attitudes and

4. William Roger Lewis and Ronald Robinson, "The United States and the Liquidation of the British Empire in Tropical Africa, 1941–1951," in *The Transfer of Power in Africa: Decolonization, 1940–1960*, ed. Prosser Gifford and William Roger Louis (New Haven: Yale University Press, 1982), 32–37.

5. G. Haggard to N. Butler, June 6, 1943, FO371/34091 A5514/3/45; minute by N. Butler, June 18, 1943, FO371/34147 A5095/93/45, PRO.

6. Minute by N. Butler, June 18, 1943, FO371/34147 A5095/93/45, PRO.

develop propaganda themes that would discourage both American isolationism and imperialism. They needed to secure American involvement but set limits to it. The goal of propagandists was to convince American opinion that the British Empire under British rule would be a valuable asset to maintaining international peace.

Propagandists discovered that on the issue of empire, as with India, the "strategy of truth" method was overburdened. The historian Arnold Toynbee optimistically summed up the method when he predicted that in the United States, "the better instructed minority of the public will probably adopt the government's policies on their merits and will then help to commend them to the electorate as a whole." Others were less confident. D. M. MacDougall, sent to the United States by the Colonial Office, reported back that there was a problem finding American individuals or groups "able and willing to speak for us."[7] Propaganda themes had to be developed that would win the backing of opinion leaders and appeal to the public at large. At the heart of this task lay the crucial question of whether imperial policy would have to be changed in order to create attractive imperial propaganda.

In reaction to the widespread belief that something must be done about American anticolonialism, Alexander Cadogan took the first step toward the creation of a high-level response to the problem. In September 1942, following the "Quit India" movement, Cadogan outlined the potential dangers for postwar cooperation in a letter to the MOI's Cyril Radcliffe. Cadogan believed that American collaboration with Britain in establishing a stable world order rested on respect for the British Empire. Without that respect, the United States might seek to impose its leadership on Britain. Cadogan suggested that London policymakers plan a large-scale program to "enlighten" American opinion about the value of the British Empire.[8]

Radcliffe agreed with Cadogan's analysis. He remarked on the need for an informed study of American opinion in order to develop adequate propaganda. He recommended that a committee representing the Foreign Office, the MOI, the Colonial Office, the India Office,

---

7. Minute by Toynbee, June 1943, FO371/34091 A5514/3/45; D. M. MacDougall to N. Sabine, January 12, 1943, CO875/18/19, PRO.
8. Cadogan to Radcliffe, September 29, 1942, CO875/19/2, PRO.

and the Dominions Office be organized to "secure a proper Survey of the field, the resistances, the causes and the possible lines of approach." The departments and the War Cabinet supported action. By the new year, the Committee on American Opinion and the British Empire was formed. Richard Law, the minister of state at the Foreign Office and one of the few senior officials with extensive experience in the United States, acted as chair. Alan Dudley, formerly of the British Library of Information in New York, served as secretary. The goal of the Law Committee, as it came to be known, was to secure American support for the maintenance of the British Empire by presenting Britain and its empire as a valuable partner of the United States.[9]

The committee's statement of aims masked the controversy among its members over British imperial policy and the role U.S. opinion should play in determining that policy and its presentation. The Law Committee organizers hoped to establish a forum for working out compromises on propaganda policy with those departments, such as the Dominions Office, the India Office, and the Colonial Office, which were inclined to disregard American opinion. Beginning with the assumption that U.S. public opinion might have a significant say about the future of the British Empire, the Foreign Office wanted British imperial policy to be drawn up with American attitudes in mind. The empire departments argued that good propaganda was not always good policy. Few members would agree with Lt. Col. B. Rowe, a visitor from the War Office, who spoke from an out-of-Whitehall world of market analysis. Rowe declared that "just as a commercial firm finding a resistance to its product would alter that product so we must be prepared to alter our product." At the end of a meeting held in the committee's second month of existence, the question was raised "whether it was not essential to know why we wish to retain the Empire." The question was briefly discussed with no reasons recorded, and the meeting terminated.[10]

9. Radcliffe to Cadogan, October 9, 1942, FO371/30685 A9422/1684/45; Dudley, introductory memorandum for the Interdepartmental Committee on American Opinion and the British Empire, FO371/30865 A10559/1684/45, PRO.

10. Dudley to Law, January 28, 1943, and covering memorandum, January 27, 1943, FO371/34086 A1070/3/45; minutes of the first meeting of the Committee on American Opinion and the British Empire, December 30, 1942, FO371/34086 A78/3/45; report on the joint meeting of subcommittees, February 23, 1943, FO371/34086 A1783/3/45, PRO.

Of the departments represented on the Law Committee, the Dominions Office had the least to say. Although the Commonwealth was considered a vital component of the presentation of the empire, the Commonwealth countries, seeking to establish independent relations with the United States, were not all that cooperative. Harold Butler, the head of the BIS, complained from Washington: "Until Australia and Canada pay homage to the system known as the British Commonwealth, America will never be seriously tempted to believe."[11] The dominions' independent stance annoyed those who wanted the Commonwealth countries to promote the British Empire by demonstrating their willing attachment to it.

After their experiences of the previous year, the India Office and the Government of India, notably the viceroy, Lord Linlithgow, saw India as a British domain to be protected from Americans, including personal representatives of President Roosevelt and war correspondents. The viceroy considered the Foreign Office "weak-kneed" for not taking a strong stand with the United States. The Foreign Office, for its part, deplored the Government of India and the India Office's lack of consideration for the effect of their statements on American opinion.[12]

The Colonial Office, which administered fifty-five territories with an estimated population of 60 million, had two serious objections to the Law Committee goal. One official questioned whether the "British Empire" could be a partner to the United States because of "the unformed nature of the Empire vis-à-vis foreign affairs." Rather than envisioning far-flung colonies in the Caribbean, the Middle East, and Southeast Asia sharing a common foreign policy, the Colonial Office thought regional councils would strengthen the ability of the colonies to deal with foreign governments. The colonial secretary, Oliver Stanley, used the notion of regional councils to strengthen the British colonial government, not the position of the colonial peoples. The Colonial Office's qualification of the term "British Empire" did show up the Law Committee's working assumption that the territories of

11. H. Butler to Law, July 22, 1943, FO371/34093 A7707/3/45; minute by Dudley, May 13, 1943, FO371/34090 A4475/3/45, PRO.
12. D. Monteath (IO) to Cadogan, October 17, 1942, FO371/30685 A9610/1684/ 45; Scott, October 20, 1943, FO371/34094 A9834/3/45, PRO; Linlithgow to Amery, May 1943, LI/1/809, India Office.

the empire had a common interest, which was and would be directed by London. The second reservation held by the Colonial Office was that in any propaganda that grouped the colonies with the dominions and India, the colonies would become "Cinderella," the ragged stepsister of the imperial family. The resulting contrast between the wealth and development of the dominions and the poverty and dependence of the colonies would encourage increased criticism of the colonial system.[13] With these contradictory agendas unresolved, the Law Committee launched a study of American opinion and how it could be influenced.

Ambassador Halifax's position on the problem of the British Empire and American opinion represented the dominant British view of early 1943. He believed that the solution was a simple matter of explanation. Halifax attributed American anticolonialism to a false analogy with the Philippines and the historical memory of the thirteen colonies. Halifax wrote to Anthony Eden that it was possible to take a strong stand on the issue and have it accepted in the United States. To official statements on India, for instance, he suggested adding something about British dedication to assisting India to achieve her full destiny and to helping the "Indians in overcoming their own difficulties." "It really is a question of presentation rather than policy," he explained, "and as the old lady, when reproached by the parson for bowing at the name of the devil, said: 'Politeness costs nothing, and you never know.' "[14] Like many of his contemporaries, Halifax believed that a bow to the American devil in matters of presentation would solve the problem of American criticism of Britain's empire policy.

A report on American attitudes toward India, presented to the Law Committee by two India Office civil servants, endorsed Halifax's interpretation. Sent to the United States to evaluate British propaganda efforts, Sir Frederick Puckle and A. H. Joyce reported on "metropolitan American thinking" based on their visits to New York and Washington. They concluded that American opinion, characterized

13. Minute by Gent, January 11, 1943, CO875/19/3; Minute by Jeffries, May 7, 1943, CO875/19/12, PRO.
14. Interview with Halifax, May 22, 1943, Fischer Papers; Halifax to Eden, October 12, 1942, Reel 2, 4.15, Halifax Papers.

by "ignorance and interest," was easily manipulated by Indian nationalist propaganda and could and should be educated by the
British. American attitudes, according to Puckle and Joyce, were
"typically adolescent towards the grown-up British Empire."[15]

Graham Spry agreed with Puckle and Joyce that American opinion
on the British Empire had its roots in a tradition of rivalry and nationalism. In the spring of 1943, the Law Committee assigned Spry
the task of conducting an extensive survey of American opinion
about the British Empire. Spry was selected because of his journalism
background, his experience as Cripps's assistant and work done in
the United States the previous year, and because the committee believed that, as a Canadian, Spry would be less likely to arouse American suspicions of British propaganda. Spry did not complete his
study until 1944; he introduced some of his findings in a preliminary
report to the Law Committee in the summer of 1943, however. He
thought that American interest in India was not dependent upon Indian nationalist propaganda or anti-British traditions. Nor did he
agree entirely with Puckle's conclusions about American ignorance
and the efficacy of "education." Spry saw the Americans as "power-
minded." He defined U.S. interests as dependent upon economic conditions and security considerations.[16]

Though Spry's initial conclusions were accepted by a few British
officials, most of the members of the Law Committee preferred Halifax's and Puckle's recommendation to focus on presentation and
education rather than on policy. They could avoid the more difficult
task of reassessing imperial policy by relying upon, in the words of
Cyril Radcliffe, the "imaginative use of the arts of explanation." The
Law Committee pulled together an analysis of the favorable and unfavorable aspects of American opinion on the British Empire. Out of
these deliberations emerged two propaganda themes that drew upon
the complexity and war-effort themes of 1942 but presented them in
terms of postwar cooperation.

The theme "white men in tough places" celebrated success, indi-

15. "The Puckle-Joyce Report on Publicity in the United States," August 12, 1943,
FO371/34148 A7522/93/45, PRO.
16. Spry, "Some preliminary and personal impressions concerning American politics and economics and their relation to the British Empire," June-July 1943, FO371/
34098 A7129/3/45, PRO.

vidual initiative, and courage, all listed as "qualities which excite American admiration" in a Law Committee study.[17] Propagandists found inspiration in the era of Theodore Roosevelt, an era they believed Americans looked back upon with "intellectual disapproval that competes with an emotional pride in the trumpet-notion of 'manifest destiny.' " British leaders themselves longed for the spirit of cooperation in the remark "What's the Constitution between friends?" attributed to the Republican Roosevelt. The adoption of TR-esque rhetoric would allow propagandists to present empire-building as a robust, moral crusade. "Americans are used to seeing pictures of their own 'covered wagon' days," reasoned Law Committee members, "and they would quickly take to the idea of the 'frontier' in the British Empire." Drawing a parallel between the American pioneers and such imperial explorers as Cecil Rhodes and Rajah Brooke, propagandists envisioned a "saga" film treatment of individual stories of "hardship and difficulty overcome, of native confidence gained, of land made productive, of superstition banished and disease conquered."[18]

Lord Halifax championed this theme, and through his influence it found its way into the January 1944 issue of *Fortune* magazine. The *Fortune* editorial declared that the British system of empire "grew from the same irresistible urge that drove Americans across the face of a continent." The BIS pamphlet *The British Commonwealth and Empire* drew parallels between American westward expansion, British settlement of the dominions, and the organization of the new lands into American "territories" and British "colonies." The American people had ceased calling the lands of their many frontiers an empire, explained the pamphlet, but the British, whose frontier was overseas, stuck with the name.[19]

17. "White men in tough places," used to describe films about the empire, is quoted from the committee report. The discussion of these themes is drawn from the preliminary report of Subcommittee I of the Committee on American Opinion and the British Empire, Part I, "Favorable Factors in American Opinion: Qualities Which Excite American Admiration," January 27, 1943, FO371/34086 A1070/3/45, PRO.

18. Ibid. Richard Slotkin explores the parallels between empire epics and American westerns in *Gunfighter Nation: The Myth of Frontier in Twentieth-Century America* (New York: HarperCollins, 1992), 265–271.

19. Editorial, "The British Empire and the United States," *Fortune*, January 1944, 94–95; BIS, *The British Commonwealth and Empire*, May 1944, OWI Overseas

The British wanted the U.S. public to identify the empire with the historical myth of continental expansion rather than with the historical myth of colonial independence. Analysts of American opinion blamed the "atrocious" teaching of history in the United States for the widespread anticolonialism. "Teachers (especially history)" appeared on the "enemies list" of imperial critics. Little history was taught in American schools, explained Graham Spry to the Law Committee: "What was taught was the doctrine of American nationalism." Propagandists discussed improving the American education curriculum and the revising of textbooks. The Colonial Office recommended the establishment of a chair of colonial history at an American university.[20] These methods of influencing American opinion aimed at long-term results. In the hope of having a more immediate effect, propagandists chose a theme designed to counter the "ancient grudge" rooted in the "doctrine of American nationalism."

If Americans identified with "white men in tough places," they would line up on the side of the British as opposed to the side of the colonial peoples. In the wartime context, the theme carried the underlying message of the propaganda on India: the danger of violent mobs and chaos, the inability of the Indians to govern themselves, and the need for the British to maintain order. The committee members recognized that this appeal rested "at its lowest on race prejudice which most Americans intellectually repudiate, but actively practice."[21] The theme united the British and Americans as whites who conquered, settled, and developed the nonwhite world. At a time when the daring Japanese attack on Pearl Harbor and the powerful Indian challenge of British rule should have indicated the assertion of nonwhites in a changing world, propagandists turned to an adventure story of empire-building, which perhaps, in the Hollywood tradition, would lead to the climactic scene in which the white men

Branch, Bureau of Overseas Intelligence Central Files, 1941–1945, Great Britain, RG 208, Entry 367, Box 316, NA.

20. "Breakdown of Anti-British Groups and Individuals in U.S.A.," April 1943, Spry Papers, Vol. 46–13, NAC; Law Committee, January 17, 1944, FO371/38522 AN402/16/45, PRO; MacDougall report, March 12, 1943, CO875/18/12, PRO.

21. "Favorable Factors in American Opinion," preliminary report of Subcommittee I of the Committee on American Opinion and the British Empire, January 1943, FO371/34086 A1070/3/45, PRO. The role of racism in World War II is discussed in John W. Dower, *War without Mercy: Race and Power in the Pacific War* (New York: Pantheon Books, 1986), 3–14, and in Thorne, *Allies of a Kind*, 7–11.

stopped fighting each other to join together against an attack by nonwhites. The theme did present difficulties, recognized the Law Committee, by promoting "old-fashioned" notions of imperialism and offending progressive elements in the United States and Britain. Cyril Radcliffe thought that a choice would have to be made between an emphasis on adventure and an emphasis on benevolence.[22]

The theme of partnership, by portraying the British Empire as a benevolent entity, was designed to counter the American view of the empire as an oppressor and exploiter of subject peoples. The qualities embodied in this theme, which supposedly appealed to Americans, were righteousness, freedom, and technological progress. The committee observed that Americans endowed their international ventures with righteousness, a quality the committee defined as "the combination of force with a moral idea." Americans should be made to understand that this quality also motivated Britain's imperial policy. Freedom—which committee members maintained was a British idea, although many Americans claimed it as their own invention—meant protection of minorities in the imperial context. The committee built upon the complexity theme by arguing that in some instances, the need to save native minorities from oppression by native majorities had delayed the development of self-government. Technological progress, illustrated by irrigation systems, railroads, and tropical medicines, demonstrated advancements made for the colonial peoples.[23]

Like "white men in tough places," this theme could correct unflattering stereotypes on the backs of others. Propagandists wanted to revise American images of colonies "ruled from the top by gin-sodden whites who refer slyly to the white man's burden and have large bank balances." A film plot described by Noel Sabine of the Colonial Office illustrated the propagandists' vision of the partnership theme:

It is about a District Officer whose work in an African district is hampered by the activities of a witch doctor who sets the people against him. (We have here the advantage of being able to see all

22. Minutes of the Law Committee meeting, February 8, 1943, FO371/34086 A1502/3/45, PRO.
23. The partnership theme already had been adopted by the MOI for domestic audiences; see "Favorable Factors in American Opinion," FO371/34086 A1070/3/45, PRO.

of the development work the D.O. is doing—getting a school going, a hospital built, and so on, quite naturally during the course
of the story.) The D.O. tries to undermine the influence of the
witch doctor by calling his bluff over the power of his medicine
by defying it himself. This he does and it has an effect for a short
time, but only a short time; for the witch doctor tells people that
the medicine does not affect the white man, but that they had
better be very careful about its effects on them. So the problem is
to get a black man to defy it. The hero of the story then is a native
African schoolmaster whom the D.O. induces to defy the medicine
and break the power of the witch doctor.[24]

Unlike "white men in tough places," the partnership theme united
whites and "progressive" nonwhites against "backward" nonwhites.
   Through the partnership theme, propagandists hoped to reach
women, church and missionary groups, and African Americans—
audiences likely to be alienated by various aspects of "white men in
tough places." Propagandists appealed to what they considered the
humanitarian strains in American thought. In part, they responded
to what they saw as the idealization of Asians by the influential novelist Pearl Buck and the writer Clare Boothe Luce. They planned to
assure these audiences of their concern for the colonial peoples under
their care. The MOI sent articles to women's pages saluting Canadian and South African women for their "equal and free part" in
wartime service. It also placed thirteen articles "dealing with the activities of the colored peoples in the Empire" with the Associated
Negro Press in the early months of 1944.[25]
   In order to portray the British Empire as ever dedicated to progress
and solicitous toward its subject peoples, propagandists had to justify
the length of time required to prepare the subject peoples for self-
government. They sought to correct the American impression that
independence movements resembled the struggle of the thirteen colonies by stressing the "natives' " lack of "civilization." Denis Brogan

24. MacDougall to Sabine, "Colonial Propaganda in America," March 12, 1943,
CO875/18/12; Sabine to MacDougall, March 25, 1943, CO875/18/19, PRO.
   25. Report of joint meeting of the subcommittees, February 22, 1943, FO371/
34086 A1783/3/45, PRO; extracts from notes of Frederick Puckle's visit to MOI,
January 22, 1943, L/I/808, India Office; Bentley to Darvall, June 27, 1944, FO371/
38557 AN2632/34/45, PRO.

of the BBC advised the committee to appeal to American farmers, considered to be isolationists, with a description of Indian farming methods. "The American farmer, if he realised that a great deal of India's economic troubles come from superstitious farming and from the sacredness of cows," suggested Brogan, "might be shaken in his conviction of British sin." The British used the Hindu veneration of the sacred cow and other beliefs and practices that symbolized the "backwardness" and "exotic" nature of colonial cultures to illustrate obstacles in the path of progress. Ideally for propagandists, such a cow caused war correspondent Raymond Clapper's plane to drastically alter its runway landing on a trip in India. When Clapper mentioned to Lord Halifax that he felt he should write about the strikes and disorder following the "Quit India" movement, the ambassador suggested instead a story about the cow on the airfield.[26]

One BIS pamphlet used a parable of the evolution from egg to tadpole to frog to illustrate the political evolution of the Empire and Commonwealth. New Guinea was in the egg stage; Jamaica, Ceylon, Southern Rhodesia, and Burma had little of the tadpole's tail left; and the "highly civilized" dominions were at the most advanced stage.[27] Although the colonies appeared as larval amphibians rather than Cinderella, this characterization confirmed the fears of the Colonial Office that the comparison of the colonies with the dominions would not enhance the progressive image.

The partnership theme implied cooperation between ruler and ruled within the empire. Propagandists hoped this concept would be substituted for the American idea of trusteeship. Lord Hailey, one of the most prominent spokesperson-experts on the empire, argued that the British acted as responsible trustees of "backward peoples." To support his argument and to draw a parallel to the American experience, he cited the U.S. Supreme Court cases of the 1830s in which the chief justice defined the federal government's role regarding the Cherokee nation as that of a trustee.[28]

Colonial Secretary Stanley was more direct about Britain's rejection of American plans for international trusteeships. The BBC used

26. Brogan to Dudley, January 25, 1943, FO371/34086 A1143/3/45, PRO; "Memoranda," August 28, 1942, Personal Files, Container 23, Clapper Papers.

27. BIS, *The British Commonwealth and Empire*, May 1944, OWI Overseas Branch, 1941–1945, Great Britain, RG 208, Entry 367, Box 316, NA.

28. Louis, *Imperialism at Bay*, 12.

a speech by Stanley in March 1943 to indicate the one area that the British excepted from their overall message of Anglo-American co-operation. The BBC commentator approved of the goal of Britain's colonial policy: "complete self-government and freedom from outside control." Stanley argued that the experience of "highly competent experts," the subjection of colonial administration to the "criticism and control by a democratic power," and the "desire of the colonial people themselves" justified British control of their colonies. To illustrate the last point, Stanley observed that "West Indian Negroes" would not "welcome the regime of an international committee," an oblique reminder to the Americans that their treatment of "dependent peoples" was not always an admired standard.[29]

Propagandists used the partnership theme to show the British Empire's contribution to international cooperation. They found their ideal spokesman in Gen. Jan Smuts, the Afrikaner lawyer and former guerrilla leader who was the prime minister of South Africa. Following upon the heels of *Life*'s "Open Letter," Smuts, speaking before the House of Commons, described the British Commonwealth and Empire as the greatest experiment of organized freedom in the world. The BBC used Smuts and South Africa as the symbol of the indomitable British Empire by referring to the resolution of the former conflict between Britain and the Afrikaners. "We found a way out from those troubles in South Africa that looked so appallingly, so insuperably difficult," announced the BBC, "and we can do it again, whether it is a question of social problems, or imperial problems, or international problems."[30] The broadcast did not refer to the African National Congress (ANC) (organized in 1912), which at its 1943 conference announced *The Africans' Claims in South Africa*. The *Claims* cited the Atlantic Charter and called for voting rights, land reform, and an end to discriminatory laws. In the same year, a new pressure group in the ANC, founded by young professionals including Anton Lembede, Nelson Mandela, Walter Sisulu, and Oliver Tambo, called for African self-reliance. The ANC's demands later were crushed by the introduction of apartheid in 1948. In Smuts, propagandists had selected a spokesperson whose country's government would move toward greater racial domination. His praise for

29. FBIS, "Weekly Review," March 13, 1943, RG 262, Entry 32, Box 4, NA.
30. Ibid., October 24, 1942, RG 262, Entry 32, Box 3, NA.

the British Empire intertwined the themes of "white men in tough places" and partnership.[31]

Smuts's description of the Empire and Commonwealth could be used by British commentators and by American friends and critics alike. Former president Herbert Hoover stated that he wanted nothing to happen to the British Empire, "one of the most outstanding and successful experiments in democratic government."[32] Freda Kirchwey of the *Nation* used it to describe the Commonwealth, distinct from the empire, as a "cooperative group of free nations."[33] The British began to use the Commonwealth as a symbol of partnership between self-governing nations that retained economic and security links with the central power.[34]

Even Churchill recognized the value of referring to the Commonwealth when mentioning the empire. At a party for congressmen at the Washington embassy, the prime minister noticed that his repeated references to the British Empire caught the attention of Senator Arthur Vandenberg. Churchill corrected himself by adding the "British Commonwealth of Nations" and announced, "We keep trade labels to suit all tastes."[35] Using the notion of a free, cooperative body, Richard Law suggested to his London committee's Washington embassy counterpart that propaganda should illustrate how the dismantling of the British Empire conflicted with the idea of the United Nations. "It was impossible to make one world by creating hundreds of little worlds," said Law. "The British Commonwealth was a model United Nations."[36]

31. Leonard Thompson, "The Parting of the Ways," in *Transfer of Power*, ed. Gifford and Louis, 426; FBIS, "Weekly Analysis," October 26, 1942, RG 262, Entry 32, Box 4, NA.

32. Although pleased by the former president's statement, Angus Malcolm of the Foreign Office noted that Hoover's audience, the University Club of New York, was not one "where a great many people need converting"; February 5, 1943, FO371/34086 A1373/3/45, PRO.

33. Other interviews with William Shirer and John Gunther were more critical of the British Empire; see *PM*, February 16, 1943.

34. A. P. Thornton, "The Transformation of the Commonwealth and the 'Special Relationship,' " in *The "Special Relationship,"* ed. Louis and Bull, 369–371.

35. Halifax, *Fullness of Days*, 283.

36. The Washington embassy counterpart to the Law Committee was chaired by George Sansom and known as the Sansom or Washington Committee. It was attended by Aubrey Morgan, Graham Spry, John Foster, Isaiah Berlin, Paul Scott-Rankine, and Paul Gore-Booth. Draft minute of a meeting of the Committee on American Opinion and the British Empire, June 14, 1943, FO371/34091 A5904/3/45, PRO.

In 1943, propaganda policy reflected the hope of policymakers that American criticism of British imperial policy was the result of misunderstandings. Propagandists assumed it was necessary merely to "enlighten" the Americans about the similarities between their own empire and the British Empire, the benefits Britain provided for its colonial peoples, and Britain's dedication to eventual self-government. Propagandists had responded to American criticism based on the Atlantic Charter and the Four Freedoms with assurances that the British shared these principles. The phrasing of poll questions reflected an interest in principles as well. A 1943 OWI study asked Americans if the British treated the people in their colonies fairly or unfairly. Of the 75 percent who had an opinion, 38 percent said the British were fair, and 31 percent, representing the more educated sector of the population, said the British were unfair.[37] These findings somewhat confirmed propagandists' distaste for the U.S. educational system.

Although the Law Committee thought the partnership theme would garner American support for their imperial system, some members worried about the charge of self-interest. They thought they could not deny that self-interest was a factor in their imperial policy, given the prime minister's "we hold what we have" stance. The committee's secretary, Alan Dudley, argued that an appeal to self-interest would be effective because it would alert people's fears while promising to soothe them. Linking the self-interest approach to the partnership theme, Dudley insisted, "We have to show Americans that the Empire is good *for them*, and that in addition it is good for the British peoples and the world at large." He explained, "American sentiments are guided by American interests." The committee rejected Dudley's cautious suggestion for an appeal to self-interest.

---

37. This study was based on interviews with 3,600 Americans and was conducted by the OWI in collaboration with the National Opinion Research Center, University of Denver. The final interpretation was prepared by Allan Nevins of Columbia University; see "American Attitudes toward the British," Memorandum No. 65, Surveys Division, Bureau of Special Services, OWI, August 21, 1943, Oscar Cox Papers, Box 100, FDRL. The Foreign Office received a preliminary report from the OWI with the reminder that the OWI was "most anxious that this material should be regarded as most secret"; May 27, 1943, FO371/34128 A5064/34/45, PRO.

They referred to it as the "profit motive" and declared it to be out of date.[38]

Spokespersons for the empire nevertheless began to appeal to American interests within the framework of the partnership theme. The American propaganda analyst for the FBIS reviewed the February 1943 broadcast made on behalf of the empire by two "character witnesses" from the dominions—Richard F. Casey, formerly the Australian minister to Washington, and Walter Nash, New Zealand's representative in Washington. He noted a more constructive defense of empire made by the use of the positive symbol of a postwar world free from fear and want: "Casey calls for 'an expanding world economy, with everyone sharing its fruits.' But such a world involves responsibilities as well. 'Nations must be willing to give up some part of their nationalism in the common interest.' . . . The present implications of the doctrine of post-war responsibility are drawn by Mr. Nash: Americans who demand independence for India must be willing to assume their share of responsibility for 'world security, if that security was in any way endangered by granting India independence.' "[39] With the "doctrine of post-war responsibility," Casey and Nash attempted to define the U.S. role in the postwar world by using a little "Four Freedoms" rhetoric but resting their appeal on American economic and security interests.

Throughout 1943 British propagandists began to emphasize appeals to interests over appeals to principles. They discovered that Americans remained anticolonial in principle and that Britain could not successfully defend the empire on principles. Americans might be capable of holding up their promise of independence to the Philippines without acknowledging their strategic and economic interests in the Pacific colony. But when the British tried to copy this practice, they aroused American suspicions of British duplicity. The British might talk about partnership and gradual self-government; the Americans were thinking about oil, tin, and rubber. British officials with more experience in the United States, as opposed to some of the

38. Alan Dudley, "British Empire Public Relations: The Definition of a Theme," February 16, 1943, FO371/34086 A1738/3/45; Dudley, "Summary of 'Notes' by the Washington Committee," April 14, 1943, FO371/34089 A1738/3/45; report of the joint meeting of the subcommittees, February 22, 1943, FO371/34086, PRO.

39. FBIS, "Weekly Review," February 20, 1943, RG 262, Entry 32, Box 4, NA.

London members of the Law Committee, argued that appeals to American economic and strategic interests, wrapped in principles, could be used to define American responsibilities in terms that protected British interests.

An April 1943 survey conducted by the OWI confirmed their views. The poll question asked:

	Yes (%)	No (%)	Don't Know (%)
After the war is over, do you think we ought to keep Guadalcanal and other territories in the Pacific that we have conquered?	61	24	15
Do you think we should keep any bases in Africa after the war?	61	27	12

These findings pleased the Foreign Office because Americans were thinking like an international imperial power and because if Americans wanted to acquire territories and bases, they would be hard pressed to object in principle to Britain maintaining its possessions. Although they welcomed the poll results, British officials remained concerned that an imperialist United States might become too acquisitive. For instance, the Foreign Office ruefully observed, few Americans seemed to realize that Guadalcanal had belonged to the British Empire.[40]

Policymakers noted that the U.S. government wanted to annex territory for bases but did not want to be considered imperialist. In December 1942, upon President Roosevelt's request, the U.S. Joint Chiefs of Staff had drawn up a master plan for an international police force. Their global security system called for the transfer of some British and French possessions in the Pacific to the United States.[41] Although the State Department talked of international trusteeships, the U.S. military planned to acquire new bases. The British did not want to discourage plans for a security system. They did, however, want to participate in it with their empire intact. They presented a security system as one in which the British Empire would serve as a

40. OWI preliminary report, May 27, 1943, FO371/34128 A5064/34/45, PRO.
41. Louis, *Imperialism at Bay*, 266.

valuable partner, not one in which the United States would replace Britain. The switch from principles to interests also reflected Britain's changing status. An appeal to principles might work among equal powers. An appeal to interests reflected the bargaining weakness of a declining power.

In the last years of the war, Britain's presentation of the empire and Commonwealth as a strong and equal partner of the United States faltered as it became increasingly obvious that the empire was not strong and equal. The Americans' vast resources of matériel and manpower overshadowed Britain's diminishing capability to contribute to the war effort. As Britain became more dependent upon the United States, policymakers feared the Americans would demand a greater say over the future of the empire as the price for American assistance. To meet this unfavorable situation, propagandists did not alter their central theme of the empire as a strong partner, nor did they abandon the "strategy of truth." They maintained both strategies by placing Anglo-American cooperation in a context of postwar uncertainty marked by the growth of Asian nationalism and the rise of the Soviet Union.

The reinterpretation of American opinion was reflected in the fifty-four-page study presented by Graham Spry to the Law Committee in May 1944. Spry based his analysis on reports prepared by government departments, including those represented on the Law Committee, the Washington embassy, British consuls, the BIS, and the wartime missions, such as the Raw Materials Mission. He interviewed British officials and American officials, as well as private citizens in Washington and throughout the United States, from May to November 1943.[42] Many of his observations were not new. They reflected the viewpoints of British officials who had spent the war years in various regions of the United States or of Americans themselves. What was new was the weight given these views by a high-level London committee.

Spry reported that American economic, strategic, and political expansion had become the central element in U.S. relations with the British Empire. Like others before him, Spry acknowledged the role

42. Spry to Sansom, November 10, 1943, Spry Papers, Vol. 46–15, NAC; minutes of Committee on American Opinion and the British Empire, January 17, 1944, FO371/38522 AN402/16/45, PRO.

of historical ties and the "ancient grudge" in shaping a fundamental contradiction in American attitudes between rivalry and nationalism on the one hand and a sense of respect and community on the other. Americans now were interested in empires "for their own sake." Therefore, the "ancient grudge" and the importance of principles in the sense of Anglo-American community were of secondary importance. Spry concluded that American attitudes about the future, not the past, should be the basis of British propaganda.

Spry's conclusions applied to policymaking as well as propaganda. "The successful pursuit of British interests is dependent on our taking legitimate American interests and opinions into account," summarized the Law Committee secretary, Alan Dudley. Then, "representation and explanation can be used effectively in America to support and explain our position. If not," warned Dudley, "no amount of whitewash is likely to remove the differences which would arise."[43] Propaganda or "whitewash" would work only if it was based on imperial policies likely to be favored by Americans. It would not be enough to merely "enlighten" American opinion, believed Spry and Dudley. Americans would be persuaded by what was done as well as by what was said.

Spry presented the Law Committee with a more sophisticated analysis of the role of public opinion in the United States.[44] First, he noted that public opinion was the *presumed* foundation of representative government. Spry qualified this presumption by stating that public opinion in general seldom decisively affected policy. The pressure on government policy came from lobbies, pressure groups, and organized political forces that also had an influence on public opinion. Spry urged propagandists to focus their efforts on organized groups and to specialize their appeal to opinion leaders. "It was difficult," objected the Foreign Office's David Scott, "to distinguish between the voice of the tobacco lobby from the great voice of America." Spry suggested that the British monitor pressure groups in order to

43. Dudley, "Conclusions Drawn from the Spry and Puckle Reports," August 16, 1944, FO371/38524 AN3260/16/45, PRO.
44. Although not discussed in his report to the committee, Spry used studies of public opinion by American social scientists Harold Lasswell, Bernard Berelson, Paul Lazarsfeld, and Donald Slesinger. The Washington embassy supplied him with studies on American reading and radio listening habits; Spry Papers, Vol. 109–19, NAC.

be prepared for their positions on issues of importance.[45] As for the possibility of influencing the ordinary American, Spry knew that "Joe America" read the picture page, the comics, and the editorials of his newspaper, and that his favorite radio program was *Fibber McGee and Molly*, followed by Bob Hope. The Canadian spared the would-be enlighteners of the Law Committee these details. Second, Spry maintained that American public opinion was chiefly a product of national, sectional, and business interests and also of political and social conditions. Interests and perceived dangers to those interests, rather than principles, determined opinion.[46]

Spry drew distinctions—between the public and pressure groups and between principles and interests—to analyze American opinion toward the British Empire. He noted that the Commonwealth did not present a serious problem, except when it was perceived as an economic bloc. The public needed to be informed about the independence of the dominions, but on the whole, Americans believed that the people of the dominions, like the British people, were "just like us." India, on the other hand, was a serious problem because American attitudes, though actively hostile only among a minority, were focused, emotional, and cut across all classes. He touched on earlier propaganda themes with the observation that by 1944, more Americans recognized the "complexities of the Indian problem." Not surprisingly, as one of its promoters, Spry stated that the Cripps mission had successfully demonstrated Britain's good intentions. He went on to say that Gandhi's behavior, his fast, and his "readiness to negotiate with Japan" had reduced the volume of American objections. He concluded that although American opinion on India appeared to be favorably disposed, a crisis like another Bengal famine could reactivate American criticism.[47]

Unlike India, the colonies aroused a less strident response from the American public which, if pressed, thought colonies should be free, but on the whole was not interested. Spry reported that American interest in the colonies was limited to international relations special-

45. "Report of the Meeting of the Committee on American Opinion and the British Empire," January 17, 1944, FO371/38522 AN402/16/45, PRO.
46. Spry, "American Relations with the British Empire," May 1, 1944, 1–3, FO371/38523 AN1577/16/45, PRO.
47. Ibid., 22–24.

ists, business organizations, and other groups, including churches and missionaries, labor organizations, and black intellectuals and the black press who had specific interests in certain regions of the empire. Spry used the oil industry as his chief example of pressure-group influence on U.S. policy. After World War I, as a result of a "propaganda campaign against 'imperialism,' " U.S. oil companies had successfully lobbied the State Department to acquire American access to Iraqi oil fields.[48]

Spry attempted to find out if the British could expect a repeat performance of American oil-company expansion into the British Empire following World War II. He asked the British representative of the Petroleum Mission in New York several questions about the plans of American oil companies. He wanted to know the status of American oil reserves, American plans for exploration (particularly within the empire), and whether private companies would claim participation in British-controlled oil fields as compensation for oil shipped to Britain under Lend-Lease. The Petroleum Mission representative replied that the British and American companies would do very well if the governments left them alone. As an example, he cited the State Department's activities in Mexico on behalf of an American oil company that left the British "out in the cold." American oil companies regretted this policy, because they feared retaliation by the British. Both sides wanted access to South America and the Middle East. American companies, the Petroleum Mission representative added, would not use Lend-Lease as leverage.[49]

In contrast to this amiable picture, the notorious five senators, upon return from their world tour, argued that the United States was running out of oil because of generous Lend-Lease supplies to Britain, which was hoarding its ample supply in the Middle East. Spry noted that this charge fell on the fertile soil of an American public enduring wartime gasoline and heating-oil rationing. Spry warned that if the U.S. Petroleum Administration, under the crusty Harold Ickes, implemented its policy of participation in the oil industry, the U.S. government would become directly involved in Saudi Arabia, Iraq, or

48. Spry at meeting of Sansom Committee, June 8, 1943, FO371/34091 A5904/3/45, PRO; see Fiona Venn, *Oil Diplomacy in the Twentieth Century* (New York: St. Martin's Press, 1986), 59–63.

49. Spry to Gore-Booth, June 25, 1943, and "Interview with Mr. Wilkinson, Petroleum Mission," July 7, 1943, Spry Papers, Vol. 46, NAC.

Jordan.[50] The oil issue involved many of the elements by which public opinion influenced policy in the United States: conditions, interests, and the predisposition of the public.

Other pressure groups were less powerful than the American oil industry but potentially troublesome. The issue of Palestine aroused American Jews, who were split over the question of a Jewish state but united in opposing British policy preventing Jewish immigration into Palestine. Isaiah Berlin reported that American Jews had two main methods of influencing American policy: through mass pressure, such as voting, and through influential individuals, such as Henry Morgenthau, Felix Frankfurter, and Bernard Baruch. Berlin noted that the U.S. government had been able to withstand the pressure but that officials were worried over "how far the situation can be met with words."[51]

Some areas of the British Empire were not the subject of much controversy. The Anglo-American Caribbean Commission, for instance, enjoyed amicable relations. The British Section reported that the Caribbean colonies were not subjected to any takeover but to "informative penetration" by American officials in search of data.[52] The general public, however, showed little interest in Britain's Caribbean possessions.

Spry, nevertheless, thought it would be easy for the American administration to make international trusteeships widely popular. The American people did not seek new territories for themselves, but they would support the acquisition of bases for security reasons, especially if there were commercial advantages to be gained. Spry noted a growing insecurity in American attitudes resulting from the abhorrence of communism and the rise of the Soviet Union as a continental power, the Pearl Harbor attack, and a fear of Asian nations, captured in the old expression "yellow peril." The U.S. government had responded to this latter fear by suspending the civil rights of 100,000 Japanese Americans, two-thirds of them U.S. citizens, and herding them into relocation centers away from the West Coast. "Insecurity arousing in the mass mind the basic emotion of fear, may have many unpre-

50. Spry, "American Relations with the British Empire," May 1, 1944, 50, FO371/38523 AN1577/16/45, PRO.
51. Isaiah Berlin, "Re: Jews," November 13, 1943, Spry Papers, Vol. 46–15, NAC.
52. "Anglo-American Relations Inside the AACC," July 1943, Spry Papers, Vol. 46–17, NAC.

dictable and strange results," Spry concluded. "Obviously, it is a new weapon which very diverse interests may use to influence the direction of American opinion."[53] Spry suggested the British could use and benefit from the "new weapon" of American insecurity in three areas: racial tension, the economy, and strategic concerns.

He observed that increasing racial tension in the United States had the potential to influence American attitudes toward the empire in a variety of ways. His analysis was based on conversations with black and white Americans and on news reports of the 1943 Detroit riots, Ku Klux Klan activity, and sit-ins organized by the Congress of Racial Equality (CORE), an organization of activists inspired by Gandhi's nonviolent civil disobedience. Spry reported that African Americans closely monitored developments in the colonial empire. Don Jones of the National Association for the Advancement of Colored People (NAACP) told him that the war had put the Chinese, the Indians, and the Africans in the same camp, and that black Americans supported "the fight for freedom wherever it may be taking place."[54]

Spry saw a similarity between the attitudes of American blacks and the Indian Congress Party. Both claimed that after loyally serving their respective governments in the First World War, they had not been granted promised freedom and equality. This time they demanded their rights. In another comparison, Spry calculated that in the 1942 U.S. elections, the total vote cast as a percentage of the total population was smaller in eight southern states than the percentage of Indians who voted in the British India elections of 1937. The Law Committee discussed the favorable impression black American GIs had of Britain's lack of segregation policies. Richard Law asked Spry whether it would be helpful to Britain's image if black soldiers compared their reception in Britain to their treatment at home. Spry thought not. As an observer of American society, Spry sympathized with the cause of black Americans. As a propagandist, he was concerned with the powerful elements in white public opinion.[55]

---

53. Spry, "American Relations with the British Empire," May 1, 1944, 30, FO371/35823 AN1577/16/45, PRO.

54. U.S. tour, June 17, 1943, Spry Papers, Vol. 22, NAC.

55. U.S. tour, July 15, 1943, ibid.; "Report of the Meeting of the Committee on American Opinion and the British Empire," January 17, 1944, FO371/38522 AN402/16/45, PRO.

Spry thought that the racial problems in the United States could be useful to Britain in two ways. First, he noticed that some Americans were aware that the "negro issue" made "a discouraging comparison with colonial issues." The issue subdued or shamed liberal critics of British imperial policy. Second, the extent of racial tensions in the United States contributed to some identification between white Americans and the British over "the problem of colour and of dependent peoples." In essence, Spry built on the complexity theme and on the "white men in tough places" theme by seeing racial issues as a way to get the majority of Americans to identify with the British. Spry did not think that racial unrest in the United States should become a subject of propaganda. He did think that its awkwardness and the uncertainty of many Americans as to the future of race relations in the United States were useful to the British.[56]

Spry suggested that the second new influence on American attitudes toward the British Empire was a growing interest in commercial and investment opportunities, particularly in the fields of civil aviation, shipping, and communications. Commercial rivalry, in the past a serious obstacle to Anglo-American cooperation, was likely to intensify in the postwar period. The danger of American economic nationalism seemed heightened because, in the words of Alan Dudley, "the United States [was] no longer so much the land of opportunity as a land looking for opportunity."[57] In their search for opportunities abroad, Americans eyed the British Empire. Spry suggested that Americans should be encouraged to see that under British administration, with its system of law and order and the provision of basic government facilities, capitalist enterprise could flourish. The alternative might be Gandhi's apparent rejection of industrial development in his call for the people of India to return to traditional crafts. Moreover, Spry raised the specter of internal disturbances or, citing China as an example, the possibility that Asian nations might attempt to shut out Westerners.[58]

56. Spry, "American Relations with the British Empire," May 1, 1944, 23, FO371/38523 AN1577/16/45, PRO.
57. Dudley, "The Essentials of an American Policy," March 21, 1944, FO371/38523 AN1538/16/45, PRO.
58. Spry drew on a point made by Denis Brogan of the BBC; Brogan to Dudley, January 25, 1943, FO371/34086 A1143/3/45; Spry, "American Relations with the British Empire," May 1, 1944, 23, FO371/38523 AN1577/16/45, PRO. On Gandhi as "enemy of machine civilizations," see Charles Chatfield, ed., *The Americanization of Gandhi* (New York: Garland, 1976), 42–43.

Propagandists viewed a 1944 *Fortune* article with great satisfaction because the Luce publication advocated that the empire be maintained under British rule. The article discussed the opportunities for Americans in an empire within "which an orderly evolution can be achieved towards freedom under law rather than revolution outside the law":

> The crying need—and the condition for orderly transition to Commonwealth status—is economic development. The trouble, said the *Economist* recently, has been not too much economic exploitation in the best sense of that word, but too little. Britain now has a ten-year $200 million subsidy scheme for the colonies, and hopes to draw in much more British and foreign private capital. . . . And, as Eric Johnston [U.S. Chamber of Commerce president] has pointed out colonial investment might be a broad outlet for American and British cooperation.[59]

Anglo-American cooperation over "economic exploitation in the best sense of that word" was the theme chosen to adjust British propaganda to American international imperialism.

The Colonial Office did not seem to accept this view. In 1944 the Colonial Office maneuvered 120 million pounds sterling out of the Treasury for colonial development and welfare. In large part, to respond to American criticism, Secretary Stanley wanted a "dynamic programme" that demonstrated "our faith and our ability to make proper use of our wide Colonial possessions." The MOI's "Guidance on the Colonial Empire" stated that policies emphasizing political advancement were unrealistic where "poverty, ignorance and disease" prevailed. In matters of economic development, the "Guidance" stated, British colonial policy aimed to plan in the interests of the inhabitants themselves. The first priority was agriculture: improving the fertility of the land, fighting diseases of plants and livestock, and training people in advanced methods of farming. Although the "Guidance" was written with a "raising-them-up-to-civilization" paternalism, its concern for colonial peoples showed up the lack of consideration for the inhabitants of the British Empire in the prop-

59. The Foreign Office, pleased with the *Fortune* editorial (January 1944), praised the Washington embassy for providing the editors with the proper background; FO371/38522 AN466/16/45, PRO.

aganda themes designed to appeal to the United States. The BBC's "consistent low-pressure campaign" employed the partnership theme. "From such evidences of native support for the war effort on the one hand and British concern for native welfare on the other," reported the FBIS, "the BBC provides a steady and largely convincing background for the intermittent official proclamations of London's colonial policy."[60]

This effort would be wasted on the sector of American public opinion that judged foreign affairs by its marketing potential. In September 1944 the Ivey and Ellington advertising agency sent suggestions to the radio commentator Cecil Brown for his news analysis broadcasts. Their client, Phillies cigars—"More Phillies Go to Men in the Services Than Any Other Cigar"—sponsored Brown's program "Sizing Up the News." Neal Ivey complained to Brown that he spent too much air time talking about Germany. As far as the American public was concerned, the war in Germany was about over, and therefore, Ivey reminded Brown, "it is our job to reach the masses of people with comment on events in which they are interested." He continued, "I think there are literally thousands and thousands of people in this country who wonder why we have American soldiers in India. Are they there to police the natives who would rebel against the British? . . . Why has the progress of the American armies been so rapid, and why has the progress of British armies been so slow? . . . Are we going to continue to give Great Britain and France and Italy millions of dollars of free goods which they will use commercially to freeze American goods out of the markets of Europe and the rest of the world?"[61]

Brown took up the subject of Lend-Lease and the British Empire in his September 20 broadcast, but not as Ivey had suggested. He reported that the war for India, Burma, and Singapore was costing American men and money, and that therefore the United States had some say about its future. Brown did not talk about markets but about the United Nations and the movement toward freedom. Five

60. Louis and Robinson, "The U.S. and the Liquidation of the British Empire in Tropical Africa," in *The Transfer of Power in Africa*, ed. Gifford and Louis, 38–39; MOI and Political Warfare Executive Special Issues Committee, "The Commonwealth and Empire in Overseas Publicity," August 22, 1944, R34/693 BBC WAC; FBIS, "Weekly Review," January 22, 1944, RG 262, Entry 32, Box 4, NA.
61. Neal Ivey to Cecil Brown, September 18 and 19, 1944, Box 1, Brown Papers.

days later, he made a scathing on-air reply to the advertising agent's assertion that the European war was over. Brown announced that to the man at the front, it must seem like "some sort of grim joke" to hear that Americans at home already had wrapped up the German war. "To a soldier," Brown stated, "death is just as uninviting on the homestretch to victory as it is at the beginning of the road back." Brown proved once again that he did not take well to news management. According to advertising studies, Brown appealed to the "Waldorf-Astoria elite," not to the "masses" or, in other words, the smokers of Phillies cigars, who would prefer to hear criticism of the British because it related to domestic economic matters.[62]

Graham Spry knew that British propaganda should appeal to business interests. He stated that the political debate over the crucial issue of economic prosperity in the 1944 election centered on the relation of industry to the state. He noted that economic prosperity had been "codified by the Republican Old Guard as 'free enterprise' and 'the American way of life.' " The parties would compete over who controlled and benefited from the wartime boom. Spry, who noted that Roosevelt had thrown the New Dealers to the "business lions," tentatively identified the president with Secretary of State Cordell Hull's liberal economic policy. Although he complained that the American version of trade was limited to selling only, Spry said that British hopes rested on "assisting those in the American Administration with liberal views to strengthen their influence and to encourage them in the faith that their public and legislature will follow them."[63] Faced with the alternatives of internationalist imperialism and isolationism, Spry seemed to be advising propagandists to target a specific group of opinion leaders and hope for a religious experience.

Spry more confidently offered strategic considerations as a major influence on American attitudes toward the empire. The security theme declared that cooperation between the two Atlantic powers must be the cornerstone of the postwar order. Although this theme had its supporters in London, its strongest recommendation came out of the Washington embassy.[64] When Lord Lothian had made the

62. Ivey to Brown, April 25, 1944, Box 1; radio scripts for "Sizing Up the News," September 20 and 25, 1944, Box 6, Brown Papers.

63. Spry, "American Relations with the British Empire," May 1, 1944, 38, FO371/38523 AN1577/16/45, PRO.

64. Dudley, "Summary of 'Notes' by the Washington Committee," April 14, 1943, FO371/34089 A3480/3/45, PRO.

case for the Destroyers for Bases Deal in 1940, he had argued that British policy and the Royal Navy had enforced the Americans' celebrated Monroe Doctrine and the peace in the Atlantic throughout the nineteenth century. He wanted Americans to adjust their interpretation of the Monroe Doctrine from a declaration of anti-imperialism and hemispheric autonomy to a symbol of Anglo-American cooperation. Propagandists hoped this theme would counter isolationism and convince Americans that Britain's imperial link to Canada and the Caribbean should be considered a strategic asset. They identified the security theme as the "Lothian thesis," in honor of its most prolific advocate.[65]

Robin Cruikshank found the Lothian thesis in Walter Lippmann's 1943 bestselling book, *U.S. Foreign Policy: Shield of the Republic,* which claimed that American and British strategic interests were intertwined. Propagandists were delighted when Lippmann's book appeared in cartoon form in the *Ladies' Home Journal.* The cartoons showed the nineteenth-century Royal Navy enforcing the Monroe Doctrine as well as protecting U.S. Pacific territories, including Alaska, Hawaii, and the Philippines, from the bucktoothed, evil genie of Japanese imperialism. Lippmann also revitalized the complexity theme in his March 1945 column, "Pandora's Box," on colonial issues at the approaching U.N. conference. First, he pointed out that the United States was a colonial power that did not apply a general formula to its governing of the Philippines, Alaska, Hawaii, the Panama Canal zone, Puerto Rico, and the Virgin Islands. Therefore, the United States, as ruler of a small colonial empire, should not seek to impose a single formula on the "great structure of the British Commonwealth" or the French Empire.[66]

Sir Norman Angell, author and Nobel Peace Prize winner, described the cooperation of American and British Empire forces around the world in a June 1944 issue of the *Saturday Evening Post.* He quoted Thomas Jefferson's support for Britain's 1823 proposal of cooperation in the enforcement of the Monroe Doctrine principles: "Great Britain is the nation which can do us the most harm of any

---

65. See Halifax's view of the Lothian thesis in Reynolds, *Lord Lothian and Anglo-American Relations,* 58.
66. Cruikshank, "Publicity and Policy in the United States," December 3, 1943, FO371/38505 AN430/6/45, PRO; Walter Lippmann, "Can the U.S. Have Peace after this War?" *Ladies Home Journal,* August 1943, 24–31; Walter Lippmann, "Pandora's Box," *New York Herald Tribune,* March 20, 1945, 21.

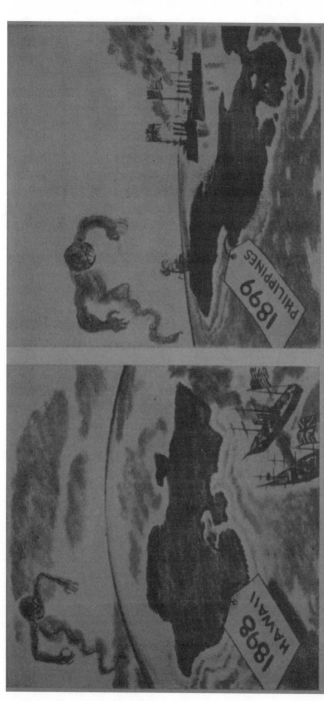

9 The Stars and Stripes were there to protect the Hawaiian Islands when they were annexed as part of the republic (1898). But the real force, which was still relied upon in case of attack (see hovering, scowling Japanese genie), was England's command of the sea. The American frontier was thus extended into the mid-Pacific, 3000 miles west of San Francisco.

10 The Japanese genie—leering, clutching talons outspread—watched the United States take over the Philippine Islands, ceded at the end of the war with Spain. U. S. A. thereby became a Pacific power with property in Japan's back yard. Philippines, nearly 5000 miles west of Honolulu, are 1700 miles from Yokohama. In the Atlantic, U. S. now held Cuba.

Two panels from the *Ladies' Home Journal* cartoon version of Walter Lippmann's *U.S. Foreign Relations* showed the Royal Navy protecting U.S. possessions in the Pacific at the turn of the century. British propagandists wanted Americans to understand that the time had come for the United States to return the favor. (Illustration by Joel King for *Ladies' Home Journal*)

one, or all on earth; and with her on our side we need not fear the whole world. With her then, we should most sedulously cherish a cordial friendship; and nothing would more tend to knit our affections than to be fighting once more, side by side, in the same cause."[67] Angell did not diminish Jefferson's timely words by noting that the Monroe government had rejected Britain's proposal. Propagandists sought to sow the seeds of twentieth-century cooperation in the nineteenth century by revising history. The message was that Britain had taken the responsibility for maintaining the peace in the nineteenth century. Propagandists reminded Americans that it was now their turn.

Robin Cruikshank agreed with Spry's argument that the way to present the British Empire to Americans was to emphasize interdependence. In his 1944 statement of propaganda policy, the MOI's head of the American Division stated that the United States's increasing awareness of power relationships made the country appreciate the strategic value of the empire. Cruikshank outlined how the prominent theologian Reinhold Niebuhr had explained why the friction between the two nations got in the way of cooperation: "Each tends to take its own type of power, with its characteristic virtues and vices for granted and to condemn the other. Americans have taken their own 'dollar imperialism' in South America and elsewhere for granted, while deprecating our political imperialism in India or Africa, and vice versa."[68] Propagandists would stress, like Niebuhr, how the two systems complemented each other. The theologian's later discussion of the moral responsibility of the United States as the leader of the free world repeated wartime propaganda themes urging American responsibility.

The security, economic, and racial themes advocated by Spry, Cruikshank, and the Law Committee were incorporated into propaganda. An MOI guideline of August 1944 stated that spokesmen

---

67. Sir Norman Angell, "What the British Empire Means to America," *Saturday Evening Post*, June 17, 1944, 51, 102; Campbell to FO, FO371/38558 AN3199/34/45, PRO.

68. On a ten-week visit in the spring of 1943, Niebuhr, at the request of the OWI, spoke to British and Allied groups in Britain; Richard Wightman Fox, *Reinhold Niebuhr: A Biography* (New York: Pantheon, 1985), 217. Cruikshank, "Britain's Publicity in the United States: A Policy for 1944," May 8, 1944, FO371/38556 AN2063/34/45, PRO.

should "project the Commonwealth and Empire as a source of material, political and strategic strength to the United Nations, and as a source of benefit to the world at large."[69] The propaganda line on the Soviet Union continued to be cautious but played up uncertainty about the future. Spry suggested that American concern arose from fears that India, if independent of Britain and the West, might adopt some "aggressive faith" and embark upon a policy of war aligned with China or dominated by the Soviet Union.[70] The consul general in Chicago, W. H. Gallienne, reporting on typical questions and answers at public meetings, gave his standard answer to questions on Russia and the Baltics: "Who can tell what Russia's attitude is likely to be after the war? No-one, because it depends on what sort of peace we make, how safe the world is likely to be, how much responsibility the United Nations will take; in fact, whether military considerations must remain of paramount importance."[71] The British were aiming to present a clear-cut view of the postwar world. On the one side, the British Empire and Commonwealth was a loyal safeguard of democratic values and capitalist enterprise. On the other side, the Soviet Union and Asian nations were at best unknown quantities; at worst, they were forces of disruption in a Western-defined peace.

The thrust of British "education" efforts had shifted. During 1942 the British sought to enlighten the American public about Britain's responsibilities as an imperial power, the complexities faced in governing diverse territories, and the obligations of partnership. From 1943 on, the British sought to enlighten the American public about the United States's responsibilities as a world power. Spry reported, "The mass of the people seem singularly ill-prepared for world responsibilities," although he noted that "perhaps, the mass of the British people were little better prepared for these responsibilities a century or more ago."[72] Propagandists sought to make Americans

69. "The Commonwealth and Empire in Overseas Publicity," MOI and PWE Special Issues Committee, August 22, 1944, R34/693, BBC WAC.

70. Spry, "American Relations with the British Empire," May 1, 1944, 23, FO371/38523 AN1577/16/45, PRO.

71. Gallienne reported that questions on Russia were most difficult because his sympathies were at odds with "the line" he must take; July 12, 1944, FO371/38577 AN2906/34/45, PRO.

72. Spry, "American Relations with the British Empire," May 1, 1944, 5, FO371/38523 AN1577/16/45, PRO.

see themselves as world leaders by promoting the "doctrine of responsibility." As always, the British hoped to create a climate of opinion that made it easier for "friendly Americans" to adopt policies favorable to Britain.

They were more successful with opinion leaders than with the American public. In the spring of 1945, Sir Frederick Puckle reported to the India Office that Americans still continued to be offended by "the idea of one people ruling over another." In March a public-opinion poll asked if four imperial powers treated their colonies fairly.[73]

	Fairly (%)	Unfairly (%)	No opinion (%)
Do you think Britain treats			
its colonies . . .	32	39	29
France . . .	29	15	56
Holland . . .	41	8	51
United States . . .	86	4	10

Those who had an opinion about France and Holland were much more likely to think them fair than not and believed the United States to be the most fair. As in a similar poll of 1943, many more Americans tended to have an opinion about the British Empire than about the other European empires. A slightly higher percentage than in 1943 considered the British unfair. Although the wording limits the question to fairness, one can conclude that as far as this aspect of British imperialism was concerned, propagandists had not made any progress with their American audience.

The State Department's Office of Public Affairs, echoing the British, concluded that the American public must be educated on the worth of its ally. According to a March 1945 study, the most widespread criticism of the Churchill government related to the British Empire, that Britain placed imperial interests ahead of the all-out war effort in the Pacific and Middle East, that it refused independence to India, and that it failed to allow Jewish immigration into Palestine.

73. Puckle to India Office, FO371/44561 AN1561/24/45, PRO; Joseph Grew, memorandum for the president, March 28, 1945, "Latest Opinion Trends in the U.S.," PSF Departmental Correspondence, Box 91, File: State Department 1945, FDRL.

Economic concerns included British use of imperial preference to keep out U.S. trade, and the promotion of British interests in oil, aviation, and shipping at the expense of American interests. The report stated that the public was insufficiently informed about the nature of British colonial government and American interest in British economic revival.[74]

There was evidence that the British had made headway with opinion leaders. From 1943 on, increasing numbers of articles and books advocated American cooperation with the British Empire. A State Department-sponsored symposium on postwar relations with Britain undertaken by thirty-four groups from university faculties showed unanimous support for continued close cooperation with the British Commonwealth in the interests of peace and security. Nearly all of the groups preferred the policy of international supervision over colonial administration. Some favored direct international administration, but most regarded it as impractical for the immediate future.[75] The university groups supported the State Department position.

British influence on the U.S. government was by no means an unqualified success. The State Department's formula for trusteeships was agreed to by Roosevelt and Soviet premier Joseph Stalin at the Yalta Conference in February 1945, to the outrage of Churchill. In April, when delegates from fifty nations met to set up the United Nations Organization at the San Francisco conference, the Americans acted on their longstanding policies but moved closer to the British view of the postwar world. The Americans forced the British to concede to the provisions for colonial accountability to an international organization. They chose, however, to support the goal of self-government rather than independence. The BBC's background guidance for the conference debates on territorial trusteeships noted the double standard being pursued by the United States as it sought one system for everyone else and another for itself, so that its control over strategic bases would not be accountable to any international body. The background guidance observed that the Americans were

---

74. "Public Attitudes on Foreign Policy: Recent Attitudes towards Britain," March 22, 1945, RG 59, Office of Public Opinion Studies, 1943–1965, Box 1, NA.
75. "Public Attitudes on Foreign Policy: Post-war Relations with Britain," February 26, 1945, ibid.

going to lengths to avoid "the stigma of imperialism."[76] Just as the British government had grappled with the difference between American government rhetoric and policy, so now did the U.S. administration on the issue of empire.

American suspicion of the Soviet Union and the potential instability in the colonial world led the U.S. government to side with the British on many issues against the strong anticolonial sentiment of many of the San Francisco conference participants. William Roger Louis argues that American anticolonialism was defused because British leaders contained the debate to the area of international trusteeship and suggests that Americans feared a revolutionary situation in India.[77] Propagandists did contain the debate with themes such as "white men in tough places," partnership, and complexity. They focused attention on the practical difficulties of administration and, as they did, encouraged many Americans to identify with the British administrators rather than with the colonial peoples. But the containment of the debate over anticolonialism was only part of the British propaganda policy. Once Spry and others established that the British Empire was a source of conflict rooted in Anglo-American rivalry over interests, British propagandists broadened the context of the debate over the empire to global proportions. The British defined a postwar world in which order and stability would be difficult to maintain in any event and impossible without the partnership of the British Empire.

Many of the propaganda themes of the campaign for empire had common threads. The complexity theme presented the multitude of languages, religions, and cultures that made up India. Propagandists used Gandhi's religious views and behavior to portray him as an impractical mystic, a dangerous child, and a tool of fascists. They deliberately nurtured American apprehension of an Indian revolution. The "sacred cow" aspect of the partnership theme was used to illustrate the "backward" nature of the colonial peoples. "White men in tough places" identified clearly the racial distinction between the ruler and the ruled. Spry linked Americans' fear of racial tension at

76. Louis, *Imperialism at Bay*, 457–459; "Background to the San Francisco Conference," May 9, 1945, E1/259, BBC WAC.

77. Louis, *Imperialism at Bay*, 568, and Thorne, *Allies of a Kind*, 598–599; Louis, "American Anti-Colonialism and the Dissolution of the British Empire," in *The "Special Relationship,"* ed. Louis and Bull, 266.

home to their fear of Asian nationalism abroad. All of the themes set the United States and Britain together and apart from much of the rest of the world. As Christopher Thorne indicated in his book's title, *Allies of a Kind*, Britain and the United States subordinated rivalry to maintain white predominance in Asia. The British had begun by seeing the United States as a continental empire with subject races. They ended by encouraging Americans to see themselves as a global caretaker of many subject races.

The triumph of "white men in tough places" emerged as the entire postwar world showed the potential to be a tough place, with only the United States, assisted by Britain, able to provide law and order. As the MOI official in New Delhi had observed, Americans held a "conviction about the inherent right of free peoples to control their own destinies." This conviction, however, dissipated when nationalist independence movements or possibly the Soviet Union threatened international stability. The contradiction between anticolonial principles and imperial behavior, noted by British analysts of American opinion as characteristic of the American "empire," was subsumed by the doctrine of responsibility.

The economics of imperial propaganda was presented less clearly during the war, largely because it was the most delicate of all the areas of friction confronting the British. Propagandists did link the partnership theme to technological advancement and development. They declared that a prosperous empire was essential for a healthy international economy. Although Americans were anxious about the international economy, many did not identify American with British interests in its maintenance. In the words of Turner Catledge as he stepped off the plane in India, they put the American taxpayer first.

6 Lend-Lease:
The Indirect Strategy

The steady drift of public opinion into this mood of War Debts, with all the stubborn prejudices involved, and all the unhappy associations of past history on both sides, is ominous. It may gravely affect all the post-war economic settlements.

— ROBIN CRUIKSHANK, DECEMBER 3, 1943

In December 1943 Robin Cruikshank described Lend-Lease as one of the issues that made Britain the most vulnerable in its relations with the United States. Lend-Lease, he warned, was becoming a modern euphemism for war debts. The linking of Lend-Lease to war debts was dangerous on a number of counts. Propagandists did not want Americans to be reminded of Britain's failure to pay off its World War I debt of $4.7 billion to the United States. After years of making annual payments of more than $100 million, Britain had defaulted in the 1930s, like many of its fellow debtors incapacitated by the Great Depression. Moreover, the British preferred that Lend-Lease aid not be considered in terms of loans and debts because they would be hard pressed to pay it back. Cruikshank feared that Americans believed they alone paid the bill for the war. He predicted the situation would change from bad to worse as the war progressed and Americans began to consider postwar economics. By making obvious Britain's dependence on the United States, Lend-Lease was the issue most likely to thwart the propagandists' goal of establishing a "partnership on equal terms."

To present Britain as an equal partner who did not have to pay back Lend-Lease, propagandists at first attempted to convince the American public that the British pulled their weight in financing the war. They stressed the concepts of the pooling of resources and "reverse Lend-Lease" or "reciprocal aid," the terms for the supplies the British provided for American forces. After several months, when opinion polls consistently showed that a large majority of the American public believed Lend-Lease should be repaid, propagandists concluded that this policy was not effective.

They discovered that the "strategy of truth" was not altogether useful in discussing Lend-Lease. Statistics showed that the American contribution in money and matériel far outweighed Britain's. Although both countries contributed about 4.75 percent of their national incomes to Lend-Lease, the U.S. total of more than $27 billion was almost five times that of Britain's $5.7 billion.[1] Policymakers nevertheless hesitated to abort the "strategy of truth" on the issue Americans most suspected the British of trying to deceive them.

Instead of tackling the issue of Lend-Lease head on, the British employed an indirect strategy with a two-pronged approach. First, they worked to set the agenda for discussion on Lend-Lease by providing American opinion leaders with information incorporating propaganda themes. Propagandists attempted to build up the image of Britain as a sturdy ally with temporary economic troubles. Americans were supposed to conclude that assistance to the British ally was in their vital interest during and after the war. Second, high-level negotiators put their energies into winning over their American counterparts. Once they had negotiated an economic settlement, it was hoped, the U.S. government would build up the required public support. The combined propaganda effort strove to create the best possible political climate for the Roosevelt Administration to act generously on the issue of aid to Britain.

The Lend-Lease Act of March 1941 was the subject of heated controversy in the United States. Lord Lothian, the British ambassador,

---

1. H. Duncan Hall, *North American Supply* (London: HMSO, 1955; rpr. New York: Kraus International Publications, 1984), 432–433.

had initiated the political debate with his announcement in November 1940 that his country needed help from the United States to continue the war. One year earlier, the U.S. neutrality acts had been amended to allow Britain to purchase American goods and arms on a "cash-and-carry" basis. An embattled Britain welcomed the amendment, but the "cash-and-carry" provision required that it expend its dollar and gold holdings of $2.1 billion. In order to conserve its dollars, Britain prohibited certain imports from the United States and thus deprived American agricultural producers of an important market. It also started an export drive to earn more dollars, which led to heightened competition between the United States and Britain in third markets, particularly Latin America. Britain's use of controls and discrimination drew protests from the United States.[2]

In December 1940, Churchill notified Roosevelt that Britain soon would no longer be able to pay cash for supplies. Roosevelt proposed lending goods to the British, thereby circumventing the neutrality laws and American aversion to World War I.-style loans. The president declared during a fireside chat that the United States would become the "arsenal of democracy." At a press conference on December 17, FDR explained the principle of Lend-Lease by announcing that he wanted to eliminate "the silly, foolish, old dollar sign" from the issue of aid to Britain. He compared the situation to that of a person whose neighbor's house was on fire. The person loaned the neighbor his hose and when the fire was out, the neighbor returned it, or if the hose had been damaged, the neighbor replaced it. The story of a person motivated by generosity and calculated self-interest in protecting his own house from a spreading fire appealed to American listeners.[3]

The Roosevelt administration carefully steered the Lend-Lease bill through Congress. The secretary of the Treasury, Henry Morgenthau, and the secretary of War, Henry Stimson, assigned their talented assistants, Oscar Cox and John J. McCloy, to oversee the bill's

---

2. Alan P. Dobson, *U.S. Wartime Aid to Britain, 1940–1946* (New York: St. Martin's Press, 1986), 16.

3. Franklin D. Roosevelt, *The Public Papers and Addresses of Franklin D. Roosevelt, Vol. 1940: War—And Aid to Democracies*, compiled by Samuel I. Rosenman (New York: Macmillan, 1941), 607. The fire-hose analogy is discussed in Warren Kimball, *The Most Unsordid Act* (Baltimore: Johns Hopkins University Press, 1969), 77, 123.

passage. Isolationists made their last great stand to preserve American neutrality at the congressional hearings. They objected that the Lend-Lease Act gave the president too much power. Under the terms of the bill, the president was permitted "to sell, transfer title to, exchange, lease, lend, or otherwise dispose of" defense articles to "any country whose defense the President deems vital to the defense of the United States."[4] Isolationists feared the president, with this new power, would take the United States into the war.

At hearings in January 1941, Administration officials argued that Britain was the United States's defender against Hitler. U.S. officials had pressured the British to prove that their need was desperate. London reluctantly provided Morgenthau with a detailed statement of Britain's dollar position, which he used to defend the need for Lend-Lease. Morgenthau also promised Congress that Britain would sell its assets in the United States. In March the administration demanded a good-faith sale from Britain. London offered the British-owned American Viscose Company as a sacrifice. It was sold to American bankers for $54 million, about one-half its worth.[5]

The British watched the congressional proceedings anxiously. Although the MOI wanted to promote the bill, Churchill took the Roosevelt administration's position that it was better to let the Americans handle it themselves. The one contribution the prime minister made was a speech directed at the American public on the night the House of Representatives passed the bill. He said, "Give us the tools and we'll finish the job."[6] Churchill used "give" where FDR used "lend." The British wanted a gift of supplies in return for fighting Nazi Germany. Although propagandists tried, they would not be able to convince the U.S. public that Lend-Lease was a gift. Most Americans believed that their British neighbor should return the hose once the fire had been put out.

The Lend-Lease Act passed on March 11, 1941, by a vote that divided along partisan lines—a clear indication that Lend-Lease and American politics would not be separated. Congress appropriated $7 billion for the first year and left the repayment arrangements up to the president. Under the act, Lend-Lease had to be renewed annually,

4. *Congressional Record* 77 (March 8, 1941), 2097.
5. Reynolds, *Creation of the Anglo-American Alliance*, 163.
6. Ibid.; Sherwood, *Roosevelt and Hopkins*, 260.

which meant, in turn, yearly congressional hearings and public debates. The terms of Lend-Lease brought the British up against the complexities, partisanship, and unique demands of the American political system. More than any other issue, Lend-Lease made the Foreign Office despise U.S. constitutional requirements and long for the discreet nature of executive agreements.

The two allies agreed in principle that they wanted to prevent a return to the economic nationalism of the 1930s by establishing stable exchange rates, multilateral trade policies, and full employment. They differed over how to achieve economic internationalism. The United States desired an open economic system, which, it believed, would be most beneficial to the international community as well as to the United States. The British government hesitated to accept the U.S. formula because it believed that Britain might need currency controls and discriminatory trading policies to rebuild its economy. Throughout the war, the United States sought to use Lend-Lease as leverage to gain British acceptance of an open economic system. London's goal was to avoid any commitment by making vague pledges to work toward the establishment of a liberal economic order. In these often strained negotiations, Britain aimed at retaining as much economic independence as possible; cooperation with the United States necessarily came first, however. As Britain's top economic negotiator, John Maynard Keynes, put it, the alternative to cooperation was a trade war with the United States, and that was a war Britain would surely lose.[7]

The politics of Anglo-American economic relations centered on the nondiscriminatory clause of the Atlantic Charter and Article 7 of the Lend-Lease Master Agreement of February 1942. In August 1941, when Churchill and Roosevelt set down the Atlantic Charter principles as unofficial war aims, the United States had attempted to include the open-door principle as the fourth point. Churchill, however, had added a qualifying phrase—"with due respect for our existing obligations," which excepted Britain's imperial preference system.[8] The State

---

7. Kimball, "Lend-Lease and the Open Door," 253; Richard N. Gardner, *Sterling-Dollar Diplomacy: Anglo-American Collaboration in the Reconstruction of Multilateral Trade* (Oxford: Oxford University Press, 1956), 58.

8. The fourth point in the final agreed text of the Atlantic Charter read: "Fourth, they will endeavor, with due respect for their existing obligations, to further the

Department sought to eliminate the equivocal Atlantic Charter language in its drafting of Article 7 for the mutual aid agreement.

Article 7 served as the basic framework for postwar economic planning. It formally linked wartime agreements to future peacetime arrangements by providing that, in return for Lend-Lease aid, Britain would render appropriate benefits to the United States. Under the Lend-Lease Act of March 1941, the benefits had not been specified beyond the statement that they were to be in any form "which the President deems satisfactory." Article 7 stated that the terms and conditions of the benefits should not "burden commerce between the two countries" but should promote economic expansion. They should direct action toward the elimination of all forms of discriminatory treatment and the reduction of tariffs and other trade barriers. The article called for early discussions about the attainment of these objectives.[9] These Article 7 obligations became known as the "Consideration."

Although Britain stalled for months in an attempt to avoid giving up its option to use discriminatory practices, it finally accepted Article 7 in February 1942, after its military position had been greatly weakened by Japanese advances in the Pacific. The Cabinet's acceptance was made easier by a note from Roosevelt. The president informed Churchill that he did not expect the British government to commit in advance to ending imperial preference, just as Britain could not expect him to commit in advance to revising U.S. tariff policy. With its acceptance of Article 7 in the Lend-Lease Master or Mutual Aid Agreement, the British government pledged to enter early talks with the United States on the postwar economy.[10]

The political debates over wartime economic diplomacy took place within the British and American governments as well as between them. In London, postwar economic policymaking split into three factions. One small group, which included the Board of Trade, shared the Roosevelt administration's belief in liberal economics. A second group of Conservative Cabinet ministers strongly opposed the American policy embodied in Article 7. Leo Amery, Lord Beaver-

---

enjoyment by all States, great or small, victor or vanquished, of access, on equal terms to the trade and to the raw materials of the world needed for their prosperity."

9. Article 7 of the Lend-Lease Master Agreement of February 23, 1942, Appendix V, Hall, *North American Supply*, 512–513.

10. Dobson, *U.S. Wartime Aid to Britain*, 118–120.

brook, and Lord Cranborne thought that the Commonwealth system, including the imperial preference system, should become the British economic model. The third group consisted of the Treasury and the Foreign Office, with Keynes as its leader. It recognized that cooperation with the United States was necessary. It aimed, however, to define the nature of that cooperation to benefit British interests as much as possible. Presiding over these factions was Churchill, whose main interest was prosecuting the war and avoiding the controversies that might interfere with that effort.[11]

Resembling Churchill, FDR had as his main interest the preservation of an effective war-making alliance. Within the Roosevelt administration, there was general agreement on the goal of constructing a multilateral world economy. The secretary of the Treasury wanted to return the international economy to the gold standard and move the world financial center from London's City and New York's Wall Street to the U.S. Treasury. The secretary of state believed that a liberal economy would guarantee a peaceful world order. One of the obstacles blocking Hull's vision was the U.S. Congress' control of tariffs. Hull intended to use British concessions to gain congressional support for reduced tariffs.[12] The Roosevelt administration was eager to show that Britain was in line with U.S. postwar economic policy.

By manipulating Lend-Lease terms, the U.S. government tried to control certain British economic plans during the war. In September 1941, the administration asked for Britain's promise not to export goods received through Lend-Lease or goods replaced by Lend-Lease supplies. The Americans extracted this agreement, known as the Export White Paper, to please Congress. The agreement's severe limitations on Britain's economy remained a sore point throughout the war. In late 1942, the presence and spending habits of American GIs in Britain boosted British dollar reserves to nearly $1 billion; rising sterling debts caused its net financial situation to deteriorate, however. Oscar Cox, now Edward R. Stettinius' deputy at the Office of Lend-Lease Administration, became concerned over the approach-

11. Reynolds, *Creation of the Anglo-American Alliance*, 270–271. According to Sir Stafford Cripps, "the Prime Minister's interest in economic affairs was secondary and his grasp on them somewhat insecure"; memorandum of discussions between Sir Stafford Cripps and Herbert Feis, June 9, 1942, Frankfurter Papers, Reel 77, Subject File: Anglo-American Relations.

12. Reynolds, *Creation of an Anglo-American Alliance*, 270.

ing appropriation hearings because Congress had backed Lend-Lease on the grounds that the British had no dollars left. On Stettinius' urging, the U.S. Cabinet recommended to Roosevelt that Britain's dollar reserves be kept between $600 million and $1 billion. FDR approved the cap without consulting London.[13] The politics of Lend-Lease created tension between the United States and Britain because the Americans continually took the upper hand.

The Roosevelt administration dominated the propaganda line on Lend-Lease as well. Redvers Opie, the Washington embassy's economic adviser, reported that the secretary of state was starting his own publicity campaign. Hull made it clear to the British that he did not want the wires crossed.[14] The Americans were not amenable to a revision of terminology. British attempts to drop the label "lend-lease," with its implication of a temporary loan, by substituting "mutual aid" and "reciprocal aid" for "reverse lend-lease" proved futile. U.S. propaganda, as designed by the OWI, defended Lend-Lease against the segment of the public who wanted to fight an "isolationist" war without allies. It countered American fears that Lend-Lease deprived the U.S. military of vital supplies and the American people of food and matériel in order to feed and supply foreigners. Americans were worried about what happened to U.S. supplies once they were shipped and how the Allies were going to repay the United States after the war.

OWI propaganda announced that Lend-Lease was not an act of charity but a means of defending America. It informed the public about reverse Lend-Lease, praising the willingness of the Allies to extend aid to the United States within the limits of their resources. The OWI aimed to persuade the public that the United States would not be repaid in money or property. "We receive payment daily in the effort and blood which our Allies expend against the common foe," explained the OWI, "and our repayment after the war will be mainly in cooperative efforts to build a better and more peaceful world."[15] The United States would be repaid when the final settlement included the economic objectives set forth in the Atlantic Char-

---

13. Alan Dobson, *The Politics of the Anglo-American Economic Special Relationship, 1940–1987* (New York: St. Martin's Press, 1988), 39.

14. R. Campbell to Mr. Ronald, October 22, 1942, INF1/683, PRO.

15. Abe Feller (OWI) to Eugene Rostow (State), January 2, 1943, "Lend Lease: Information Objectives and Policies," RG 59, Records of the Office of Assistant Secretary and Undersecretary of State Dean Acheson, Box 3, File 1, NA.

ter. Although American propaganda paralleled Britain's on the pooling of resources, it differed significantly by treating Lend-Lease as a pledge for postwar economic prosperity.

The Roosevelt administration monitored public opinion on Lend-Lease closely. In February 1943, the OWI reported that newspaper and radio comment on Lend-Lease had been favorable and that reverse Lend-Lease received increasing attention. The report concluded, however, that the idea that Lend-Lease was a "glorified hand-out" still persisted. It also suggested that more emphasis should be placed on the postwar benefits of Lend-Lease as a long-term goodwill asset. Oscar Cox asked Hadley Cantril of the Office of Public Opinion Research to request that George Gallup run Lend-Lease questions on a regular basis so that trends could be measured. The polls in early 1943 showed that Lend-Lease had high public recognition but that Americans expected to be repaid.[16]

(1) Do you happen to know what the Lend-Lease program is?

	Yes (%)	No (%)
January 7, 1943	73	27
March 10, 1943	80	20

(2) Asked of those who said yes: Do you favor or oppose continuing the Lend-Lease program?

	Favor (%)	Oppose (%)	No opinion (%)
January 7, 1943	83	9	8
March 10, 1943	89	7	4

(3) Asked of those who knew what Lend-Lease was: Do you think the nations now getting Lend-Lease materials from us will repay us for these materials either in money or in goods, or will not repay us at all?

	Will repay (%)	Will not repay (%)	No opinion (%)
January 7, 1943	30	58	12
March 10, 1943	28	60	12

16. OWI Intelligence Report, February 12, 1943, PSF Subject File, Box 174, FDRL; Cantril to Cox, March 26, 1943, Oscar Cox Papers, Lend-Lease Files, Box 100, FDRL.

(4) Asked of those who knew what Lend-Lease was: Do you think they should repay us?

	Yes (%)	No (%)	No opinion (%)
January 7, 1943	74	19	7
March 10, 1943	74	21	5

Cox noted that these results showed there was still room for improvement on the repayment issue.

When the Foreign Office's American Department officials received the results of the January poll, they agreed that there was need for education of the American public. One official complained that the Gallup question, suggesting possible repayment in money, reintroduced "the dollar sign where it does not belong." He wrote, "The Americans" were "grossly ignorant" of the Lend-Lease Act's "Consideration" clause.[17] Yet when British propagandists developed a campaign, they ran into several roadblocks. Not only did they have to accommodate American economic policies and politics, they also found that their own government wanted them to promote Lend-Lease without saying much about it.

When faced with a tough propaganda problem, the British government created an interdepartmental committee to coordinate policy. In 1942 the deputy prime minister, Clement Attlee, the minister of information, Brendan Bracken, and the minister of production, Oliver Lyttleton, were assigned the task of handling American allegations of abuse of Lend-Lease. The ministers set up the Informal Interdepartmental Committee on Publicity in the North American Economic and Supply Field, chaired by Robin Cruikshank of the MOI's American Division. Other members included Angus Malcolm from the Foreign Office, Lord Moore from the War Cabinet's Joint American Secretariat, William Edwards from the Ministry of Production, and representatives of the Treasury, the Board of Trade, and the Ministry of Food. A counterpart committee, called the Economic Operations Committee, was organized in the Washington embassy under Harold Butler, the minister who headed the British Information Services.[18] The organization of machinery, however, did not solve the problem of creating an effective propaganda policy.

17. February 3, 1943, FO371/34127 A1155/34/45, PRO.
18. Members of the Economic Operations Committee included Isaiah Berlin;

In London, both the Treasury and the Foreign Office put obstacles in the way. The Treasury did not want any publicity on reciprocal aid or reverse Lend-Lease, explained E. W. Playfair to D'Arcy Edmondson of the BIS in May 1942. Reverse Lend-Lease "would be a good point if we were able to say that we were doing the same for the Americans as they for us," wrote Playfair. "This, however, would not be true now, nor is it likely to be true in the future."[19] The Treasury did not want the American public to know that the British were selling some goods to the United States for dollars while the United States was sending products to the British under Lend-Lease. The propagandists ignored this scruple in their promotion of reverse Lend-Lease. The "strategy of truth" was a policy of using selected information with the undesirable facts left out.

Cruikshank believed that the MOI and the BIS should complement the Roosevelt administration's linkage of Lend-Lease to plans for the postwar international economy by supporting the principles of the Atlantic Charter and Article 7. He did not receive encouragement from the Foreign Office's Nevile Butler. "The difficulty," Butler replied, "is that our ability to spread the light is severely handicapped because we cannot fully practice what we preach."[20] Butler noted that Britain supported free trade in principle, but the postwar economy might require continued rationing and controls. The Foreign Office and the Treasury wanted to keep their options open as much as possible. Butler ultimately advised Cruikshank to continue with the "pooling of resources" theme. London policymakers preferred to avoid raising issues related to Article 7 and long-term economic policy. This left propagandists little to go on.

American analysts of propaganda at the FBIS observed this dilemma in the BBC's broadcasts promoting congressional renewal of the Lend-Lease Act in January 1943. One FBIS analyst noted that the BBC had two tasks. It tried to correct the American attitude that U.S. forces alone were winning the war by reporting that Britain was doing its share. At the same time, it had to request further assistance from America without appearing to beg. The BBC seemed to be cop-

---

Charles Campbell and Jack Winocour of the BIS Washington branch; Aubrey Morgan and D'Arcy Edmondson of New York BIS; Redvers Opie, economics expert at the embassy; and K. Jopson of the Board of Trade. BT28/1059; BT28/1060, PRO.

19. E. W. Playfair to D. Edmondson, May 6, 1942, FO371/32557 W6748/6748/49, PRO.

20. Butler to Cruikshank, August 11, 1943, FO371/34137 A5788/57/45, PRO.

ing with its problem, noted the FBIS analyst, by making indirect references to Lend-Lease. The BBC frequently presented Lend-Lease as a U.N. issue. For example, it announced that the Russians needed all the aid the British and the Americans could send to them, thereby uniting the Western Allies as donors. Another common practice was to blame German propaganda for trying to split the Allies by inciting controversy over Lend-Lease. This tactic attempted to put Lend-Lease critics in league with the enemy. One BBC speaker, H. V. Hudson, the former director of the MOI's Empire Division, described Lend-Lease as one of the instruments of cooperation in the postwar period. "Can anyone doubt," Hudson asked, "that this practice of working together on man-to-man terms, of fitting into a joint plan of action, will help to mold the outlook and behavior of the United Nations after the war?" The FBIS analyst noted that, with these presentations, the BBC treated Lend-Lease as part of the rational management of Allied resources rather than as charity from the United States to Britain.[21]

When Congress debated the renewal of Lend-Lease, propagandists coordinated a broad show of British and American support. The BBC scheduled a broadcast to the United States introduced by Averell Harriman, the head of the U.S. Lend-Lease Mission in London, and featured Herbert Agar of the London OWI interviewing British spokesmen. The British also provided U.S. officials with information for their public statements on Lend-Lease. For Stettinius' January 24, 1943, statement on reciprocal aid, London pulled together a packet with information obtained from the British Treasury, the Harriman Mission, the U.S. forces in Britain, and the MOI. In his speech, Stettinius announced that thanks to reciprocal aid, U.S. expenditures for its troops in Britain for the month of December 1942 had totaled a mere $25,000. Dean Acheson's collection of background material for his appearance before a congressional hearing on Lend-Lease included an article on reciprocal aid written by the MOI American Division's Joan Skipsey. She listed some of the items provided for the Americans by the British: "Bangalore torpedoes, Bayonets, Beer, Belts, Bicycles; steel and asbestos Nissan hutting in thousands; mobile laundries by the hundred, lifebelts and lighters by the thousand; training facilities for keeping United States pilots in perpetual fighting

21. FBIS, "Weekly Review," January 23, 1943, RG 262, Entry 32, Box 4, NA.

trim; millions of blankets, thousands of pounds of nuts and bolts, and all the bread consumed by the American forces in the United Kingdom."[22] To British ears, this list seemed generous, given their straitened resources. To most Americans, unacquainted with life in wartime Britain, nothing was too good for their soldiers away from home, and anything the British could offer would be, at the most, only adequate.

As usual, the BBC relied upon American spokesmen. In March 1943, Ivan Peterson, London correspondent for the *Philadelphia Inquirer*, assured U.S. audiences that the British people were not feasting on American steaks and that the Food Ministry was not profiting from the sales of Lend-Lease food. Peterson asserted that everything the Americans had done through Lend-Lease was being repaid by what the British were doing for the Americans. In conclusion, Peterson implied that the British had already paid their share, when he reminded Americans that their allies "not only held the fort until we got ready; they took an awful beating in the process, and provided a pattern for us in all humility to follow."[23] Peterson voiced what propagandists felt about their country's lone stand against Germany. The appeal failed to recognize that humility was not a characteristic common to Americans when tax dollars were at stake.

Propagandists did try to present reverse Lend-Lease or reciprocal aid as value for money. The BBC interviewed a U.S. Army officer who said, "Ever since we arrived we've seen innumerable signs that Lend-Lease isn't a one-way affair." In the fall of 1943, propagandists gave the mutual aid theme multimedia coverage. The main event was the British government's release of a White Paper on mutual aid. Lord Halifax, on a visit to the U.S. Eighth Army while in England, spoke to the United States over CBS. His speech, which opened with praise for the "fine fighting spirit" of "your boys," observed that American troops lived in quarters built by the British and ate British as well as American food: "The fact is that the original idea of Lend-Lease has grown into something much bigger—into the idea of Mutual Aid, of pooling all our resources for the common job. Today

22. "Reciprocal Aid Publicity," February 19–March 9, 1943, BT28/289, PRO; *New York Times*, March 12, 1943; Joan Skipsey, "Reciprocal Aid," RG 59, Records of the Office of Assistant Secretary and Undersecretary of State Dean Acheson, Box 3, File 1, Lend-Lease General Reference, NA.

23. FBIS, "Weekly Review," March 6, 1943, RG 262, Entry 32, Box 4, NA.

"SUPPLY . . . 'the hidden huge submerged nine-tenths of the iceberg, of which only the glittering peak is seen.'"

John Steinbeck.

American flag waves over the US Army's biggest food depot in Britain. British labor and materials equipped it to the last telephone before it was turned over to US command

A radiant heat lamp warms a soldier's foot before massage at the US Army's first rehabilitation center in a 115-acre park. US and British staff have developed for Americans a treatment with thousands of miracles to its credit in the British Army. Men come in maimed, crippled, and leave fighting fit.

Nothing left to chance, and maximum comfort for a grim job. Pilot Lieut. Charles Keefe, of Baton Rouge, Louisiana, goes aboard with British electrically heated flying jacket, parachute harness and parachute.

Below: Anglo-American cooperation hit hard at the Japs for six months from this aircraft carrier. She is the Royal Naval vessel Victorious, from which US Navy planes and pilots operated in the Pacific when America was short of carriers.

These are the US Navy pilots who fought under the ensign and crest of HM Aircraft Carrier Victorious, manned by the Royal Navy six months in the Pacific. Only the Japs counted the cost.

Above: To the theaters of war and to the invasion coasts. Britain's seamen and her finest ships have taken fighting Americans.

Right: British searchlight brings the Fortresses safely down from a deadly mission. Lieut Ernest Weigner, of Philadelphia, signals to an aircrew somewhere over England.

Below: Air-Sea Rescue brings them home too. Every airman blessing Europe has ditching equipment and knows this RAF service is on day and night watch in case he crashes in the sea.

To illustrate the British contribution to the Anglo-American war effort, a page from the BIS pamphlet *Mutual Aid* showed American servicemen relying on British equipment and supplies. (Public Record Office INF 2/18)

Britain, in relation to her national income, is contributing almost as much to the United States as the United States, in relation to her national income, is contributing to Great Britain. I am not going to weary you with figures."[24] By late 1943, propagandists had decided that the actual figures were more than wearying; they were discouraging. Instead of stating the numbers, Halifax referred his listeners to the White Paper on mutual aid and to a recent speech by President Roosevelt for the facts. The BIS released a copy of Halifax's speech to their American media clients.

British propagandists placed numerous stories and articles on reverse Lend-Lease in American publications. At the end of December, Frank Thistlethwaite of the Joint American Secretariat received a suggestion for a story from Lord Strathallan of the Ministry of Production. He replied that he would ask Robin Cruikshank if he felt "it would be a suitable topic to feed to one of his tame American journalists." He suggested to Cruikshank that the MOI place the story of how British businessmen felt handicapped by wartime controls and U.S. limitations on exports while their American rivals were profiting. He mentioned as an example an article in *Fortune* magazine that stated that American salesmanship had a great opportunity abroad, because the British paper quota for book publishing was at 37 percent of the prewar level, whereas the American quota remained virtually unchanged. Cruikshank replied that he thought it was a good idea. The journalists he had in mind for it were James Reston of the *New York Times*, Geoffrey Parsons of the *New York Herald Tribune*, and Frederick Kuh of the *Chicago Sun*. Cruikshank himself more likely would have thought of the Americans as friends of Britain rather than "tamed." Indeed, the MOI's H. G. Nicholas later recalled that these Americans "didn't eat out of our hands."[25]

By 1943 polls showed that the public knew about Lend-Lease. Americans' awareness of Lend-Lease was not always in British in-

24. Ibid., January 30, 1943; Halifax, broadcast speech of November 20, 1943, BIS press release, OWI Bureau of Overseas Intelligence Central Files, 1941–1945, RG 208, Entry 367, Box 316, NA.
25. Thistlethwaite to Strathallan, December 31, 1943; Thistlethwaite to Cruikshank, December 31, 1943; and Cruikshank to Thistlethwaite, January 3, 1944; CAB 110/242. Evidently, Reston and Parsons had come through for Cruikshank "at the time of the Five Senators"; Cruikshank to Malcolm, May 13, 1944, FO371/38556 AN1909/34/45, PRO. Interview with Nicholas.

terests, however, because along with it went the assumption that the United States should be repaid. The low public awareness of reverse Lend-Lease meant that most Americans did not know about Britain's end of supplying the war effort. Although the Roosevelt administration continued to give lip service to the idea of pooling resources, the president responded to pressure from Congress that the war be run in a businesslike fashion by saying that the Allies would repay Lend-Lease as much as they could.[26] Congress passed Lend-Lease appropriations by wide margins, always with the stipulation that it was for the war only. After two years of conducting a propaganda campaign restricted by government policy and overshadowed by U.S. propaganda, policymakers revised their efforts.

As the Allies moved closer to victory, American and British policymakers distrusted the others' intentions. British officials were particularly concerned with plans for Stage II, the period between the defeat of Germany and the end of the Pacific War, when Britain would have to begin reconverting its economy and expand exports. They were not convinced that the U.S. government would adopt liberal policies, especially lower tariffs, and therefore wanted to retain the alternative of the imperial preference. The United States, in turn, suspected the British of wavering on Article 7 and increased its demands that Britain abandon controls and preferences. By mid-1944 the British had fulfilled their commitment to engage in economic planning talks only on the issue of international monetary policy at Bretton Woods.[27]

In 1944 British propagandists knew they were in for a difficult year. At the end of 1943, the U.S. Congress, stirred up by the five senators' allegations of Lend-Lease abuse, launched an investigation. Ralph Owen Brewster (R-Me.) linked charges of Lend-Lease misuse to issues of postwar economic competition in the areas of oil resources and civil aviation. In an article in *Collier's* magazine, Brewster warned that the British were out-maneuvering and out-trading the United States. He praised President Roosevelt's stand on Lend-Lease but noted, "No British spokesman has said: 'We aim to get rid of the silly, foolish, old pound-sterling sign.' " Brewster concluded that Anglo-American collaboration was necessary for future peace; he urged, however, that Americans be as hardheaded as the British in their international policy.[28] Senator Brewster's article alerted the British that it would become increasingly difficult to discuss Land-Lease without facing the larger postwar economic issues.

Robert Brand, the banker-statesman, warned that the entire British government must attend to American public opinion. Brand spoke from experience. He had served the British government in Washington during the First World War as a member of the British Mission. He was back during the Second World War as head of the Food Mission from 1941 to 1944 and as the Treasury's representative from 1944 to 1946. Brand wrote Sir John Anderson, chancellor of the Exchequer, that the U.S. government was more directly and immediately influenced by public opinion than any other government in the world. He described the apprehension felt by government officials who had to be cross-examined by congressional committees, and how difficult it was for them to present any British position that might be unpopular. Brand alluded to the firehose analogy. If the president could not repeat his miracle of Lend-Lease, he continued, American attitudes were bound to be determined by their views of Britain's war effort. He wanted the American public to be informed about Britain's mobilization, the sacrifice of its export trade, and its economic difficulties: "What we want the American people to feel is that the British and American nations are like two comrades, who have fought a good fight together. The one is badly wounded and fainting from loss of blood. The other is unwounded. By a blood gift to his comrade the latter can restore him quickly and in a few hours not feel the loss of the blood he has given."[29] Brand pleaded for the utmost publicity to be given to promoting the British war effort in the United States. He noted that he was sure Brendan Bracken was doing something about influencing opinion, but the results were not satisfactory. Anderson asked the Foreign Office for its views on Brand's analysis of American opinion. Foreign Secretary Eden replied

28. Owen Brewster, "Don't Blame the British—Blame Us," *Collier's,* December 25, 1943, 21.
29. Brand remained concerned about public opinion but became more resigned that it could not be changed. Brand to Sir John Anderson, August 23, 1944, Brand to Anderson, January 3, 1945, File 197, Brand Papers.

that Britain's "American friends need facts and figures so that our people can set them to work on our behalf."[30]

Propagandists, however, had discovered that providing their American friends with information was not enough. When they surveyed American opinion in early 1944, they noted that although the public appeared to have accepted the concept of postwar international cooperation in political terms, it had not accepted the concept in economic terms. On economic policy the British seemed to be moving left, increasingly interested in social welfare and employment. The Americans seemed to be moving right, away from the New Deal and toward a policy of aggressive international economic expansion. Cruikshank summed up the implications of these shifting attitudes: "Unfortunately these matters touch the Americans on their least attractive side. The normal business ethics of the U.S. are not noble, or magnanimous, and with the existent prejudice—brought out by the Five Senators—that we are slick guys, resolved to outsmart the ingenuous American sucker, piled on top of the American illusion that we are a respectable old firm now fallen on seedy days, trouble is inevitable." Cruikshank warned that this melodrama, in which the hero, "the simple, good-hearted American, the country boy," is cheated by that city slicker, "the cunning, crafty John Bull," could enjoy a long run because it advanced political and economic interests. American politicians and businessmen calculated that they could get better terms in any agreement, Cruikshank noted, if beforehand they portrayed U.S. negotiators as "simpletons who are sure to be fleeced."[31]

The British, therefore, needed to counter this story with a good one of their own. William Edwards, a former railway executive with experience in public relations and head of the Industrial Information Division of the Ministry of Production, had been sent to the United States in late 1943 to investigate propaganda regarding Lend-Lease. He concluded that the British had not been convincing about their total mobilization. He suggested that this failure was the result of security restrictions on statistics and technical information, as well as the result of what he termed the "excessive publicity" Americans

30. Eden to Anderson, September 7, 1944, FO371/38512 AN3460/6/45, PRO.
31. Malcolm, FO371/38577 AN2678/34/45; Cruikshank, "Publicity and Policy in the United States," December 3, 1943, FO371/38505 AN430/6/45, PRO.

had given to their own war production. Like many of the propagandists who had backgrounds in public relations or journalism, Edwards urged an open and frank discussion of Britain's trade and economic problems. First, the British economy was based on a large volume of imports. It was traditionally the world's and especially the United States's best customer. Second, in order to maintain its balance of payments, Britain needed to export. During the war Britain had sold its foreign investments, sacrificed its export trade, and lost its shipping and international insurance trade. Britain would emerge from the war as a debtor nation. The message that Edwards suggested should accompany this bleak outlook was that Britain could not be a strong military power in the postwar world unless it was a strong economic power.[32]

The MOI's Frank Darvall urged that propaganda policy broaden its strategy. He deplored the North American Supply Council Information Division's current strategy of refuting each specific allegation made against Lend-Lease. For example, when the syndicated columnist Drew Pearson reported that under Lend-Lease, U.S. officers in Accra had to rent American trucks from the British for $25 a day, or Austine Cassini in the *Washington Times-Herald* announced that through Lend-Lease, the British secured bathroom fixtures for King Ibn Saud, the Supply Council issued a dry rebuttal explaining official accounting procedures. A report on the "Answers to Charges" in August 1944 concluded that the rebuttals were seldom printed.[33] Darvall pointed out that publicizing reciprocal aid was not effective because American reporters resisted using these stories and because the facts countered the message Britain wanted to put across. For instance, Darvall noted that Lend-Lease from the United States

32. Edwards, "Suggested Objectives of Information Policy in U.S.A. and Suggested Programme of Work," February 16, 1944, FO371/38506 AN731/6/45, PRO.

33. The British Supply Council followed a standard format called "Answers to Charges." Since late 1941 the Supply Council had issued 141 "Answers," which were circulated to the British consuls, the British missions, the BIS, forty U.S. government officials, and a number of journalists, including Raymond Clapper, Walter Waggoner of the *Wall Street Journal*, Henry Luce, John McCormack of the *New York Times*, Raymond Gram Swing, Drummond Christian of the *Christian Science Monitor*, and Dorothy Thompson. Also on the list was Eric Johnston, head of the U.S. Chamber of Commerce. See "Report on the Use Made of the 'Answers to Charges,' August 25, 1944, FO371/38511 AN3325/6/45; Minutes of Informal Committee on Mutual Aid, January 10, 1944, FO371/38504 AN167/6/45; Office of Information, British Supply Council, October 2, 1944, FO371/38510 AN2735/6/45, PRO.

exceeded $20 billion, of which 40 percent went to Britain or British forces; British reciprocal aid to the United States scarcely exceeded $2 billion. Cruikshank observed that Darvall's memorandum brought them all up "against the hard brick wall of reality."[34]

Cruikshank drew up a publicity plan called "What Britain Has Done" to serve as the general directive for British propagandists in the United States. The directive had three sections: the magnitude of the war effort, the effect of the war effort on Britain's external economy, and the effect of the war effort on Britain's civilian economy. Cruikshank, as always, stressed the human and emotional elements needed in propaganda themes. He wanted Americans to know about the harsh effect of mobilization on families. The father might be moved to a factory in the North while the mother worked in a defense plant in the South. The younger children were in day nurseries; grown children were in uniform away in Italy or France. Nearly three out of four British boys and girls between the ages of fourteen and seventeen worked in vital industries. Forty-five percent of all women between the ages of fourteen and sixty-five were in the forces, in civil defense, or in war-related work. Cruikshank instructed propagandists, when they announced that one in three munitions workers was female, to describe a woman's typical day from blackout to blackout. Finally, the war effort had absorbed two out of three of the adult population, meaning that British trade industry had been virtually abandoned and family life sacrificed. Cruikshank recalled the "comrades at arms": "Ideally, what I would like for the next lap in our race is a finely phrased statement of Mutual Aid that would have about it something of the glow and exaltation of a shared adventure, of a selfless comradeship in peace, of that kind of affirmation of unity which, at least for a season, silences the cynical and shames the sordid wranglers over pennies and cents."[35]

While the MOI and the BIS planned a human interest campaign

34. Thistlethwaite agreed that attention should be concentrated on the larger aspects of the war, but he wanted to continue publicity on reciprocal aid to balance the Roosevelt administration's promotion of Lend-Lease; Darvall to Malcolm, June 24, 1944, and Thistlethwaite to Darvall, July 17, 1944, FO371/38510 AN2492/2800/6/45, PRO.

35. Cruikshank, "What Britain Has Done," July 17, 1944, FO371/38557 AN2864/34/45; Cruikshank to N. Butler, March 6, 1944, FO371/38506 AN937/6/45, PRO.

on the British war effort, high-level officials prepared to negotiate the economic policies of Stage II. Walter Lippmann explained his understanding of this aspect of the propaganda strategy to Robert Brand: "Keynes told me last night that he wanted to keep the whole subject dull and important, so that the general public will accept the views of the experts on their authority, rather than try to understand them and form an independent judgment." Lippmann, not surprisingly, given his views on opinion management, endorsed this plan. Brand answered that although he agreed with Keynes, the matter would eventually come before Congress, and then an informed opinion would be necessary. Brand was especially worried about the banking community. Lippmann, admitting that he had not been as serious as he should have been, replied that Brand was right. He urged Brand not to rely solely on Washington officials but to cultivate American bankers as well. The British negotiators—Keynes, Brand, and Sir Wilfred Eady, a veteran Treasury official—conducted what Nevile Butler referred to as "educational work" among U.S. officials.[36] The policymakers wanted to provide their American friends, especially Walter Lippmann and Raymond Gram Swing, with the information they needed to put across the British case.

The propagandists' plan for a subtle campaign to prepare for the Quebec conference to be held in September 1944, was shaken by a National Association of Manufacturers story published in early August. The American business group reported that high-level talks were underway over continuing Lend-Lease to Britain after the defeat of Germany, until the surrender of Japan and possibly longer. The report stated that the primary purpose of the plan under discussion was to support Britain's domestic economy, at a cost to the American taxpayer of $2.5 billion and more yearly, above war costs. The British were claiming, the story concluded, that this assistance was absolutely necessary.

American friends informed Cruikshank that this disclosure was bad for the British and would create their toughest public relations problem since 1940. Cruikshank told his fellow propagandists that the situation would deteriorate the closer the Allies came to victory.

36. Lippmann to Brand, September 24, 1943; Brand to Lippmann, September 27, 1943; Lippmann to Brand, September 29, 1943, Box 58, Lippmann Papers; N. Butler to E. L. Hall-Patch, August 11, 1944, FO371/38558 AN3137/34/45, PRO.

London policymakers decided not to address the National Association of Manufacturers story directly. They instead pursued their policy of not referring specifically to the Lend-Lease negotiations. Richard Law warned against taking any aggressive action: "If it becomes an election issue it is not inconceivable that the President, who may have a desperate fight on his hands, would throw us to the wolves." Minister of State and member of the British Mission, E. L. Hall-Patch, described the propaganda campaign as second only in importance to the actual fighting, its success the "equivalent of a resounding military victory." He cautioned that "the 'putting across' should be done in such a way that the hand of the 'crafty British propagandist' is not disclosed. It will be a great test for the BIS in America and I feel they will realise the importance of success. We are playing for very high stakes, and it is up to the BIS to play the hand with every bit of skill they possess."[37]

London policymakers sent out a secret directive to senior BIS officials and the consul generals setting out the themes of propaganda during the negotiations for Stage II. It directed propagandists to assure the Americans that the defeat of Japan would demand Britain's immediate attention during Stage II. Nevertheless, the directive explained, Britain must begin to reconvert and resume some expansion of its export trade. The MOI supplied propagandists with the figures and arguments they needed to make this case. The directive warned that these figures and arguments should not appear to be connected in any way to official negotiations: "It will be appreciated that, if any suspicion were aroused amongst Americans that the British were lobbying for support on this question, infinite harm would be done. On the other hand, used with discretion and tact, publicity of this sort at the present time can immensely facilitate official discussions on the level of supplies from the U.S. to the U.K. by helping to create a friendly and sympathetic American public opinion." London policymakers followed up this secret directive with the release of two White Papers, one on mutual aid and one on the British war effort. The war effort paper's immense size earned it the ill-fated nickname "Moby-Dick" in the MOI's American Division.[38]

---

37. Minutes of Informal Interdepartmental Committee on Publicity, August 15, 1944, BT28/1060; Cruikshank, August 9, 1944; minute by R. Law, August 17, 1944; and minute by Hall-Patch, August 12, 1944, FO371/38558 AN3137/34/45, PRO.

38. "Lend-Lease in Stage II," September 1944, FO371/38512 AN3564/6/45;

British policy seemed to have paid off at the second Quebec conference in September 1944, when Churchill obtained Roosevelt's support for continued assistance.[39] FDR agreed that Lend-Lease should continue in the first year of Stage II, then expected to last from fifteen months to two years, at a level of $3.5 million for military supplies and $3 million for nonmilitary supplies. Roosevelt also agreed to ease the export restrictions on Britain.

Morgenthau, Roosevelt's chief adviser at Quebec, supported a generous Lend-Lease agreement for several reasons. He had achieved his goal of establishing the dollar as the top international currency at the Bretton Woods conference in July. His talks in London in August with the chancellor of the Exchequer, John Anderson, had convinced him that Britain was approaching bankruptcy. Like many American visitors to London, Morgenthau was struck by the total mobilization of British society and the devastation caused by the war. At Quebec, moreover, Churchill had accepted Morgenthau's plan for the deindustrialization and dismemberment of Germany. Although the prime minister had been anxious enough over the Stage II agreement that he had asked Roosevelt if he were expected to beg like Fala (FDR's dog), the British were pleased with the results.[40] They apparently had forgotten that Lend-Lease remained a political issue.

A long line of opposition to the Quebec agreements formed. Secretary of State Hull was outraged that FDR had promised assistance to Britain without obtaining any assurance that London would abide by Article 7. Leo Crowley, the head of the Foreign Economic Administration, disagreed with Morgenthau that America's job was to rehabilitate Britain. He advocated a businesslike approach to Lend-Lease, meaning that once the war ended, Britain should pay its own way. The Joint Chiefs of Staff objected to providing Britain with Lend-Lease during the war against Japan because they wanted the Pacific to be a U.S. theater. Stettinius told the president that allowing the British to export in competition with American business would

---

minutes of meeting of the Informal Interdepartmental Committee on Publicity, December 1, 1944, FO371/38515 AN4580/6/45, PRO.

39. The Quebec Conference is discussed in Dobson, *U.S. Wartime Aid to Britain*, 185–211, Gardner, *Sterling-Dollar Diplomacy*, 180–183, and George C. Herring, "The United States and British Bankruptcy, 1944–1945: Responsibilities Deferred," *Political Science Quarterly* 86.2 (June 1971), 266–269.

40. Dobson, *Politics*, 69.

be dynamite on Capitol Hill.[41] The Morgenthau plan for Germany was rapidly discarded. The promise of Lend-Lease to Britain was whittled away. By the end of 1944, the status of the Stage II agreements was uncertain.

Robert Marett summed up the second Quebec conference as a "flop from the point of view of press relations." The British had not followed their usual policy of attempting to shape the interpretation of events on the spot. Marett observed that the conference spokesmen—Steve Early, FDR's press secretary, and Robin Cruikshank, who had flown out from London to handle the conference—had little to tell the hundreds of reporters present because most of the negotiations were kept secret: "Everyday there was a press conference in which Steve and Robin made anodyne statements about nothing in particular, being reduced to describing in detail the dresses which Mrs. Roosevelt and Mrs. Churchill were wearing, or what Churchill had for breakfast that morning. Denied their natural diet of news, the correspondents became cantankerous and complained about the facilities. It was all very disagreeable."[42]

The business columnist Ralph Robey expressed his cantankerousness in a *Newsweek* article entitled "What Goes On behind Our Backs." Robey described the Quebec agreements as "an international horsetrading story with hair-raising implications." The columnist listed two horrors. One was that through Lend-Lease the British had been able to restore their prewar financial position in the United States. The second was that Britain would continue to receive billions in U.S. aid while it began industrial reconversion to peacetime production during Stage II. He concluded with the observation that it was no surprise that the British had been so interested in the reelection of President Roosevelt.[43]

Senator Brewster returned to sound the alarm in an article for *American Magazine*, entitled "Let's Not Be Suckers Again." The magazine introduced the article with its own summary: "Our good

41. Hull to FDR, September 30 and October 2, 1944 in U.S. Department of State, *Foreign Relations of the United States, 1940–45, 1944*, vol. 3 (Washington, D.C.: U.S. Government Printing Office, 1965), 61–66; Herring, "The United States and British Bankruptcy," 266–267.

42. Marett, *Through the Back Door*, 110–111.

43. Ralph Robey, "What Goes on behind Our Backs," *Newsweek*, November 20, 1944, 72.

The second Quebec conference in 1944 was "a flop from the point of view of press relations." FDR, Clementine Churchill, Winston Churchill, Eleanor Roosevelt, and the Canadian prime minister Mackenzie King at The Citadel. (Franklin D. Roosevelt Presidential Library)

friends, the British, are already on the job to outsmart us in postwar trade. After the last war many people felt that they had gobbled the choice cuts, while American taxpayers footed the bills. And they'll slip us the check again, says Senator Brewster, unless we demand our share of global air lines, shipping, oil, and communications." According to Senator Brewster, Britain believed that if the United States continued Lend-Lease after the war, the United States would still be doing no more than its share. He observed that of the eight thousand British officials working to advance the interests of their country in the United States, several were "effective counselors of public relations." He noted that they worked closely with American propagandists to do the "excellent and necessary job in building closer friendship between the United States and Britain." While praising their work, the senator criticized a method used to increase American respect for Britain in which the "facts about how the British are putting it over on us" were suppressed. He suggested that Americans negotiate for world trade as though they were going into a "football game with a friendly rival who is out to win."[44] Both Brewster and Robey invoked the image of the manipulative John Bull that propagandists had worked long and hard to bury. More important, they had challenged the essential message that the British and the Americans had common interests.

Propagandists responded to such criticism by continuing the indirect strategy. They played up the war effort and promoted British inventions and scientific discoveries through exhibits, magazines, speeches, and photographs. London meanwhile said as little as possible about reconversion and postwar issues. Officials worked closely with the Roosevelt administration in promoting Lend-Lease and reciprocal aid. The British Supply Council and the Foreign Economic Administration set up a joint information organization on Lend-Lease in action aimed at the press and the armed forces. The U.S. Army, for instance, printed 1 million copies of the pamphlet *Invisible Weapon*, on Lend-Lease and reverse Lend-Lease for its troops.[45]

44. Owen Brewster, "Let's Not Be Suckers Again," *American Magazine*, January 1945, 24, 98.
45. "British Supply Council in North America Office of Information: Progress Report No. 12," covering six weeks to March 10, 1945; H. G. Nicholas Papers, in private hands.

As always, the propagandists preferred that Americans carry the message for them. Ernest Lindley, a long-time friend of the British with close ties to the White House, replied to Richard Robey's article in his own *Newsweek* column at the request of Oscar Cox. Lindley incorporated the main themes of British propaganda into "Lend-Lease and a Healthy Britain." He wrote that along with being the United States's trade rival, Britain was its best customer. He concluded, therefore, that a healthy Britain was advantageous to the United States.[46] To answer Senator Brewster, the British placed an article in *American Magazine* under the name of Philip Reed, the chairman of the board of General Electric, who had worked on Lend-Lease at the American embassy in London. The article, entitled "Suspicion—Greatest Enemy of the Allies," responded to each of Brewster's allegations of misuse and deviousness. It observed that each country was making plans to further its own interests but that those interests would not be advanced by refusing to cooperate with each other. "We must recognize the fact that America cannot remain healthy itself if the rest of the world is sick," the article concluded.[47] Both articles placed cooperation on Lend-Lease in the context of a healthy postwar economy.

For his part, Walter Lippmann wrote a column in March 1945 criticizing the American Bankers Association's opposition to the Bretton Woods agreements. After discussions with Keynes and Brand, Lippmann argued that the creation of the International Monetary Fund and the World Bank should be evaluated in terms of politics, not economics. Lippmann pointed out that because of political pressures, England, "the ancient center of free enterprise," was moving toward greater government control over employment and social policy, as were other European countries. He recommended that U.S. bankers accept Bretton Woods, which restored a free-enterprise system on conditions to which other governments had only reluctantly agreed, or else the United States might be left with the only free enterprise econ-

46. Early to Bill Hassett, December 9, 1944, President Roosevelt memos, Stephen Early Papers, FDRL; Ernest Lindley, "Lend-Lease and a Healthy Britain," *Newsweek*, December 4, 1944, 42.

47. Mentioned in "British Supply Council in North America Office of Information Progress Report No. 12," H.G. Nicholas Papers; Philip Reed, "Suspicion—Greatest Enemy of the Allies," *American Magazine* 140 (July 1945), 132.

omy in an increasingly collectivized world. Keynes praised Lippmann's article as the "most fundamental contribution yet."[48]

Britain's propaganda campaign for Lend-Lease had a mixed success.
Officials adopted the indirect strategy after they recognized that the
"pooling of resources" theme suffered from weak statistics and competition with the U.S. government. The two-pronged approach called
for propagandists to convince the general public that Lend-Lease be
considered part of the common war effort and a step toward a re-
constructed postwar economy. This effort to create a supportive
opinion among the public was supposed to allow the high-level negotiators to reach a favorable settlement unhampered by politics. The
British never convinced a majority of the American public that Lend-
Lease should not be repaid, but they did win the support of opinion
leaders.

A May 1945 study by the State Department found that leadership
and editorial opinion sympathized strongly with Britain's economic
difficulties. The public, however, appeared to be apathetic or at best
insufficiently informed regarding Britain's economic plight. Hadley
Cantril provided Oscar Cox with discouraging opinion poll results
on the concept of reverse Lend-Lease throughout 1943 and 1944.[49]

As far as you know, have we received any war materials and supplies from England in return for our Lend-Lease help?

	Yes (%)	No (%)	Don't know (%)
September 1943	25	40	35
October 1943	30	30	36
November 1943	37	25	38
December 1943	38	25	37
June 1944	40	27	31
December 1944	31	31	38

48. Walter Lippmann, "The Bankers and Bretton Woods," *New York Herald Tribune*, March 17, 1945, 13; Lippmann–Keynes correspondence, July–August 1944, and
March 1945, Box 82, Lippmann Papers.

49. "U.S. Opinion on the Dumbarton Oaks Proposals," May 11, 1945, RG 59,
Office of Public Opinion Studies, 1943–1965, NA; Cantril to Cox, December 27,
1944, Box 5, Oscar Cox Papers, FDRL.

The polls showed that the small improvement had ended in June 1944, at the height of Allied good feeling over the invasion of the European continent.

A January 1945 memorandum for President Roosevelt from Joseph Grew, undersecretary of state, reported that despite sympathetic treatment in the press, only one-third of the public seemed to be aware of reverse Lend-Lease furnished by Britain. When limited to the college educated and the upper economic group, the results showed that one-half were aware of reverse Lend-Lease. On the question of repayment, the report noted, 70 percent of the public thought that Britain should repay the United States in full. Among those who were unaware of reverse Lend-Lease, 85 percent favored repayment in full. Among those aware of it, 56 percent favored repayment in full. The surveys showed that those who knew about reverse Lend-Lease were less likely to demand full repayment, but only a small percentage knew about it. A Gallup poll of June 28, 1945, asked, "Do you think Britain can pay us back for Lend-Lease?" Forty-one percent answered yes, 43 percent answered no, and 16 percent had no opinion. Although two-thirds of Americans, according to surveys, thought Britain should repay Lend-Lease, 43 percent believed that Britain was unable to do so. Gallup, exercising a role as shaper of opinion as well as measurer, considered these results too poor to be published.[50]

President Harry Truman's view of Lend-Lease as solely a wartime measure reflected congressional direction and public sentiments. He terminated Lend-Lease following the Japanese surrender on August 14, 1945. He later viewed his cancellation of aid to Britain as his greatest mistake as president. For the new British Labour government, it was a traumatic blow. Its reserves were at $1.9 billion, the current year's adverse balance was $5 billion, and enormous debts were owed to members of the sterling bloc. For instance, India's sterling balance by mid-1945 was more than 1 billion pounds.[51] The cutoff of Lend-Lease was not only devastating to Britain's economic

---

50. Joseph Grew to the president, January 12, 1945, PSF Departmental Correspondence, Box 91, FDRL; William Griffin to Oscar Cox, July 4, 1945, Cox Papers, Lend-Lease Files, Box 100, FDRL.

51. Herring, "The United States and British Bankruptcy," 277; Dobson, *Politics*, 78; L. S. Pressnell, *The Post-War Financial Settlement*, vol. 1 of *External Economic Policy since the War* (London: HMSO, 1986), 217.

situation. It also signaled a rupture in the partnership the British had desired and worked to create.

On the question of British treatment of the Lend-Lease settlement, David Ogilvy at the BSC wrote from Washington that the British government was faced with three choices. One was that it could default as it had on World War I debts in the thirties, which would be a political disaster. The second was that it could pay the debts, which was impossible. The third was that it could do a better job on American public opinion by working with the U.S. government to prepare the Americans for a cancellation of the debts.[52] Ogilvy bluntly summed up the lack of options open to the British as they turned to the Americans in 1945.

Following the end of the war and the termination of Lend-Lease, British policymakers were still playing for high stakes. Ahead of them lay the negotiations for both the settlement of Lend-Lease and the arrangements for an American loan. At a meeting in Washington on August 23, propagandists agreed to continue the indirect strategy. In the hope that official negotiations would be conducted "out of the limelight," the BIS was advised to say as little as possible about Lend-Lease. They concluded that it would be wiser to leave the method of "selling" the final agreement to the administration rather than trying to "sell" it themselves.[53]

Without the unity of wartime, political debate over Lend-Lease returned to the partisanship of 1941. When President Truman mentioned that the United States should write off wartime Lend-Lease, the *New York Herald Tribune* reported, "Truman Stirs Bi-Party Row on War Debts." In an attempt to divert Americans from their preoccupation with debts, propagandists relied upon their central theme that a strong and healthy British ally was in the interests of the United States as it prepared to face the uncertainties of the postwar world. Opinion leaders, echoing British and American propaganda, responded favorably to President Truman's suggestion. Newspaper editors believed that the debts already had been paid in the "coin of victory."[54]

52. Ogilvy, "Notes on American Public Opinion in Relation to the U.K.," September 25, 1945, FO371/44608 AN3037/109/45, PRO.
53. "Publicity on Termination of Lend-Lease and on the British War Effort," August 25, 1945, BT28/1059, PRO.
54. Gardner, *Sterling-Dollar Diplomacy*, 191; H. Schuyler Foster, *Activism Re-*

A generous settlement was agreed upon in December 1945. The outstanding Lend-Lease account on which the British owed the United States approximately $4 billion was canceled. Six billion dollars' worth of surplus property and Lend-Lease located in Britain was transferred to the British for $532 million. For the Lend-Lease orders still in the pipeline, Britain was asked to pay $118 million. The British therefore owed $650 million. The Americans had wiped the slate clean of the $20-billion difference between their own and Britain's contributions to Lend-Lease. John Maynard Keynes told the House of Lords on December 18, 1945, that the settlement was "an act of unprecedented liberality." He said it expressed the "intense good will towards this country of the American people" and their desire to see Britain as a "strong and effective partner" in a troubled world.[55]

These themes were repeated in the discussion over a major U.S. loan to Britain. The Lend-Lease settlement was part of a package that included a $3.75-billion loan to be repaid over fifty years at 2 percent interest. As part of the loan agreement, Britain had to ratify the Bretton Woods agreement and enter the International Monetary Fund, accept the Article 7 framework on ending imperial preference, and commit to making sterling convertible by 1947. The terms of the loan dismayed the British government, but it was in little position to bargain.[56]

The American public split on the issue of the loan in the same way it had over Lend-Lease. Most opinion leaders approved it and most of the general public opposed it. Supporters, including the media, business organizations, and civic groups, used the economic argument that the loan would be good business for the United States.[57] Congress sided with the opinion leaders over the majority of the public by approving the loan in July with a vote of 46 to 34 in the Senate and 219 to 155 in the House. Senator Arthur Vandenberg (R-Mich.), who the British had earlier categorized as an economic na-

---

places Isolationism: U.S. Public Attitudes, 1940–1975 (Washington, D.C.: Foxhall Press, 1983), 38.

55. Gardner, Sterling-Dollar Diplomacy, 208. H. Duncan Hall concluded that with the settlement, "in the end the 'lending' was true to the old English root: laenan, to give"; Hall, North American Supply, 482.

56. Pressnell, Post-War Financial Settlement, 262–330.

57. Foster, Activism Replaces Isolationism, 39–41; Gardner, Sterling-Dollar Diplomacy, 257.

tionalist, voted for the loan because he said it was a matter of "intelligent American self-interest," although he predicted that "about 90% of my constituency will be unimpressed." He was right about his Michigan voters. According to his mail, his speech in support of the loan was the most unpopular he ever made on foreign affairs. The senator's assertion that the United States must accept economic and moral leadership in a "wandering world" echoed British propaganda themes.[58] Other congressional supporters, staunch nationalists like Vandenberg, argued that assistance to Britain was a necessary defense against communism and the Soviet challenge.[59] Although British propagandists had avoided directly referring to the Soviet Union as a threat, they had repeatedly described an uneasy postwar world in which an Anglo-American partnership must maintain order to protect their mutual interests.

The Truman administration and Congress had done what British analysts thought impossible: they had supported a generous settlement in the face of public sentiment that Lend-Lease be repaid. Nevertheless, in the months before the vote, British propagandists considered their Lend-Lease campaign a failure. In September 1945 David Ogilvy's synopsis of American opinion sparked a Foreign Office analysis of propaganda strategy. It contained the following statistics on American attitudes of importance to the British:

(1) 44% of adult Americans suffer under the delusion that most of the planes used by the RAF were made in the United States.

(2) Only 10% realize that most American troops have been carried across the Atlantic in British ships.

(3) Only 44% are aware that their country did not belong to the League of Nations.

(4) 60 million American adults have never heard of reverse Lend-Lease.

---

58. Arthur Vandenberg, *The Private Papers of Senator Vandenberg*, ed. Arthur Vandenberg, Jr. (Boston: Houghton Mifflin, 1952), 231.

59. The Truman administration hesitated to use this argument; see Foster, *Activism Replaces Isolationism*, 40; Gardner, *Sterling-Dollar Diplomacy*, 249; Richard Freeland, *The Truman Doctrine and the Origins of McCarthyism: Foreign Policy, Domestic Politics, and Internal Security, 1946–1948* (New York: Alfred A. Knopf, 1972), 68.

(5) One year after the fall of Singapore, only 52% of American adults knew that Britain had lost territory to the Japanese.

(6) 60% of American adults have never heard of the Atlantic Charter and only 4% can name even *one* of its provisions.

(7) 37% do not have the vaguest idea what the word TARIFF means, while 56% have never heard of reciprocal trade agreements.[60]

Ogilvy concluded his list with a quotation from Raymond Clapper: "Never overestimate the people's knowledge nor underestimate their intelligence."[61]

Ogilvy's report confirmed the Foreign Office's preference for directing its educational efforts toward American officials and opinion leaders. J. G. Donnelly observed that Ogilvy's statistics showed "that Democracy in practice does not yet mean that every citizen understands everything equally well and exerts an equal influence on the decisions of his government."[62] At first, propagandists had attempted to inform the public about Britain's contribution to Lend-Lease, but unfavorable facts and lack of success had persuaded them to change their approach. They promoted Britain's war effort to the public, especially the human interest side of hardship and sacrifice. To opinion leaders, they directed information stressing how British recovery would benefit the United States. They decided to keep the actual coverage of the financial negotiations "dull and important." Although this tactic presented a show of Anglo-American cooperation between governments, it also raised the "sucker alarm" among politicians and commentators who distrusted any British maneuvering behind closed doors. At least the closed doors had allowed the British delegation to make the occasionally humiliating concessions demanded by American negotiators in private. When it was over, however, the U.S. administration, as London hoped, encouraged congressional support of the settlement.[63]

60. Ogilvy, "Notes on American Public Opinion in Relation to the U.K.," September 25, 1945, FO371/44608 AN3037/109/45, PRO.

61. Raymond Clapper had been killed in a collision of U.S. bombers in the Pacific in February 1944. Olive Clapper, who wrote that her husband had agreed with the quotation, attributed it to Glenn Frank, publicist, editor, and president of the University of Wisconsin, 1925–1937. Olive Clapper, *One Lucky Woman* (Garden City, N.Y.: Doubleday, 1961), 149.

62. Donnelly, October 8, 1945, FO371/44608 AN3037/109/45, PRO.

63. G. John Ikenberry explores the role of interests, timing, power, and coalition-

In propaganda policymaking, as in Donnelly's "democracy in practice," all citizens were not equal. Since most of the public clung to their belief that Lend-Lease should be repaid, propagandists decided to appeal to their sympathies for the British people. This appeal to sympathy had not worked during the Blitz, but, as then, it did strengthen the position of friendly Americans by providing an emotional context for the case that action was in U.S. interests. Propagandists supplied opinion leaders with reasonable arguments stressing self-interest to counter critics and to exert their more than equal influence on the U.S. government. These calculated appeals hid the turmoil of propagandists, who felt that reason played little part in such transactions.

Although some London officials seemed to feel as though Britain merely had an overdraft at the bank and that repeated reminders of this shortfall in its accounts were to be regarded as bad manners, others exposed their anguish as they designed Lend-Lease propaganda. Frank Darvall of the MOI offered to reply to any bill presented by the U.S. Congress with a list of a million casualties, billions of dollars of property damage, thousands of planes, thousands of ships, etc., per head of population, as a percentage of national income. Darvall reckoned that Britain had contributed relatively more than the United States to victory. "Since, however, this has been a common war and we do not want to take away from the honor and drama of our common struggle and common victory [with] sordid accounting," concluded Darvall, "we propose to present no bill."[64] Colleagues applauded Darvall's vision of a victory without bills, but they, as did Darvall himself, knew their audience. Polls reminded them that the majority of American citizens, who might not know about the Atlantic Charter or reverse Lend-Lease, expected to be repaid.

The U.S. administration's own propaganda on Lend-Lease had in-

---

building in Anglo-American economic negotiations. See G. John Ikenberry, "A World Economy Restored: Expert Consensus and the Anglo-American Postwar Settlement," *International Organization* 46.1 (Winter 1992), 289–321.

64. Darvall's casualty figure was high as of the summer of 1944. Cruikshank's figures included 667,159 of British Empire forces, 30,314 of merchant seamen, and 109,101 civilian casualties; total: 806,574. By the end of the war he expected it to reach one million. Darvall to Malcolm, June 24, 1944, FO371/38510 AN2492/6/45, PRO.

spired public support for aid, but it had drawbacks from the British point of view. By praising the United States's productive capacity and presenting the British as impoverished, the Americans quashed propagandists' attempts to portray an equal partnership. Any sign that the British were not destitute could arouse Americans' suspicions of British duplicity. Furthermore, the administration's promotion of Lend-Lease as a guarantee of the liberal principles of the Atlantic Charter and Article 7 placed propagandists in an awkward position. They could not agree or disagree openly with the American line.

At the Foreign Office, B. E. F. Gage asserted that events and the "judicious treatment of those events" were the best ways to influence American opinion. On the issue of Lend-Lease, the strategy of truth's dependence upon policy and events proved debilitating. First, the policy had to be in place as events occurred, so propagandists could be prepared with on-the-spot interpretation. The desire of the Foreign Office and the Treasury to maintain a competitive edge by keeping their options open had made them reluctant to provide the MOI and the BIS with specific government policy. Second, propagandists had the problem of shaping a positive message out of dismaying evidence. Faced with a staggering debt and a monumental reconversion process, they also confronted the American political debate on Anglo-American economic questions, which frequently ignited old competitions for markets and raw materials. Ernest Bevin made the best of "the hard brick wall of reality" when he said, "We are broke. We have spent everything in this struggle, and I am glad we have."[65]

Though eventually pleased with the outcome of Lend-Lease, London considered the campaign a failure because there was no equal partnership. The United States, emerging as an economic superpower, was able to impose its conditions on a needy Britain in the loan negotiations as well as make a generous settlement on Lend-Lease. Propagandists now had to transform the "special relationship," no longer based upon equality, into a mutually beneficial partnership, once Britain had recovered with the help of the United States. Clearly, the work of cultivating the Americans had just begun. The realization hit hard that, in economic terms at least, winning the war had meant Britain would not win the peace.

65. Gage, October 29, 1945, FO371/44608 AN3037/109/45; Cruikshank, "What Britain Has Done," July 17, 1944, FO371/38557 AN2864/34/45, PRO.

Conclusion: The Artillery of Propaganda

> The trouble is that publicity is always treated, especially in relation to America, as though it were a separate tactical operation, designed to pursue and reach its own objectives, rather than as it were, a form of artillery which is best used to facilitate the advance of the infantry and the armour.
>
> —ALAN DUDLEY, FOREIGN OFFICE,
> OCTOBER 15, 1945

Britain's propaganda campaign to promote an Anglo-American "partnership on equal terms" achieved qualified success. Together with the Soviet Union, Britain and the United States had led the Allies to victory over the Axis. They would remain allies. The partners, however, were not equal. By 1945, Britain had lost one-quarter of its national wealth; the United States emerged the strongest and richest nation in the world.[1] The efficacy of the partnership would depend upon how the Americans exercised their immense power.

1. Bradford Perkins used "unequal partners" as the title of his essay, "Unequal Partners: The Truman Administration and Great Britain," in The "Special Relationship," ed. Louis and Bull, 43–64. On postwar Anglo-American relations see also Terry Anderson, The United States, Great Britain, and the Cold War, 1944–1947 (Columbia: University of Missouri Press, 1981); Richard A. Best, "Cooperation with Like-Minded Peoples": British Influences on American Security Policy, 1945–1949 (Westport, Conn.: Greenwood Press, 1986); Robin Edmonds, Setting the Mould: The United States and Britain, 1945–1950 (Oxford: Clarendon Press, 1986); Fraser Harbutt, The Iron Curtain: Churchill, America, and the Origins of the Cold

In the last years of the war, concerns that a victorious United States might embark upon an ambitious expansionism overshadowed fears that Americans would revert to isolationist behavior. To the OWI chief, Elmer Davis, Edward R. Murrow explained the reason for anti-American sentiments in London in March 1944: "People here—particularly the Big Boys—are going through a very difficult period, trying to adjust their views of the future, and particularly the future of their relations with Russia and America and their decrease in relative strength. They are naturally very touchy when we appear to ignore them or to act without consultation." Murrow thought that such "irritations" between the two allies would not harm the war effort, and in any case there was little that could be done about it. From the British perspective, Robert Bruce Lockhart, the head of Political Warfare Executive, noted that according to PWE and MOI sources, the Americans "were becoming intensely national and were determined to use their power." Recorded Lockhart, "The British had pushed the world around for the last hundred years and now the Americans were going to do it."[2] Policymakers in London would not accept Murrow's view that little could be done about Anglo-American relations. The British government did not relish the prospect of being pushed around; moreover, it wanted the United States to underwrite Britain's recovery and security.

The deliberate construction of the "special relationship" was, as historian David Reynolds has pointed out, the invention of a "tradition" as an instrument of diplomacy. Prime Minister Churchill pursued his vision of Anglo-American leadership with President Roosevelt. "Our friendship is the rock on which I build for the future of the world," wrote Churchill to FDR in March 1945. Although their friendship had symbolized the close ties between wartime allies, it ended with Roosevelt's death in April. Military and diplomatic officials built effective working relations with their American counterparts and hoped to continue into peacetime the combined policymaking and consultation. In the British version of collabora-

---

War (New York: Oxford University Press, 1986); Hathaway, *Ambiguous Partnership*; Henry Butterfield Ryan, *The Vision of Anglo-America: The US-UK Alliance and the Emerging Cold War, 1943–1946* (Cambridge: Cambridge University Press, 1987).

2. Murrow to Elmer Davis, March 17, 1944, Container 1, Elmer Davis Papers, Library of Congress, Washington, D.C.; March 28, 1944, Robert Bruce Lockhart, *Diaries*, Vol. 2, 291.

tion, as described by Christopher Hitchens, "the Americans were to supply the capital, and the British were to provide the class."[3] Aware that Americans might not consider this arrangement a good bargain, British officials portrayed future cooperation as essential to American interests. Propagandists spread this idea of partnership to the American people. Their campaign reflected the advantages and limitations of conducting propaganda in a democratic nation that was a wartime ally and a peacetime rival.

Anxious to shed the sinister reputation of their Great War predecessors, the staff of the interwar British Library of Information had, as Paul Gore-Booth remembered, "kept their heads down and their mouths shut."[4] When the Second World War broke out, the British government adopted discreet methods of persuading the United States to abandon neutrality, chiefly using reports of Britain's brave defense against Nazi Germany's triumphal aggression to rally Americans to the Allied cause. The so-called "no propaganda" policy failed to convince the United States to enter the war. More conspicuous efforts, however, might have bolstered isolationists and reduced support for President Roosevelt's provisions of assistance. The campaign as it was conducted did dispel some distrust and earned enough toleration from the Roosevelt administration to pave the way for an expansion in 1942.

The Ministry of Information, the British Information Services, the BBC, diplomats, and consular officers offered their presentation of news and information as a service to their American allies. They adopted the World War I precedent of relying upon American opinion leaders to convey the information (which frequently contained propaganda messages of Anglo-American cooperation) to the public. When the "strategy of truth" worked, British officials and American opinion leaders functioned as a team. As the *Christian Science Monitor*'s Erwin Canham said of his experience covering the San Francisco conference, "Just as you feel the need of knowing something, a British information officer will pop around the corner with the

3. David Reynolds, "A 'Special Relationship'? America, Britain, and the International Order since the Second World War," *International Affairs* 62 (Winter 1985–86), 2; Churchill to Roosevelt, March 17, 1945, quoted by Martin Gilbert in "The Big Two," *New York Review of Books*, February 14, 1985; Hitchens, *Blood, Class, and Nostalgia*, 37.
4. Gore-Booth, *Great Truth and Respect*, 170.

answer."[5] The British hoped that if Americans agreed with the message and approved of the method of delivery, they would consider this information not as propaganda but as an expression of shared values and interests, attractively and efficiently provided as part of the common war effort.

Britain's service of information was the product of an intricate process. Propaganda policymakers evaluated U.S. foreign policy goals, analyzed American domestic politics, identified audiences, and studied opinion in order to offer interpretations of events that resonated with the American public. They aimed to tell the Americans not only what was happening but also how to think about it and what conclusions to draw. Those conclusions were designated by British government policy. For instance, the MOI described Mahatma Gandhi's arrest and the 1942 "Quit India" movement as detrimental to the war effort and proof of the necessity of continued British rule over the subcontinent. The D-Day invasion provided an opportunity to show the Americans the strategic value of Britain as a base of operation. In these cases, the MOI planned ahead, coordinating the presentation of events with policy goals and consideration of American opinion.

Circumstances sometimes sabotaged efforts to manage the news. During the early months of 1942, military disasters belied the instruction from the head of the British Press Service that British reverses should be "countered by positive statements of the facts issued officially on the spot." American war correspondents Cecil Brown in Singapore and Eric Sevareid in India witnessed the contortions of information officials caught between the contradictions of the official line and actual events. Censorship worked to Britain's advantage during the crisis in India, but it could backfire by arousing American suspicion of British deviousness. The lack of news at the second Quebec conference, where Churchill and FDR agreed on economic arrangements for Stage II, provoked accusations that the British government had manipulated the Americans. To turn attention away from negotiations over the Lend-Lease settlement, propagandists had poured out stories of hardship and left policy explanations to the Roosevelt administration. Although certain events brought Britain too much attention, others, such as Britain's war effort, received too

5. Marett, *Through the Back Door*, 115.

little. As American military achievements dominated the news in April and May of 1945, Ronald Campbell reported from the Washington embassy that in order to get into the headlines, "we must take the trouble to dress our doings in picturesque garb."[6]

Drawing on American culture and traditions, propagandists used "facts," "dull and important" reports, and compilations of statistics, as well as "stories"—creative historical analogies, myths of heroism and adventure, and morality tales of good versus evil—to build a case for the past, present, and future of American-British partnership. British officials believed American knowledge of history to be inadequate; their job, however, was not to teach history but to construct useful versions of the past. As though they were sorting through the attic for redeemable junk, they left World War I to gather cobwebs but dusted off Teddy Roosevelt and, ironically, embraced the Monroe Doctrine as evidence of shared strategic interests. They did not ridicule or dismiss the "ancient grudge" but honored the Declaration of Independence. They celebrated and adapted such themes as "white men in tough places," linking the settlement of the American West with imperial conquest and development.

To present the theme of wartime unity against the Axis, the American Division of the MOI put the spotlight on valiant RAF pilots, bombed-out cities, and *Mrs. Miniver*'s middle-class defiance. They mustered J. B. Priestley's industrial workers with bad teeth, farmers and land girls, women at defense plants, and children who were growing up without their parents. Propagandists called forth American witnesses—the articulate Edward R. Murrow, Iowa farmers turned GIs, transatlantic visitors from politics and government, the media, churches, labor unions, and the universities—who told Americans of the fortitude of the British people. The American Division hoped dramatic representations of a new democratic Britain and an all-out war effort would upstage other images, in particular, the conniving city slicker John Bull, the decadent aristocrat, and the imperial overlord.

The ease with which American critics recalled these images indicated the persistence of friction between the two powers and presaged its reemergence in peacetime. To contain old rivalries,

---

6. G. Campbell to MOI, April 14, 1942, FO371/30669 A3535/399/45; Campbell to FO, May 9, 1945, FO371/44575 AN1409/36/45, PRO.

propagandists placed Anglo-American relations in a global context, where potential dangers would continue to unite the two allies. The description of India as a land of "backward" peoples with irresponsible nationalist leaders could be applied to other imperial territories. Under British rule, propagandists predicted, the colonial peoples would be guided and reformed from the top; without Britain, they might turn to some "aggressive faith" or break down into chaos and war. Underneath the portrayals of orderly progress and evolving democracy hummed a faint reprise of the World War I theme, "civilization vs. barbarism."

Propagandists resorted to broad themes of goodwill and common purpose when they could not obtain clear statements of policy from His Majesty's government that translated into appealing messages for their American audiences. First, divisions among policymakers over difficult postwar problems hindered the formation of a definitive approach. Even when propagandists wrung from Whitehall a much-debated policy directive, calling for the portrayal of the Empire and Commonwealth, for instance, as the embodiment of liberal reform, they could be undermined by a trenchant Churchillism. On the other hand, if several British officials spoke the same "party line," as at the 1942 Institute for Pacific Relations Conference or over the BBC, they too aroused American skepticism. Second, important differences with U.S. policy on aspects of postwar economic matters or imperial jurisdictions contradicted the message of common interests. Policymakers who wanted to maintain flexibility by not committing to a particular stance advocated vague propaganda. They did not want a straightforward statement of a major disagreement with the United States to threaten their theme of unity, nor did they want a brazenly dishonest representation of their intentions to jeopardize the "strategy of truth."

Wartime experience taught that propaganda, to be most effective, must be coordinated with policy. As "separate tactical operations" or as a simple matter of presentation, for example, Lord Halifax's "bow to the devil," propaganda might not be convincing. Americans, as Graham Spry and others pointed out, would be persuaded by what was done. In reply to the Colonial Office and the India Office's objections that imperial policies be modified to suit the Americans, David Scott of the Foreign Office pointed out, "There are clearly cases where American power to thwart may be so great as to make it essential to adopt a different policy from what we would like to follow if we could leave U.S. opinion out of the picture." Scott's view was confirmed by a 1944 OSS analysis of postwar relations: "Unless Britain follows policies which are consistent with American interests and in accord with American popular views, she must contemplate great difficulties in obtaining American cooperation."[7] Propagandists believed that if they had policies eliciting adequate U.S. support, they might, with clever interpretation, maintain some flexibility by making the policy appear even more congenial to Americans than it actually was. As Alan Dudley pointed out, the artillery of propaganda could soften the ground and weaken opposing positions to prepare the way for British policies on such controversial issues as the empire and economics.

The British propaganda campaign, run by outsiders trying in every possible way to be insiders, throws into relief the process of building foreign-policy consensus in the United States. British analysts had assumed that American public opinion was volatile and emotional. They were disappointed, therefore, when U.S. public opinion remained fairly consistent throughout the war. A majority persisted in opposing the idea of the British Empire and in believing that Americans should be compensated for Lend-Lease. Analysts struggled to reconcile the characteristics of sentimentalism and hardheadedness and of ignorance and intelligence they found in American opinion. A generation earlier, William Wiseman, then a World War I intelligence officer, had determined, "For all their idealism, the Americans are a people with shrewd common sense."[8] They also discovered that because public opinion varied according to region, party politics, business interests, gender, race, ethnicity, and religion, it was almost impossible to appeal to one group without offending others. With general propaganda messages they reached out to diverse audiences but exerted great effort into reaching different pressure groups and members of the media who they believed were most influential.

The formulation of opinion was, according to BIS official William Edwards, a "highly organized and competitive business." Propagan-

7. Scott, October 20, 1943, FO371/34094 A9834/3/45, PRO; "Britain's Security Interests in the Post-War World," September 14, 1944, Office of Strategic Services Research and Analysis #2218, NA.

8. Fowler, *British-American Relations*, 292.

dists did not plunge straight into the competition but instead attempted to shape discussion by providing American opinion leaders with their interpretations of distant events or complex crises. The Americans who collaborated with the British shared their outlook. Edward R. Murrow and Dorothy Thompson had believed the United States should take up the fight against Nazi Germany. Walter Lippmann and James Reston agreed that the United States should regard the British Commonwealth and Empire as a vital postwar ally. Isaiah Berlin later recalled, "We didn't convert anybody"; propagandists rather armed their American friends with facts, background, and narratives of cooperation.[9] These friends then helped counter such critics as Henry Luce by charging that Luce's condemnation of the British Empire was detrimental to the Allied war effort.

Propagandists recognized the significance of domestic politics in shaping American foreign policy and the need, therefore, for bipartisan cooperation. In their analysis of opinion they listed as friends and potential friends moderate Democrats and Republicans, who would endorse a collaborative foreign policy with the British Empire and Commonwealth. Their potential enemies were left-wing Democrats, the World New Dealers, and right-wing Republicans—the isolationists turned nationalists as well as internationalist-imperialists. Circumventing the repeated injunction against any appearance of interfering in American politics and the Roosevelt administration's admonishment not to recruit ethnic communities, they made indirect approaches. The MOI invited congressmen to view Britain's war effort. Propagandists avoided tributes to Anglo-Saxonism or slurs against German Americans. They approached partisan strongholds and ethnic groups through churches, labor organizations, or such regional tactics as targeting the Midwest, home to large numbers of Republicans and German Americans. Although propagandists considered African Americans to be potentially friendly, they discounted this American minority as a target audience because many of its members lacked voting rights and because they did not wish to alienate white majority opinion. They hoped that messages of unity and teamwork would deter U.S. politicians and businessmen from their habit of appeal-

9. Edwards to Christopher Warner, "Information Work in the U.S.A.," June 24, 1949, FO953/486 PAN604/40/945, PRO; interview with Isaiah Berlin.

ing to particular interest and ethnic groups by employing anti-British rhetoric, or "twisting the lion's tail."

Britain's theme of unity echoed Franklin Roosevelt's. During the war FDR's powers as chief executive grew, along with the importance of Washington as a news center. President Roosevelt, the one truly national voice in American politics, made the most of his ability to shape opinion. American presidents, as both Colonel House and Harry Hopkins had explained, preferred to handle propaganda themselves. The U.S. government allowed the British to conduct propaganda as long is it did not interfere with the administration's own efforts. British officials did not always favor the president's position, nor did they wish to be accused of partisanship, but whenever possible, they aligned themselves with administration policies.

This method of opinion formation paid off when, on the question of a generous Lend-Lease settlement, for instance, the U.S. Congress sided with Britain, the administration, and American opinion leaders instead of the public. The weapon of propaganda, used to subdue domestic politics, allowed policymakers greater freedom of action. Britain's preference for a U.S. political system with a strong executive who enjoyed bipartisan consensus was shared by internationalist Americans. The president's use of executive agreements and his powers as commander-in-chief could bypass congressional checks on an activist foreign policy. Such action did run the danger of reviving isolationist concerns about a too-powerful executive. The possibility remained as well that government leaders, in their effort to build consensus through the management of opinion, might, to paraphrase Karl Kraus, read their own propaganda in the news and believe it to be true.

For British officials, the celebration of the war's end was clouded by the realization of losses sustained and difficulties ahead. In a letter to FDR written in January 1945, Secretary of State Edward Stettinius described London's traumatic adjustment to a secondary role, enhanced by uncertainty about U.S. intentions regarding future cooperation. "On top of it all," Stettinius added, "is a state of sensitive, irritated, war-weary nerves, brought on by five years of overwork, privation and major and minor hardships." Propagandists, diplomats, and civil servants suffered a form of combat fatigue. While the military forces organized victory parades, the Foreign Office and MOI numbly monitored U.S. politics and opinion. Sterndale Bennett of the Far Eastern office wrote, "A kind of paralysis seems to descend on all our efforts." The America-watchers of the Foreign Office and the MOI were well aware that they had to adjust to a changed world; nevertheless, they were, as the American Division's H. G. Nicholas recalled, reluctant to do so.[10]

Their job seemed more formidable than ever. In his survey of the work of the MOI's American Division in late May 1945, Robin Cruikshank noted there were "now hardly any affairs of HMG which do *not* have 'American ends.' "[11] When the MOI disbanded in 1946, the Foreign Office's Information Department took over the supervision of the British Information Services, which expanded with representatives in Boston, Los Angeles, Detroit, Seattle, and Houston.[12] Propaganda, or information, or "public diplomacy" had become a permanent fixture of postwar international relations. Atomic diplomacy, the reconstruction of Europe, the beginnings of decolonization, and the containment of communism dominated the turbulent postwar period. Within a few years, the BIS would claim the British Commonwealth and Empire as a "bulwark against Communism" and inform Americans that progress in colonial development required more than supplies of cars and refrigerators.[13] The BIS continued its wartime policy of attempting to "enlighten" American attitudes within the framework of common interests.

The British campaign did succeed in laying the groundwork for postwar Anglo-American relations. Propagandists laid this foundation not by defining the "special relationship" in the sentimental terms used by Winston Churchill, although they did draw upon the emotional ties of wartime comradeship and sacrifice. Instead, they

10. Edward R. Stettinius, Jr. to FDR, January 3, 1945, PSF, Box 95, FDRL; Lockhart, *Diaries*, 266; Radcliffe to Bracken, February 21 1945, INF1/701; Sterndale Bennett, May 11, 1945, FO371/44575 AN1409/36/45, PRO; interview with Nicholas.

11. Cruikshank memo, May 29, 1945, INF1/102, PRO.

12. Caroline Anstey, "Foreign Office Efforts to Influence American Opinion, 1945–1949," Ph.D. diss., London School of Economics and Political Science, March 1984, 6–18, 34. After the war, Cyril Radcliffe returned to the bar. Robin Cruikshank took up the editorship of the *News Chronicle* from 1948 until two years before his death in 1956. Hamish Hamilton returned to his publishing business. H. G. Nicholas and Isaiah Berlin returned to the university. Mary Agnes Hamilton continued information work at the Foreign Office. William Edwards became head of the BIS from 1946–1949. D'Arcy Edmondson inherited the British Information Services in New York.

13. Edwards to M. Hamilton, "Colonial Publicity in the US," July 7, 1949, FO953/486 PAN644/40/945, PRO.

promoted partnership in terms of American interests and, in defining
American interests, projected a new role for the United States. Propagandists countered isolationist arguments and built up internationalist positions. They joined with Americans who decried the
inadequate collaboration after World War I and the failure to check
the rise of aggressors in the 1930s. They called for economic cooperation to prevent a return to Depression-era nationalism and
stressed the need for postwar stability. Senator Arthur Vandenberg
represented a satisfactory transformation of American attitudes. In
October 1939, the Michigan Republican had denounced the repeal
of the arms embargo: "In the name of 'democracy' we have taken
the first step, once more, into Europe's power politics. What 'suckers'
our emotions make of us!" At the end of 1945, Vandenberg endorsed
a loan to Britain, over the opposition of many of his constituents,
with the argument that it was a policy of "intelligent American self-
interest."[14]

To encourage the United States to assume a global leadership that
secured British interests, propagandists portrayed the partnership as
critical to the domestic well-being of the United States. "Our constant
aim," instructed the Foreign Office in 1942, "must be to do everything calculated to keep America permanently interested in the
preservation of world order as being essential to her economic prosperity." Britain endorsed an "American century" in which past imperial and economic rivalries were turned into opportunities for
collaboration. During a December 1944 dispute over postwar economic policy, the Foreign Office's J. G. Donnelly had observed:
"What the Americans did was to take their desiderata and label them
freedoms." British propagandists labeled their desiderata "responsibilities." They preached a "doctrine of responsibility," urging white,
Western nations to assist in the "orderly" development of the colonial world. While the Soviet Union was still an ally, British propaganda refrained from direct warnings about the ambitions of the
eastern power. Instead, it emphasized the need for cooperation to
meet the uncertainties of the postwar world. The campaign fulfilled
the prediction of the perspicacious Jawaharlal Nehru, who wrote in
1927 that "in order to save herself," Britain will "incite the imperialism and capitalism of America to fight by her side."[15]

14. Vandenberg, *Private Papers of Senator Vandenberg*, 3, 231.
15. "Cooperation between Great Britain and the United States," February 19,

The small army that wielded "the artillery of propaganda" had been up against great odds. "Our government will have a tough time," Robin Cruikshank had warned, if Americans' illusion that Britain had become a "poor relation" could not be corrected.[16] Correcting American illusions had proven a difficult task. Certainly, future British governments would continue to find reason to dislike the U.S. Constitution and to endure with exasperation the American way of making foreign policy. For wartime propagandists, even if the results were less than satisfactory, the mission had been worth the trouble. As scouts of the U.S. position, they had reported back to London with analyses of American power and objectives that suggested to British policymakers a revised world view. Using their reconnaissance of American political culture, propagandists took advantage of shifting roles and relationships to define and influence Americans' understanding of their global responsibilities. By appealing to American ambitions and apprehensions as the United States assumed international leadership, propagandists presented a healthy and strong Britain as a steadfast ally in a world transformed by war. They realized not the happy ending of an Anglo-American partnership on equal terms but a peace in which Britain's economic and security interests would be protected by the United States.

1942, FO371/30685 A1684/1684/45; Donnelly, December 31, 1944, FO371/44609 AN119/119/45, PRO; Nehru quoted in H. W. Brands, *India and the United States: The Cold Peace* (Boston: Twayne Publishers, 1990), 8.

16. Cruikshank, "Publicity and Policy in the United States," December 3, 1943, FO371/38505 AN430/6/45, PRO.

BIBLIOGRAPHY

Manuscript Collections

Allen, Frederick Lewis. Papers. Library of Congress, Washington, D.C.
American Defense, Harvard Group. Papers. Harvard University Archives, Cambridge, Mass.
Brand, Robert H. Papers. Bodleian Library, Oxford University, Oxford, Eng.
British Broadcasting Corporation. Papers. BBC Written Archives Center, Caversham Park, Reading, Eng.
Brown, Cecil. Papers. State Historical Society of Wisconsin, Madison, Wis.
Cadogan, Alexander. Papers. Churchill College Library, Cambridge, Eng.
Clapper, Raymond. Papers. Library of Congress, Washington, D.C.
Cox, Oscar. Papers. Franklin D. Roosevelt Library, Hyde Park, N.Y.
Davis, Elmer. Papers. Library of Congress, Washington, D.C.
Early, Stephen. Papers. Franklin D. Roosevelt Library, Hyde Park, N.Y.
Fight For Freedom, Inc. Archives. Seeley G. Mudd Manuscript Library, Department of Rare Books and Special Collections, Princeton University Libraries, Princeton, N.J.
Fischer, Louis. Papers. Seeley G. Mudd Manuscript Library, Department of Rare Books and Special Collections, Princeton University Libraries, Princeton, N.J.
Frankfurter, Felix. Papers. Library of Congress, Washington, D.C.
Halifax, Edward. Papers. Churchill College Library, Cambridge, Eng.
Harriman, W. Averell. Papers. Library of Congress, Washington, D.C.
Harsch, Joseph C. Papers. State Historical Society of Wisconsin, Madison, Wis.
Hopkins, Harry. Papers. Franklin D. Roosevelt Library, Hyde Park, N.Y.
Kaltenborn, Hans von. Papers. State Historical Society of Wisconsin, Madison, Wis.
Lippmann, Walter. Papers. Manuscripts and Archives, Yale University Library, New Haven, Conn.
MacLeish, Archibald. Papers. Library of Congress, Washington, D.C.
Mead, Margaret. Papers. Library of Congress, Washington, D.C.

Ogilvy, David. Papers. Library of Congress, Washington, D.C.

Pearson, Lester. Papers. National Archives of Canada, Ottawa.

Roosevelt, Franklin D. Papers: Official Files, Presidential Secretary Files, Presidential Personal Files, Franklin D. Roosevelt Presidential Library, Hyde Park, N.Y.

Russell, Richard B. Papers. Richard B. Russell Library for Political Research and Studies, University of Georgia Libraries, Athens, Ga.

Sevareid, Eric. Papers. Library of Congress, Washington, D.C.

Spry, Graham. Papers. National Archives of Canada, Ottawa.

Wiseman, Sir William. Papers. Manuscripts and Archives, Yale University Library, New Haven, Conn.

Ziemer, Gregor. Papers. State Historical Society of Wisconsin, Madison, Wis.

Unpublished Government Documents

London, England
  Public Record Office (Kew):
    Board of Trade (BT)
    Cabinet Office (CAB)
    Colonial Office (CO)
    Dominions Office (DO)
    Foreign Office (FO)
    Ministry of Information (INF)
    Prime Minister's Office (PREM)
  India Office Library:
    India Office (IO)
Ottawa, Canada
  National Archives of Canada:
    Department of External Affairs
Washington, D.C.
  National Archives:
    Office of Strategic Services, Research and Analysis Reports
    RG 44, Records of the Office of Government Reports
    RG 59, Department of State
    RG 208, Records of the Office of War Information
    RG 262, Foreign Broadcasting Intelligence Service

Published Government Documents

Congressional Record. 1940–1945. Washington, D.C.

Mansergh, Nicholas, ed. *The Transfer of Power, 1942–1947: Constitutional Relations between Britain and India*, Vol. 1, *The Cripps Mission, January–April 1942*. London: HMSO, 1970.

"Report of the Committee on Alleged German Outrages Appointed by His Bri-

tannic Majesty's Government and Presided over by Right Honorable Viscount Bryce, Formerly British Ambassador at Washington." London: HMSO, 1915.
United States Army. Military Intelligence Branch, Executive Division, General Staff. *Propaganda in Its Military and Legal Aspects.* 1919.
U.S. Congress. Senate. Committee on Foreign Relations. *Hearings on the Extension of the Lend-Lease Act, S. 813.* 78th Cong., 1st sess., March 1943.
U.S. Department of State. *Foreign Relations of the United States 1940–1945.* Washington, D.C.

Interviews by Author

Sir Isaiah Berlin, Washington, D.C., November 10, 1988
Graham Hutton, London, Eng., August 17, 1988
Herbert G. Nicholas, Oxford, Eng., August 16, 1991
Dean Rusk, Athens, Ga., June 26, 1991
Arthur Schlesinger, Jr., New York, N.Y., March 31, 1994
Eric Sevareid, Washington, D.C., June 21, 1991
Irene M. Spry, Ottawa, June 29, 1990

Articles

Allen, Frederick Lewis. "Notes on an English Visit." *Harper's,* January 1944, 117–128.
Angell, Sir Norman. "What the British Empire Means to America." *Saturday Evening Post,* June 17, 1944, 216.
Brewster, R. Owen. "Don't Blame the British—Blame Us." *Collier's,* December 25, 1943.
———. "Let's Not Be Suckers Again." *American Magazine,* January 1945.
Editorial. "The British Empire and the United States." *Fortune,* January 1944, 94–95.
Gilbert, Martin. "The Big Two." Review of *Churchill and Roosevelt: The Complete Correspondence,* ed. Warren Kimball. *New York Review of Books,* February 14, 1985.
Harbutt, Fraser. "Churchill, Hopkins, and the 'Other' Americans: An Alternative Perspective on Anglo-American Relations, 1941–1945." *International History Review* 8 (May 1986), 236–262.
Herring, George C. "The United States and British Bankruptcy, 1944–1945: Responsibilities Deferred." *Political Science Quarterly* 86.2 (June 1971), 260–280.
Ikenberry, G. John. "A World Economy Restored: Expert Consensus and the Anglo-American Postwar Settlement." *International Organizations* 46.1 (Winter 1992), 289–321.
Kimball, Warren F. "Lend-Lease and the Open Door: The Temptation of British Opulence, 1937–1942." *Political Science Quarterly* 86.2 (June 1971), 232–259.

Lindley, Ernest. "Lend-Lease and a Healthy Britain." *Newsweek,* December 4, 1944, 42.

Lippmann, Walter. "The Bankers and Bretton Woods." *New York Herald Tribune,* March 17, 1945, 13.

———. "Can the U.S. Have Peace After This War?" *Ladies Home Journal,* August 1943, 24–31.

———. "Pandora's Box." *New York Herald Tribune,* March 20, 1945, 21.

McCombs, Maxwell E., and Donald L. Shaw. "The Agenda-Setting Function of Mass Media." *Public Opinion Quarterly* 36 (Summer 1972), 176–187.

Nelson, Richard. "Propaganda." In *Handbook of American Popular Culture,* vol. 3, edited by M. T. Inge, 1011–1126. New York: Greenwood Press, 1981.

Parker, Sir Gilbert. "The United States and the War." *Harper's,* March 1918, 521–531.

Reed, Philip. "Suspicion: Greatest Enemy of the Allies." *American Magazine,* July 1945, 140.

Reynolds, David. "Competitive Cooperation: Anglo-American Relations in World War II." *Historical Journal* 23 (March 1980), 233–245.

———. "Roosevelt, the British Left, and the Appointment of John G. Winant as United States Ambassador to Britain in 1941." *International History Review* 4 (August 1982), 394–413.

———. "A 'Special Relationship'? America, Britain, and the International Order since the Second World War." *International Affairs* 62 (Winter 1985–86), 1–21.

Robey, Richard. "What Goes On Behind Our Backs." *Newsweek,* November 20, 1944, 72.

Shapiro, Robert Y., and Benjamin Page. "Foreign Policy and the Rational Public." *Journal of Conflict Resolution* 32 (June 1988), 211–247.

Wilson, Trevor. "Lord Bryce's Investigation into Alleged German Atrocities in Belgium, 1914–1915." *Journal of Contemporary History* 14 (July 1979), 369–381.

Books and Dissertations

Acheson, Dean. *Present at the Creation: My Years at the State Department.* New York: W. W. Norton, 1970.

Addison, Paul. *The Road to 1945: British Politics and the Second World War.* London: Jonathan Cape, 1975.

Aldgate, Anthony, and Jeffrey Richards. *Britain Can Take It: The British Cinema in the Second World War.* Edinburgh: Edinburgh University Press, 1994.

Almond, Gabriel. *The American People and Foreign Policy.* New York: Praeger, 1960.

Anderson, Terry. *United States, Great Britain, and the Cold War, 1944–1947.* Columbia: University of Missouri Press, 1981.

Anstey, Caroline. "Foreign Office Efforts to Influence American Opinion, 1945–

1949." Ph.D. diss., London School of Economics and Political Science, March 1984.

Balfour, Michael. *Propaganda in War, 1939–1945: Organizations, Policies, and Publics in Britain and Germany*. Boston: Routledge and Kegan Paul, 1979.

Barker, Elisabeth. *The British between the Superpowers, 1945–1950*. Toronto: University of Toronto Press, 1983.

Barnouw, Erik. *The Golden Web: A History of Broadcasting in the United States, 1933–1953*, vol. 2. New York: Oxford University Press, 1968.

Becker, Carl. *How New Will the Better World Be? A Discussion of Post-war Reconstruction*. New York: Alfred A. Knopf, 1944.

Bell, Coral. "The Special Relationship." In *Constraints and Adjustments in British Foreign Policy*, edited by Michael Leifer, 103–119. London: George Allen and Unwin, 1972.

Beloff, Max. "The Special Relationship: An Anglo-American Myth." In *A Century of Conflict, 1850–1950: Essays for A. J. P. Taylor*, edited by Martin Gilbert, 151–171. London: Hamish Hamilton, 1966.

Bentley, Phyllis. *"O Dream, O Destinations": An Autobiography*. London: Victor Gollancz, 1962.

Berle, Adolf A. *Navigating the Rapids, 1918–1971: From the Papers of Adolf A. Berle*. Edited by Beatrice Bishop Berle and Travis Beal Jacobs. New York: Harcourt Brace Jovanovich, 1973.

Berlin, Isaiah. *Personal Impressions*. New York: Viking Press, 1981.

Bernays, Edward L. *Biography of an Idea: Memoirs of a Public Relations Counsel*. New York: Simon and Schuster, 1965.

Best, Richard A. *"Cooperation with Like-Minded Peoples": British Influences on American Security Policy, 1945–1949*. Westport, Conn.: Greenwood Press, 1986.

Blakey, George. *Historians on the Homefront: American Propagandists for the Great War*. Lexington: University of Kentucky Press, 1970.

Bliss, Edward, Jr. *Now the News: The Story of Broadcast Journalism*. New York: Columbia University Press, 1991.

Blum, John M. *From the Morgenthau Diaries: Years of War, 1941–1945*. Boston: Houghton Mifflin, 1975.

——. *V Was for Victory: Politics and American Culture during World War II*. New York: Harcourt Brace Jovanovich, 1976.

Brands, H. W. *India and the United States: The Cold Peace*. Boston: Twayne Publishers, 1990.

Briggs, Asa. *The War of Words*. Vol. 3 of *The History of Broadcasting in the United Kingdom*. London: Oxford University Press, 1970.

Brown, Cecil. *Suez to Singapore*. New York: Random House, 1942.

Bryce, James. *The American Commonwealth*. 2 vols. New York: Macmillan, 1910.

Burk, Kathleen. *Britain, America, and the Sinews of War, 1914–1918*. Boston: George Allen and Unwin, 1984.

Cain, P. J., and A. G. Hopkins. *British Imperialism: Crisis and Deconstruction, 1914–1990.* London: Longman, 1993.

Calder, Angus. *The Myth of the Blitz.* London: Jonathan Cape, 1991.

———. *The People's War: Britain, 1939–1945.* New York: Pantheon Books, 1969.

Callahan, Raymond A. *Churchill: Retreat from Empire.* Wilmington, Del.: Scholarly Resources, 1984.

Campbell. Gerald. *Of True Experience.* New York: Dodd, Mead, 1947.

Canning, Paul. *British Policy towards Ireland, 1921–1941.* Oxford: Clarendon Press, 1985.

Cantril, Hadley. *Gauging Public Opinion.* Princeton: Princeton University Press, 1944.

———. *The Human Dimension: Experiences in Policy Research.* New Brunswick, N.J.: Rutgers University Press, 1967.

Cantril, Hadley, and Mildred Strunk, eds. *Public Opinion, 1935–1946.* Princeton: Princeton University Press, 1951.

Cardiff, David, and Paddy Scannell. " 'Good Luck, War Workers!': Class, Politics, and Entertainment in Wartime Broadcasting." In *Popular Culture and Social Relations,* edited by Tony Bennett, Colin Mercer, and Janet Woollacott, 93–116. Milton Keynes, Eng.: Open University Press, 1986.

Carroll, Wallace. *Persuade or Perish.* Boston: Houghton Mifflin, 1948.

Chadwin, Mark Lincoln. *The War Hawks of World War II.* Chapel Hill: University of North Carolina Press, 1968.

Chandler, Alfred D., ed. *The Papers of Dwight David Eisenhower: The War Years.* Vol. 1. Baltimore, Md.: Johns Hopkins University Press, 1970.

Chatfield, Charles, ed. *The Americanization of Gandhi.* New York: Garland Publishing, 1976.

Churchill, Winston S. *The Grand Alliance.* Boston: Houghton Mifflin, 1950.

———. *Winston S. Churchill: His Complete Speeches, 1897–1963.* Vols. 6 and 7. Edited by Robert Rhodes James. New York: Chelsea House, 1974.

Clapper, Olive. *One Lucky Woman.* Garden City, N.Y.: Doubleday, 1961.

Clark, William. *From Three Worlds.* London: Sidgwick and Jackson, 1986.

———. *Less Than Kin: A Study of Anglo-American Relations.* London: Hamish Hamilton, 1957.

Clymer, Kenton J. *Quest for Freedom: The United States and India's Independence.* New York: Columbia University Press, 1995.

Cohen, Bernard C. *The Press and Foreign Policy.* Princeton: Princeton University Press, 1963.

———. *The Public's Impact on Foreign Policy.* Boston: Little, Brown, 1973.

Cohen, Warren I. *The American Revisionists: The Lessons of Intervention in World War I.* Chicago: University of Chicago Press, 1967.

———. *Empire without Tears: America's Foreign Relations, 1921–1933.* New York: Alfred A. Knopf, 1987.

Cole, Wayne S. *Roosevelt and the Isolationists, 1932–1945.* Lincoln: University of Nebraska Press, 1983.

——. *Senator Gerald P. Nye and American Foreign Relations*. Minneapolis: University of Minnesota Press, 1962.

Colville, John. *The Fringes of Power: Downing Street Diaries, 1939–1955*. New York: Norton, 1986.

Costigliola, Frank. *Awkward Dominion: American Political, Economic, and Cultural Relations with Europe, 1919–1933*. Ithaca: Cornell University Press, 1984.

Culbert, David Holbrook. *News for Everyman: Radio and Foreign Affairs in Thirties America*. Westport, Conn.: Greenwood Press, 1976.

Cull, Nicholas John. *Selling War: The British Propaganda Campaign against American Neutrality in World War II*. New York: Oxford University Press, 1995.

Czitrom, Daniel J. *The Media and the American Mind: From Morse to McLuhan*. Chapel Hill: University of North Carolina Press, 1982.

Dallek, Robert. *Franklin D. Roosevelt and American Foreign Policy, 1931–1945*. New York: Oxford University Press, 1979.

Darwin, John. *Britain and Decolonisation: The Retreat from Empire in the Postwar World*. New York: St. Martin's Press, 1988.

Dimbleby, David, and David Reynolds. *An Ocean Apart: The Relationship between Britain and America in the Twentieth Century*. London: Hodder and Stoughton, 1988.

Divine, Robert A. *Second Chance: The Triumph of Internationalism in America during World War II*. New York: Atheneum, 1967.

Dobson, Alan. *The Politics of the Anglo-American Economic Special Relationship, 1940–1987*. New York: St. Martin's Press, 1988.

——. *U.S. Wartime Aid to Britain, 1940–1946*. New York: St. Martin's Press, 1986.

Dower, John. *War without Mercy: Race and Power in the Pacific War*. New York: Pantheon Books, 1986.

Eckersley, Roger. *The BBC and All That*. London: Snapson, Low, Marston, 1946.

Edmonds, Robin. *Setting the Mould: The United States and Britain, 1945–1950*. Oxford: Clarendon Press, 1986.

Ferrell, Robert H. *Woodrow Wilson and World War I, 1917–1921*. New York: Harper and Row, 1985.

Foster, H. Schuyler. *Activism Replaces Isolationism: U.S. Public Attitudes, 1940–1975*. Washington, D.C.: Foxhall Press, 1983.

Fowler, W. B. *British-American Relations, 1917–1918: The Role of Sir William Wiseman*. Princeton: Princeton University Press, 1969.

Fox, Richard Wightman. *Reinhold Niebuhr: A Biography*. New York: Pantheon, 1985.

Frankfurter, Felix. *From the Diaries of Felix Frankfurter*. New York: W. W. Norton, 1975.

Freeland, Richard. *The Truman Doctrine and the Origins of McCarthyism: For-*

eign Policy, Domestic Politics, and Internal Security, 1946–1948. New York: Alfred A. Knopf, 1972.

Fussell, Paul. *Wartime: Understanding and Behavior in the Second World War.* New York: Oxford University Press, 1989.

Gallup, George. *The Gallup Poll: Public Opinion, 1935–1948.* New York: Random House, 1972.

Gallup, George, and Saul Forbes Rae. *The Pulse of Democracy: The Public Opinion Poll and How It Works.* New York: Simon and Schuster, 1940.

Gardner, Lloyd. *Architects of Illusion: Men and Ideas in American Foreign Policy, 1941–1949.* Chicago: Quadrangle Books, 1970.

———. *Safe for Democracy: The Anglo-American Response to Revolution, 1913–1923.* New York: Oxford University Press, 1984.

Gardner, Richard N. *Sterling-Dollar Diplomacy: Anglo-American Collaboration in the Reconstruction of Multilateral Trade.* Oxford: Oxford University Press, 1956.

Gifford, Prosser, and William Roger Louis. eds. *The Transfer of Power in Africa: Decolonization, 1940–1960.* New Haven: Yale University Press, 1982.

Gilbert, Martin. *Finest Hour, 1939–1941,* and *Road to Victory, 1941–1945.* Vols. 6–7. of *Winston S. Churchill.* Boston: Houghton Mifflin, 1986.

Gore-Booth, Paul. *With Great Truth and Respect.* London: Constable, 1974.

Gorham, Maurice. *Sound and Fury: Twenty-one Years in the BBC.* London: Percival Marshall, 1948.

Grant, Mariel. *Propaganda and the Role of the State in Inter-War Britain.* Oxford: Clarendon Press, 1994.

Grigg, P. J. *Prejudice and Judgement.* London: Jonathan Cape, 1948.

Gruber, Carol S. *Mars and Minerva: World War I and the Uses of Higher Learning.* Baton Rouge: Louisiana State University Press, 1975.

Hachey, Thomas E., ed. *Confidential Dispatches: Analyses of America by the British Ambassador, 1939–1945.* Evanston, Ill.: New University Press, 1974.

Halifax, Edward. *Fullness of Days.* New York: Dodd, Mead, 1957.

Hall, H. Duncan. *North American Supply.* London: HMSO, 1955. Reprint. New York: Kraus International Publications, 1984.

Hamilton, Mary Agnes. *Uphill All the Way: A Third Cheer for Democracy.* London: Jonathan Cape, 1953.

Harbutt, Fraser. *The Iron Curtain: Churchill, America, and the Origins of the Cold War.* New York: Oxford University Press, 1986.

Harriman, W. Averell, and Elie Abel. *Special Envoy to Churchill and Stalin, 1941–1946.* New York: Random House, 1975.

Harvey, Oliver. *The War Diaries of Oliver Harvey.* Edited by John Harvey. London: Collins, 1978.

Hathaway, Robert. *Ambiguous Partnership: Britain and America, 1944–1947.* New York: Columbia University Press, 1981.

———. *Great Britain and the United States: Special Relations since World War II.* Boston: Twayne Publishers, 1990.

Heinrichs, Waldo. *Threshold of War: Franklin D. Roosevelt and American Entry into World War II.* New York: Oxford University Press, 1988.

Herman, Edward S., and Noam Chomsky. *Manufacturing Consent: The Political Economy of the Mass Media.* New York: Pantheon, 1988.

Hess, Gary. *America Encounters India, 1942–1947.* Baltimore: Johns Hopkins University Press, 1971.

Hilderbrand, Robert C. *Power and the People: Executive Management of Public Opinion in Foreign Affairs, 1897–1921.* Chapel Hill: University of North Carolina Press, 1981.

Hitchens, Christopher. *Blood, Class, and Nostalgia: Anglo-American Ironies.* New York: Farrar, Straus and Giroux, 1990.

Hitler, Adolf. *Mein Kampf.* Boston: Houghton Mifflin, 1971.

Hughes, Barry. *The Domestic Context of American Foreign Policy.* San Francisco: W. H. Freeman, 1978.

Hyde, H. Montgomery. *Room 3603: The Story of the British Intelligence Center in New York during World War II.* New York: Farrar, Strauss, 1963.

Iatrides, John O. *Revolt in Athens: The Greek Communist "Second Round," 1944–1946.* Princeton, N.J.: Princeton University Press, 1972.

Irion, Frederick. *Public Opinion and Propaganda.* New York: Thomas Y. Crowell, 1952.

Isaacs, Harold. *Scratches on Our Minds: American Images of China and India.* New York: J. Day, 1958.

Jonas, Manfred. *Isolationism in America, 1935–1941.* Ithaca: Cornell University Press, 1966.

Jowett, Garth S., and Victoria O'Donnell. *Propaganda and Persuasion.* Beverly Hills: Sage Publications, 1986.

Karl, Barry D. *The Uneasy State: The United States from 1915–1945.* Chicago: University of Chicago Press, 1983.

Katz, Daniel. "Britain Speaks." In *Propaganda by Short Wave.* Edited by Harwood L. Childs and John B. Whiton. Princeton: Princeton University Press, 1942.

Kennedy, David. *Over Here: The First World War and American Society.* New York: Oxford University Press, 1980.

Kimball, Warren, ed. *Churchill and Roosevelt: The Complete Correspondence.* 3 vols. Princeton: Princeton University Press, 1984.

——. *The Most Unsordid Act.* Baltimore: Johns Hopkins University Press, 1969.

Knightley, Phillip. *The First Casualty: From the Crimea to Vietnam: The War Correspondent as Hero, Propagandist, and Myth Maker.* New York: Harcourt Brace Jovanovich, 1975.

Koppes, Clayton R., and Gregory D. Black. *Hollywood Goes to War: How Politics, Profits, and Propaganda Shaped World War II Movies.* Berkeley: University of California Press, 1990.

Krome, Frederic James. " 'A Weapon of War Second to None': Anglo-American

Film Propaganda during World War II." Ph.D. diss., University of Cincinnati, 1992.

Lal, Chaman. *British Propaganda in America.* Allahabad, India: Kitab Mahal, 1945.

Lasswell, Harold. *Democracy through Public Opinion.* Menasha, Wis.: George Banta Publishing, 1941.

——. *Propaganda Technique in World War I.* 1927. reprint. Cambridge: MIT Press, 1971.

——. *Public Opinion and British-American Unity.* Princeton: American Committee for International Studies, 1941.

Lasswell, Harold, Daniel Lerner, and Hans Speier, eds. *Propaganda and Communication in World History.* 3 vols. Honolulu: University Press of Hawaii, 1979.

Leigh, Michael. *Mobilizing Consent: Public Opinion and American Foreign Policy, 1937–1947.* Westport, Conn.: Greenwood Press, 1976.

Lerner, Daniel. *Psychological Warfare against Nazi Germany: The Sykewar Campaign, D-Day to V-E Day.* Cambridge: MIT Press, 1971.

Leutze, James R. *Bargaining for Supremacy: Anglo-American Naval Cooperation, 1937–1941.* Chapel Hill: University of North Carolina, 1977.

Levering, Ralph B. *The Public and American Foreign Policy, 1918–1978.* New York: William Morrow, 1978.

Lindbergh, Anne Morrow. *War Within and Without: Diaries and Letters of Anne Morrow Lindbergh, 1939–1944.* New York: Harcourt Brace Jovanovich, 1980.

Link, Arthur S. *Woodrow Wilson: Revolution, War, and Peace.* Arlington Heights, Ill.: AHM Publishing, 1979.

Lippmann, Walter. *Public Opinion.* New York: Free Press, 1965.

——. *United States Foreign Policy: Shield of the Republic.* Boston: Little, Brown, 1943.

——. *United States War Aims.* Boston: Little, Brown, 1944.

Lockhart, Robert Bruce. *Comes the Reckoning.* London: Putnam, 1947.

——. *The Diaries of Sir Robert Bruce Lockhart.* 2 vols. Edited by Kenneth Young. London: Macmillan, 1980.

Louis, William Roger. *Imperialism at Bay, 1941–1945: The United States and the Decolonization of the British Empire.* New York: Oxford University Press, 1978.

Louis, William Roger, and Hedley Bull, eds. *The "Special Relationship": Anglo-American Relations since 1945.* Oxford: Clarendon Press, 1986.

Luce, Henry. *The American Century.* New York: Farrar and Rinehart, 1941.

MacDonald, C. A. *The United States, Britain, and Appeasement, 1936–1939.* New York: St. Martin's Press, 1981.

MacDonnell, Francis. *Insidious Foes: The Axis Fifth Column and the American Home Front.* New York: Oxford University Press, 1995.

MacLeish, Archibald. *A Time to Act: Selected Addresses.* Boston: Houghton Mifflin, 1943.

Macmillan, Harold. *War Diaries: Politics and War in the Mediterranean, January 1943–May 1945*. London: Macmillan, 1984.

Marchand, Roland. *Advertising the American Dream: Making Way for Modernity, 1920–1940*. Berkeley: University of California Press, 1986.

Marett, Robert. *Through the Back Door: An Inside View of Britain's Overseas Information Services*. Oxford: Pergamon Press, 1968.

Marwick, Arthur. *The British and the Second World War*. London: Thames and Hudson, 1976.

McKercher, B. J. C. *The Second Baldwin Government and the United States, 1924–1929: Attitudes and Diplomacy*. New York: Cambridge University Press, 1984.

McLaine, Ian. *Ministry of Morale: Home Front Morale and the Ministry of Information in World War II*. London: George Allen and Unwin, 1979.

Messinger, Gary S. *British Propaganda and the State in the First World War*. New York: Manchester University Press, 1992.

Millis, Walter. *Road to War: America, 1914–1917*. Boston: Houghton Mifflin, 1935.

Mock, James R., and Cedric Larson. *Words That Won the War: The Story of the Committee on Public Information, 1917–1919*. Princeton: Princeton University Press, 1939.

Moore, R. J. *Endgames of Empire: Studies of Britain's India Problem*. Delhi: Oxford University Press, 1988.

Morgan, Kenneth O. *The People's Peace: British History, 1945–1989*. Oxford: Oxford University Press, 1990.

Mueller, John E. *War, Presidents, and Public Opinion*. New York: John Wiley, 1973.

Nicholas, H. G., ed. *Washington Despatches, 1941–1945: Weekly Political Reports from the British Embassy*. London: Weidenfeld and Nicolson, 1981.

Nicolson, Harold. *The War Years: Diaries and Letters, 1939–1945*. Edited by Nigel Nicolson. New York: Atheneum, 1967.

Ogilvy, David. *Blood, Brains, and Beer*. New York: Atheneum, 1967.

Ogilvy-Webb, Marjorie. *The Government Explains: A Study of the Information Services*. London: George Allen and Unwin, 1965.

O'Grady, Joseph P., ed. *The Immigrant's Influence on Wilson's Peace Policies*. Lexington: University of Kentucky Press, 1967.

Page, Benjamin I., and Robert Y. Shapiro. *The Rational Public: Fifty Years of Trends in Americans' Policy Preferences*. Chicago: University of Chicago, 1992.

Perkins, Bradford. *The Great Rapprochement: England and the United States, 1898–1905*. New York: Atheneum, 1968.

Persico, Joseph E. *Edward R. Murrow: An American Original*. New York: McGraw Hill, 1988.

Peterson, H. C. *Propaganda for War: The Campaign against Neutrality, 1914–1917*. Norman: University of Oklahoma Press, 1939.

Ponsonby, Arthur. *Falsehood in War-Time*. New York: E. P. Dutton, 1928.

Pressnell, L. S. *The Post-War Financial Settlement*. Vol. 1 of *External Economic Policy Since the War*. London: HMSO, 1986.

Pronay, Nicholas, and D. W. Spring, eds. *Propaganda, Politics, and Film, 1918–1945*. London: Macmillan, 1982.

Qualter, Terence H. *Opinion Control in Democracies*. New York: St. Martin's Press, 1985.

Reston, James. *Deadline: A Memoir*. New York: Random House, 1991.

Reynolds, David. *The Creation of the Anglo-American Alliance, 1937–1941: A Study in Competitive Cooperation*. Chapel Hill: University of North Carolina Press, 1982.

———. *Lord Lothian and Anglo-American Relations, 1939–1940*. Philadelphia: American Philosophical Society, 1982.

———. *Rich Relations: The American Occupation of Britain, 1942–1945*. New York: Random House, 1995.

Rhodes, Benjamin D. "Sir Ronald Lindsay and the British View from Washington, 1930–1939." In *Essays in Twentieth-Century American Diplomatic History Dedicated to Professor Daniel Smith*, edited by Clifford L. Egan and Alexander W. Knott, 62–89. Washington, D.C.: University Press of America, 1982.

Rogerson, Sidney. *Propaganda in the Next War*. London: B. Bles, 1938.

Roosevelt, Franklin D. *The Public Papers and Addresses of Franklin D. Roosevelt*. Compiled by Samuel I. Rosenman. New York: Macmillan, 1941.

Rosenberg, Emily. *Spreading the American Dream: American Economic and Cultural Expansion, 1890–1945*. New York: Hill and Wang, 1982.

Ryan, Henry Butterfield. *The Vision of Anglo-America: The U.S.-U.K. Alliance and the Emerging Cold War, 1943–1946*. Cambridge: Cambridge University Press, 1987.

Sanders, Michael, and Philip Taylor. *British Propaganda in the First World War, 1914–1918*. London: Macmillan, 1982.

Sevareid, Eric. *Not So Wild a Dream*. New York: Atheneum, 1976.

Sherwood, Robert. *Roosevelt and Hopkins: An Intimate History*. New York: Harper Brothers, 1948.

Short, K. R. M. "Cinematic Support for the Anglo-American Detente, 1939–1943." In *Britain and the Cinema in the Second World War*, edited by Philip Taylor, 121–143. New York: St. Martin's Press, 1988.

———, ed. *Film and Radio Propaganda in World War II*. Knoxville: University of Tennessee Press, 1983.

Slotkin, Richard. *Gunfighter Nation: The Myth of Frontier in Twentieth Century America*. New York: Harper Collins, 1992.

Smith, R. Franklin. *Edward R. Murrow: The War Years*. Kalamazoo, Mich.: New Issues Press, 1978.

Sperber, A. M. *Murrow: His Life and Times*. New York: Freundlich Books, 1986.

Sproule, J. Michael. "Social Reponses to Twentieth Century Propaganda." In *Propaganda: A Pluralistic Perspective*, edited by Ted Smith III, 5–22. New York: Praeger, 1989.

Squires, James Duane. *British Propaganda at Home and in the United States: From 1914 to 1917.* Cambridge: Harvard University Press, 1935.

Steel, Ronald. *Walter Lippmann and the American Century.* Boston: Little, Brown, 1980.

Steele, Richard W. *Propaganda in an Open Society: The Roosevelt Administration and the Media, 1933–1941.* Westport, Conn.: Greenwood Press, 1985.

Stoler, Mark A. *The Politics of the Second Front: American Military Planning and Diplomacy in Coalition Warfare, 1941–1943.* Westport, Conn.: Greenwood Press, 1977.

Taylor, Philip M. *The Projection of Britain: British Overseas Publicity and Propaganda, 1919–1939.* Cambridge: Cambridge University Press, 1981.

Thomson, Oliver. *Mass Persuasion in History: An Historical Analysis of the Development of Propaganda Techniques.* Edinburgh: Paul Harris, 1977.

Thorne, Christopher. *Allies of a Kind: The United States, Britain, and the War against Japan, 1941–1945.* New York: Oxford University Press, 1978.

———. *Border Crossings: Studies in International History.* Oxford: Basil Blackwell, 1988.

Thorpe, Frances, and Nicholas Pronay. *British Official Films in the Second World War: A Descriptive Catalogue.* Oxford, Eng.: Clio Press, 1980.

Tree, Ronald. *When the Moon Was High: Memoirs of War and Peace, 1897–1942.* London: Macmillan, 1975.

Vandenberg, Arthur. *The Private Papers of Senator Vandenberg.* Edited by Arthur Vandenberg, Jr. Boston: Houghton Mifflin, 1952.

Vaughn, Stephen. *Holding Fast the Inner Lines: Democracy, Nationalism, and the Committee on Public Information.* Chapel Hill: University of North Carolina Press, 1980.

Venkataramani, M. S., and B. K. Shrivastava. *Quit India: The American Response to the 1942 Struggle.* New Delhi: Vikas Publishing, 1979.

Venn, Fiona. *Oil Diplomacy in the Twentieth Century.* New York: St. Martin's Press, 1986.

Ward, Alan J. *Ireland and Anglo-American Relations, 1899–1921.* London: Weidenfeld and Nicolson, 1969.

Watt, D. C. *Succeeding John Bull: America in Britain's Place, 1900–1975.* Cambridge: Cambridge University Press, 1984.

West, W. J., ed. *Orwell: The War Commentaries.* New York: Pantheon Books, 1985.

Wheeler-Bennett, John. *Special Relationships: America in War and Peace.* London: Macmillan, 1975.

Wiebe, Robert. *The Search for Order, 1877–1920.* New York: Hill and Wang, 1967.

Willert, Arthur. *The Road to Safety: A Study in Anglo-American Relations.* London: Derek Verschoyle, 1952.

———. *Washington and Other Memories.* Boston: Houghton Mifflin, 1972.

Winant, John G. *Letter from Grosvenor Square.* Boston: Houghton Mifflin, 1974.

Winkler, Allan. *The Politics of Propaganda: The Office of War Information, 1942–1945.* New Haven: Yale University Press, 1974.

Woods, Randall Bennett. *A Changing of the Guard: Anglo-American Relations, 1941–1946.* Chapel Hill: University of North Carolina Press, 1990.

Zwick, Jim, ed. *Mark Twain's Weapons of Satire: Anti-Imperialist Writings on the Philippine-American War.* Syracuse, N.Y.: Syracuse University Press, 1992.

INDEX